Shaman's Path

Shaman's Path

HEALING, PERSONAL GROWTH, & EMPOWERMENT

Compiled & edited by
Gary Doore

SHAMBHALA
Boston & London
1988

Shambhala Publications, Inc.
Horticultural Hall
300 Massachusetts Avenue
Boston, Massachusetts 02115

"What Is a Shaman?" and "Shamanic Counseling" © 1988 by Michael Harner. "Ecstasy and
Sacrifice" © 1988 by Rowena Pattee. "Shamanism: A Religious Phenomenon?" © 1988 by
Åke Hultkrantz. "Seeing Is Believing: The Four Worlds of the Shaman" © 1988 by Serge
King. "Shamanic Trance Postures" © 1988 by Felicitas D. Goodman. The Bridge, an
Essential Implement of Hmong and Yao Shamanism" © 1988 by Jacques Lemoine. "Neo-
Shamanism and the Modern Mystical Movement" © 1988 by Joan B. Townsend. "The Inner
Life of the Healer: The Importance of Shamanism for Modern Medicine" © 1988 by Larry
Dossey. "Shamans: The First Healers" © 1988 by Stanley Krippner. "The Wounded Healer:
Transformational Journeys in Modern Medicine" © 1988 by Jeanne Achterberg. "Modern
Shamanism: Integration of Biomedicine with Traditional World Views" © 1988 by Lewis E.
Mehl. "Shamanic Approaches in a Hospital Pain Clinic" © 1988 by Frank Lawlis. "Sacred
Places in Nature: One Tool in the Shaman's Medicine Bag" © 1988 by Jim Swan. "The
Shamanic Journey: Observations from Holotropic Therapy" © 1988 by Stanislav Grof.
"Shamanic Tales as Ways of Personal Empowerment" © 1988 by Jürgen W. Kremer.
"Shaman's Journey, Buddhist Path" © 1988 by Joan Halifax. "To Paint Ourselves Red" ©
1988 by Brooke Medicine Eagle. "Shamans, Yogis, and Bodhisattvas" © 1988 by Gary
Doore.

9 8 7 6 5 4 3 2

Printed in the United States of America
Distributed in the United States of America by Random House
and in Canada by Random House of Canada Ltd.

Library of Congress Cataloging-in-Publication Data
Shaman's path.
    1. Shamanism.   2. Shaman.   3. Healing—Religious
aspects.   I. Doore, Gary.
BL2370.S5S525   1988   291.6'2   87-32233
ISBN 0-87773-432-1 (pbk.)

Contents

Contents

Acknowledgments

I AM INDEBTED to the many people who gave so generously of their time, talents, and expertise in the process of locating contributors and identifying important topics to be covered. Special thanks go to Michael Harner for inspiration and encouragement during all stages of the book's development, and for much useful advice. Thanks are due as well to Timothy White and Dennis Dutton of *Shaman's Drum* for their suggestions, and to Ruth-Inge Heinze, who put me in touch with several of the authors whose articles are included here. I am also grateful to Emily Sell and Kendra Crossen at Shambhala Publications for their help in bringing this information to the growing audience of those who have recognized the relevance of the shaman's path today.

About the Contributors

JEANNE ACHTERBERG, Ph.D., is Associate Professor and Director of Research in the Department of Rehabilitation Science, and Clinical Professor of Psychology and Physical Medicine at the University of Texas Health Science Center. She is co-author, with G. F. Lawlis, of *Imagery of Cancer* and *Bridges of the Bodymind*, and author of *Imagery in Healing: Shamanism and Modern Medicine* (Boston: Shambhala, 1985).

GARY DOORE, Ph.D. (d. Phil., Oxford), is currently an editor for *Yoga Journal* in Berkeley, California. He has published numerous articles on comparative philosophy and religion in such journals as *Mind*, *Philosophy*, and *Religious Studies*.

LARRY DOSSEY, M.D., is former Chief of Staff, Medical City Dallas Hospital, and the author of numerous publications in the field of holistic health. His books *Space, Time and Medicine* (Boulder: Shambhala, 1982), *Beyond Illness* (Boulder: Shambhala, 1984), and *Mind Beyond Body* (forthcoming), reflect his concerns about the interface of human consciousness with health and illness, and attempt to anchor the holistic health movement in a scientifically respectable theory of mind and consciousness.

BROOKE MEDICINE EAGLE, M.A., is a visionary, healer, writer, singer, and ceremonial leader. Her work draws heavily from her native background, as well as from numerous other spiritual sources. She travels internationally, teaching and leading outdoor adventure quests. Her visions and spiritual journeys have been documented in *Shaman's Drum*, in *East/West Journal*, and in Joan Halifax's *Shamanic Voices*.

FELICITAS D. GOODMAN, Ph.D., is a psychological anthropologist. Until her retirement in 1979 she taught at Denison University. She is the founder and director of Cuyamungue Institute and the author of several books, most recently of *How About Demons: Possession and Exorcism in the Modern World* (Bloomington: Indiana University Press, 1988). A comprehensive work about trance postures is in preparation.

STANISLAV GROF, M.D., is scholar in residence at Esalen Institute. He has done research on LSD psychotherapy in Czechoslovakia and the United States, and with his wife, Christina, has recently pioneered a new nondrug method of transpersonal psychotherapy called holonomic integration. His books include *Realms of the Human Unconscious: Observations from LSD Research* (New York: Dutton, 1976), *LSD Psychotherapy* (Pomona, Calif.: Hunter House, 1980), and *Beyond the Brain* (Albany: State University of New York Press, 1985).

JOAN HALIFAX, Ph.D., is a medical anthropologist and former director of the Ojai Foundation. She has worked with healers and shamans throughout the world and now travels widely, teaching shamanism. She is co-author, with Stanislav Grof, of *The Human Encounter with Death*, and author of *Shamanic Voices* and *Shaman, The Wounded Healer*.

MICHAEL HARNER, Ph.D., has pioneered the contemporary teaching of shamanism, shamanic healing, and shamanic counseling in modern society, both in the United States and abroad. He is president of the Foundation for Shamanic Studies in Norwalk, Connecticut, as well as co-chairman of the Anthropology Section of the New York Academy of Sciences. His books include *The Way of the Shaman, The Jívaro, Hallucinogens and Shamanism*, and a novel, *Cannibal*, which he co-authored.

ÅKE HULTKRANTZ, Ph.D., is professor at the Institute of Comparative Religion at the University of Stockholm, Sweden. He has done fieldwork among the Lapps, the Shoshoni and Arapaho Indians of Wyoming and Idaho, and the Northern Plains Indians. His numerous books include *Belief and Worship in Native North America* (Syracuse, N.Y.: Syracuse University Press, 1981) and *The Study of American Indian Religions* (Crossroad Publishing Company and Scholar's Press, 1983).

SERGE KING, Ph.D., is director of the Order of Huna International in Kilauea, Hawaii. Adopted and trained from an early age by a Hawaiian master shaman, he views the shaman from the Polynesian perspective as an "adventurer," in contrast to the "warrior" model of other traditions. His many publications include *Imagineering for Health* (1981), *Kahuna Healing* (1983), and *Mastering Your Hidden Self* (1985), all published by Quest Books in Wheaton, Illinois.

JÜRGEN W. KREMER, Ph.D., is a member of the Executive Faculty and Director of Clinical Inquiry Concentration, Saybrook Institute, San Francisco. He is currently writing a book on tales of power and the narrative universe, as well as a book of shamanic stories.

STANLEY KRIPPNER, Ph.D., is Professor of Psychology and Director of the Center for Consciousness Studies at the Saybrook Institute in San

Francisco, where he teaches "The Psychology of Shamanism" and other courses. A pioneer in parapsychology and consciousness research since the 1960s, he has investigated shamanic states of consciousness and their current relevance as a therapeutic tool. Among his recent books are *The Realms of Healing*, revised edition (Millbrae, Calif.: Celestial Arts, 1987), *Healing States* (New York: Simon & Schuster, 1987), and *Human Possibilities* (New York: Anchor, 1980).

FRANK LAWLIS, Ph.D., is Professor of Psychology at North Texas State University and also on the attending staff at Medical Arts Hospital, Dallas. He is co-author with his wife, Jeanne Achterberg, of the book *Bridges of the Bodymind*, and is currently working on a book based on his experiences at pain clinics.

JACQUES LEMOINE, Ph.D., is Director of the Center for the Anthropological Study of Southern China and the Indochinese Peninsula at the French National Research Center in Paris. His books include *Yao Ceremonial Paintings* (Bangkok, 1978), and *Entre la maladie et la mort: Le chamane hmong sur les chemins de l'Au-dela* (Bangkok, 1987).

LEWIS E. MEHL, M.D., Ph.D., is a Cherokee Indian and expert on Native American healing techniques. In addition to his current post as Clinical Assistant Professor at Stanford University School of Medicine, where he teaches behavioral medicine, Dr. Mehl also practices shamanic holistic medicine at the Center for Recovery from Illness in San Francisco. He is the co-author of *Hypnosis, Healing and Physical Illness* (New York: Irvington Press, 1988) and the author of *Mind and Matter* (San Francisco: Mindbody/Health Resources Press, 1986).

ROWENA PATTEE, Ph.D., is the director of the Creative Harmonic Institute, Mount Shasta, California, a center for meditation, shamanism, and sacred science and arts. She also teaches "Shamanic Art and Ritual Healing" and "Myths and Symbols" at the California Institute of Integral Studies in San Francisco. Her recent book is *Moving with Change* (London: RKP Arkana, 1986) with companion *I Ching* hexagram cards produced by Golden Point Productions. She has produced five films and video tapes and has exhibited her sacred art widely in the United States and Europe.

JIM SWAN, Ph.D., is a psychologist, entertainer, and section editor for *Shaman's Drum* magazine. His studies of traditional shamanic wisdom include work with Sun Bear and Rolling Thunder, as well as designing the environmental health education plan for the government of American Samoa. He appears in the forthcoming feature movie *Tucker*, directed by Francis Ford Coppola and produced by George Lucas.

JOAN B. TOWNSEND, Ph.D., teaches anthropology at the University of Manitoba, Winnipeg. She has conducted sociocultural and ethnohistoric research among the Tanaina Athapaskan Indians of southwestern Alaska. For several years she has conducted research and taught graduate seminars in Anthropology of Religion, focusing on the whole spectrum of new religious movements and New Age activities in the West, including neo-shamanism.

Shaman's Path

Introduction

The loud "boom, boom, boom" of the insistent drumbeat seemed to be pushing me toward some sort of crisis, pounding my ordinary reality into a heap of fragments. Tension was mounting, it was difficult to breathe, and I could feel my palms breaking into a cold sweat. Energy seemed to be draining out of my body from some unseen wound, and I began to shiver involuntarily, worried that my heart was about to stop. Perhaps I was dying. "This the the the end!" I thought, feeling the panic rising as a sinister voice in my head kept suggesting that the monotonous drumming was somehow part of a cosmic plot to destroy me.

And then I felt myself suddenly starting to fall into a gravity well or vortex of some kind, sucked downward with incredible energy. I seemed to be floating on a river of liquid light that was entering an enormous cavern in the center of a mound of reddish-brown earth somewhere in the desert to the south. Then I was in the waterfall, plunging headlong down through a black tunnel whose walls were studded with crystals gleaming with deep red and earthen hues.

At the base of the waterfall I swam up into a deep pool, then began to float along on the current of the underground river, flanked by a huge fish with a long snout and rows of sharp teeth—a gigantic green beast whose scales resembled glittering emeralds. . . .

THUS BEGINS the report of an apprentice shaman's first journey to nonordinary reality, the world of spirits, in a ceremony that took place in 1985. He goes on to describe incredible adventures that involve meeting and taming a deadly serpent and a giant bear in the Lower World; entering a town of strange elfish beings; finding a wise hermit and a sacred mountain; discovering a tunnel in the center of the mountain leading to the Upper World; riding to the Upper World on the back of a flying blue dragon and arriving finally at the kingdom of the Sun God; being dismembered and burned in the solar furnace; undergoing a shattering

1

death and profound rebirth experience; and ending with a return to the Middle World of ordinary reality on earth as the drumming comes to a halt.

What makes this narrative remarkable is that it is not taken from field notes of initiation rites among native tribes in faraway, exotic lands but is instead the report of a contemporary American student of shamanism living in a modern urban center, describing an experience that occurred during a weekend workshop and drumming session he attended after having spent the previous five days in a busy office.

Why has the ancient path of shamanism captured the attention of this man as well as that of so many others in the West today? Is it merely another passing fad, or does it speak to profound spiritual needs? How does this "archaic technique of ecstasy," as Mircea Eliade describes the shaman's activity, relate to modern problems? For example, can it help in crises or difficult life transitions? Why are increasing numbers of physicians and psychotherapists becoming interested in the shaman's methods? What is the role of shamanism in personal growth and empowerment? Is it relevant to our search for meaning in the wasteland of industrialization and runaway technology? Will it help in healing the planet and preventing ecological catastrophe or nuclear holocaust?

These are just a few of the questions addressed by the leaders of the neo-shamanism movement who have contributed to this collection of previously unpublished articles—which is, I believe, the most comprehensive of its kind available today. Each of these authors is a specialist in a particular branch of shamanic study or practice, and each discusses shamanism from the standpoint of his or her own unique discipline and areas of concern. Thus the book is addressed to many different kinds of readers, both to those whose interests are theoretical as well as to those who wish to learn more about practical "core" shamanism as a tool for healing and personal growth.

Part I, "Shamans and Neo-Shamans," explores topics such as what a shaman is and who should be called a shaman, the difference between shamans and other mystical specialists such as mediums and ceremonial leaders, how a shaman is recognized, shamanic techniques for altering consciousness, shamanic cosmologies, shamanism and religion, the shamanic "journey," the origins and goals of the neo-shamanism movement, and its impact on modern society. Contributors to this section draw on their experiences among native tribal shamans as well as urban neo-shamans around the globe in helping us gain a clearer understanding of the many facets of this complex cultural phenomenon and its relevance to our situation today.

Part II, "Shamanism and Healing," examines why shamanism is generating so much interest among modern health care professionals. With many concrete examples taken from case histories of their patients, authors in this section describe shamanic methods that have proven to be effective and compatible with Western medicine. Some explain how shamanic techniques such as drumming, visualization, and storytelling have been used in treatment programs for a variety of physical problems from back pain to cancer; others describe the use of sacred places or "power spots" in shamanic healing practices; still others examine the role of shamanic techniques in modern psychotherapeutic treatment for many kinds of mental disorders. Here we get a clear view of the essential work of the shaman—relieving human suffering at its most intense physical and emotional levels.

Part III considers shamanism as a path of self-transformation. Chapters here investigate the transpersonal dimensions of shamanism, showing how its methods and assumptions are relevant beyond the treatment of pathological conditions but can also be used to unlock the higher potentials of the human mind and spirit. Authors discuss topics such as shamanic counseling, the role of shamanic stories in the process of individuation, types of shamanic body work, and the relationship between shamanism and the "contemplative" branches of the mystical tradition such as Buddhism and yoga. These writers place shamanism in the context of other spiritual paths, showing its relations to the "perennial" tradition as a whole and revealing how the complete healing sought by shamans involves the same process of spiritual transformation known to mystics of other paths—a journey that involves all aspects of the individual.

As this volume clearly demonstrates, shamanism is alive and well in contemporary society. Indeed, it is no exaggeration to say that Western culture is presently undergoing what might be called a neo-shamanic renaissance. The articles gathered here chronicle the origins and ramifications of this rebirth of shamans in our midst and seek to provide some guideposts that will help the reader investigate the phenomenon further.

Of course, intellectual explanations and analyses such as these are no substitute for personal acquaintance with shamanic techniques and experience, which is only available to those who actually set out on the shamanic journey for themselves. Nevertheless, it is my hope that the collection presented here will stimulate the reader to begin a deeper, more personal exploration of this enduring system of healing and personal empowerment.

I

Shamans and Neo-Shamans

MICHAEL HARNER begins this section with a discussion of what the term *shaman* was originally intended to mean by anthropologists, pointing out that the word was adopted because of its precise meaning, which allows us to maintain a clear distinction between shamans, mediums, and ceremonial leaders such as medicine men and women. A majority of contributors implicitly or explicitly embrace this definition and the distinction between shamans and mediums that it implies, but some prefer a broader definition that would include mediums or "channels" as well—that is, individuals who enter trance states and allow themselves to be "taken over" or "possessed" temporarily by spiritual entities for the purpose of healing or communication. For these authors, the fact that mediums may not recall later what occurred during a trance does not mean that we should exclude them from the category of shamans.

Rowena Pattee sees the primary role of the shaman as a specialist in ecstasy and sacrifice, where *sacrifice* is understood in its orginal sense of "making sacred." Like Harner, she maintains that the true shaman is one who does not allow himself or herself to be possessed by spiritual entities but, on the contrary, often seeks to cure others of such possession. Pattee regards shamanic ecstasy as basically different in nature from Christian mystical experience or from the trance states known as *samadhi* in certain Eastern spiritual traditions, a view in which she differs from some other contributors, such as Doore and Halifax (see Part III).

Åke Hultkrantz discusses the question of whether shamanism is a religious phenomenon, noting the relations between shamanism and magic and between magic and religion. He argues that shamanism can best be characterized as a complex religio-magical cultural phenomenon, but that it is best to disconnect the term *religion* from the idea of an institutionalized priesthood and considerations about sociopolitical structures served by religions. He emphasizes the ability to enter the shamanic state of consciousness as central to the shaman's vocation.

Serge King provides us with a glimpse into the "four worlds" of the

Hawaiian kahuna shaman, using his personal training from an early age in this still-living tradition to illustrate the assumptions underlying the activities of Polynesian shamans. He explains the processes involved in the kahuna shaman's ability to shift between different realities, and shows what can be accomplished by making these shifts.

Felicitas Goodman describes her research into the use of certain bodily postures in facilitating shamanic trance states. Based on experiments with student research subjects and workshop participants using over twenty different postures taken from the pictographs and sculptured images of shamans in a variety of cultures worldwide, she maintains that each of these postures produces its own unmistakable type of visionary phenomena. In examining the possible physiological mechanism by means of which the postures alter consciousness, she describes her own research in Germany, which seems to indicate that the postures increase the brain's production of theta waves and beta-endorphins—the body's own pain-killers.

Anthropologist Jacques Lemoine takes us into the world of the Hmong and Yao shamans of Southeast Asia, describing the rituals, implements, symbols, and assumptions of these shamans as they journey to the land of spirits in search of the lost souls of critically ill patients. He explains the elaborate construction of the cloth "bridge" and its place in the geography of these shamans' altars, which is used as a device for gathering the shaman's "spirit troops" and entering nonordinary reality to do battle with the spiritual powers responsible for soul loss. In this chapter we get a detailed look at native shamans at work and can sense some of the rich variety of specific methods and ideologies found in particular cultures where this ancient path still survives.

In closing this section, Joan Townsend traces the rise of the neo-shamanism movement within the development in the West of the modern mystical movement as a whole, showing its roots in the counterculture of the 1960s and arguing that for its members the movement is more than a mere fad but is a genuine source of meaning and guidance capable of taking the place of traditional religions. She discusses shamanism and the new paradigm of reality emerging from science, maintaining that neo-shamanism contains important spiritual truths and provides methods of achieving the transcendent experiences that so many Westerners are seeking. In her view, neo-shamanism represents a major trend with the potential to dramatically reshape the beliefs of our society.

What Is a Shaman?

MICHAEL HARNER

T HE WORD *shaman* comes from the language of the Tungus tribe in
Siberia. This word was specifically chosen by anthropologists and
given a precise technical definition in order to accurately describe certain
individuals in native societies who perform specific part-time functions in
the community. The advantage of having such an exact technical term is
that its meaning is not mixed up with other very broad and historically
laden words like *wizard, witch doctor, medicine man, medium,* or *psychic.*
Each of these words has certain connotations due to past usage. If we
wish to describe certain people in contemporary Western society as
shamans, we can avoid a lot of confusion by keeping in mind exactly what
the word means.

Mircea Eliade, the great scholar of comparative religion who died in
1986, set forth the definition of a shaman in his classic book *Shamanism.*[1]
According to him, among other characteristics, a shaman is a man or
woman who "journeys" in an altered state of consciousness[2] (which I have
elsewhere called *the shamanic state of consciousness,* or SSC), usually induced
by rhythmic drumming or other types of percussion sound, or in some
cases by the use of psychoactive drugs.[3]

To borrow a term from Carlos Castaneda, the shaman journeys to
"nonordinary reality" in the SSC. Such journeys are generally undertaken
in order to help other people, members of the community, in a number
of different ways. For instance, the shaman may journey for the purpose
of diagnosing or treating illnesses; for divination or prophecy; for acqui-
sition of power through interaction with "spirits," "power animals,"
"guardians," or other spiritual entities; for establishing contact with
guides or teachers in nonordinary reality, from whom the shaman may

7

solicit advice on tribal or individual problems; or for contact with the spirits of the dead. In all these activities, the shaman usually remains conscious and in control of his or her own faculties and will, and typically suffers no amnesia upon returning to ordinary reality.

Shamans and Mediums

There are, of course, traditions other than shamanism in which people change their state of consciousness or contact a personal spirit. So-called trance mediumship is one such case. But in trance mediumship (or "channeling") the spirits come to the medium, who relinquishes voluntary control to the spirits, allowing them to work through his or her body, whether this is by means of automatic writing or through possession of the vocal cords or bodily movements. As Eliade makes clear, however, these are not activities that distinguish *shamanism;* for, by definition, a shaman is a person who journeys *to* the spirits, seeking them out in their own world and remaining in control during the time spent there.[4] In some places in the world, such as the Himalayas, the shamans are often also mediums, but the fact that one person can do both does not make shamanism mediumship.

A basic difference, therefore, is that a medium is a passive instrument but a shaman is not. The medium is generally unconscious of what is happening at the time it is happening, but the shaman remains aware of what is happening at all times, interacting with the spirits as an autonomous individual, under his or her own volition. Therefore the shaman can remember later what took place in the spirit world, whereas the medium generally comes out of the altered state without substantial memory of the events that transpired during the time of possession.

The shaman journeys in nonordinary reality to what are technically called the Upper Worlds and the Lower Worlds—or, in some cases, to parts of the Middle World—for the purpose of helping others. In these journeys the shaman collects valuable information, makes contact and talks with teachers, works with power animals or guardians, helps the spirits of the dead, assists people to make the transition over to a land of the dead, and generally has adventures that he or she consciously experiences and can later recall and interpret to members of the community. Hence, being able to remember what happened in the ssc is crucial to the shaman's function in his or her society. The shamanic journey is therefore really the centerpiece of shamanism. In order to find out whether people are doing shamanism, at least in the classic sense, it is necessary to find out whether they journey—which may be very clear or very subtle—and also whether they can remember later the details of what happened to them on their journey.

It is very common for people to confuse shamanism with the type of work done by medicine men and medicine women in tribal societies. It is easy to be unclear about this because every shaman is a *kind* of medicine person, whereas not all medicine people are shamans. In fact, *most* medicine men and women are not shamans; many fill social roles more like that of priests. An important difference between a shaman and a priest is that a shaman journeys and otherwise works in another reality while in a substantially altered state of consciousness, whereas priests work basically in ordinary reality. For example, in working with spirits, the shaman sees them just as clearly as we see cars and houses and trees in ordinary reality. In fact, most of the important work of the shaman is done in nonordinary reality, where he or she talks with spirits, touches them, and so on. The priest, on the other hand—for instance, a Plains Indian medicine man—although he may have many shamanistic practices (for example, when he goes on a vision quest), nevertheless does his or her main work in ordinary reality, where he or she makes very careful rituals, offerings, and beautiful prayers to the spirits. Shamans generally do not undertake long liturgies and prayers. There are also shaman/priests—people who perform both shamanic and priestly roles at different times. Many medicine people serve both functions. For instance, the Huichol *marikame* is both a shaman and a priest, with the emphasis on one or another function varying from person to person and from situation to situation.

Yet to insist that we keep the meaning of both terms distinct and use them correctly is not in any way intended to make invidious comparisons between shamans and tribal priests. The work done by each has its own beauty and value to the community. It is only to suggest that the differences ought to be kept in mind, because it would be awkward if the meaning of a precise term like *shaman* were to become blurred, so that we could no longer use it to clarify our communications.

Our Shamanic Heritage

Of course, shamans also do other things besides making journeys to nonordinary reality. Some of these things may be thought to be rather strange to most people in our culture, such as talking with plants, animals, and all of nature. It sounds neurotic or deranged, of course, from the perspective of much of Western psychology. Nevertheless, our ancestors did it and managed to survive for three million years, whereas in the "civilized" countries of the world today, where people *don't* talk with the planet and its inhabitants, we are also faced with the possibility of nuclear destruction and ecological catastrophe. From these facts we may draw our own conclusions about which cultural assumptions are the saner.

The shamans say that we need to talk to plants and trees, animals, and rocks because our lives and our spirits are connected with theirs. In shamanic cultures all things are seen to be interrelated and interdependent—and not just what people commonly call "living" things. From a shamanic point of view, everything that exists is alive. But if all things are alive, how do we verify this? By communicating with them in the shamanic state of consciousness, and especially through the journey method.

Although the word *shaman* comes from Siberia, shamanism itself is a worldwide tradition. It has been practiced on all inhabited continents and was only eliminated from the West due to the influence of the Church, such as through the Inquisition, when many shamans were exterminated as "witches," "wizards," and so forth. In fact, it survived in the old form, using the drum for journeying, at least until the 1930s in northern Europe among the Saami or Sami (Laplanders). Shamanism is not an exclusively Eastern or Western spiritual tradition. It is simply our common human tradition that was destroyed when state churches arose, both in the East and the West.

A reason it was wiped out is that it undermines the authority of the state church, or at least the organizers or maintainers of it, to have hundreds and thousands of prophets running around loose. In shamanism everyone is his or her own prophet, getting spiritual revelation directly from the highest sources. Such people rock the boat; they are subversive. After all, if everyone is an authority, there is little possibility of creating a monopolistic business based on privileged access or right to interpret the words of a few official prophets or holy books. Whether we consider the East or the West, there have been many exterminations of shamans by the authorities of state religions of various kinds throughout so-called civilized history. Now we are in an age, at least in America and certain other countries, where the church state does not have the old kind of absolute power. In some cases, of course, it may still have some power—as in northern Scandinavia, where the Lutheran missionaries still forbid the use of the drum among the Laplanders (perhaps because they know that it works!). But in general it is legal to engage in shamanic activities now again in the West. We are coming out of hiding, out of the Dark Ages—and we are going home.

It is not that we are "playing Indian" and trying to adopt an archaic cultural style that does not suit us. Rather, we are simply attempting to "play human" by going back to the saner and healthier world view that we had before the church and the state. Evidence of progress in this return to our shamanic roots can be seen in the fact that now shamanic journeys are being labeled as "guided imagery" or "visualization" and are even accepted in some official medical circles. Nevertheless, it should be noted that the real shamanic journey goes well beyond what is called "guided imagery."

Much prejudice against shamanism still remains, based mainly on misconceptions about what it is. As I have tried to show, shamanism is really just getting back to our common human nature and reconnecting with the plants and animals and the planet itself. Therefore, when people in Western civilization profess that shamanism would be unsuitable for them, they are actually saying—probably without knowing it—that getting spiritually in touch with the planet, other people, all species, and their own hearts and souls is not for them. But I don't think they mean to say that. Instead it seems more likely that they are simply ignorant of what shamanism really is.

The Shaman's Role in the Community

Besides making journeys, seeing, and changing states of consciousness, the shaman is a person who, in a sense, is a public servant. Shamanism is not primarily a system for self-improvement—although that can be one of its uses. In a tribal society the main work of the shaman is for others. If one has shamanic powers and abilities, and if relatives and friends ask for help, the shaman cannot deny it to them. The shaman is not trying only or mainly to achieve self-enlightenment. Shamanism is people directly helping others. It is a kind of spiritual activism in which one works with the powers that connect human beings to the incredible power of the universe—a work that involves journeying and shifting back and forth between realities.

The shaman does not do this kind of work all the time. For the Westerner, who typically has a full-time profession, it is easy to picture the shaman as practicing shamanism for eight hours a day, every day. In fact, however, the shaman is necessarily a part-timer, doing ordinary work such as farming or hunting, food-gathering or weaving, and moving over into nonordinary reality to do shamanism "on call," as it were, in a disciplined and controlled way.

This reason for this is that shamans are in a unique situation: they typically work with constant drumming in order to remain in the ssc, and in that state of consciousness the work is very intensive. It is not possible even to eat a meal. So it is inconceivable that one could be in this kind of altered state of consciousness all day on a regular basis. The shaman must be a part-timer.

Another interesting feature of tribal shamanism is that no shaman of any worth describes himself or herself as a shaman. One reason for this is humility: a recognition that the power involved is not one's own to proclaim but is, as it were, "on loan" from the universe. Thus shamans consider themselves humbly to be farmers or mothers of hunters or whatever. Yet they are different; they do shamanic work. When darkness comes it is easier for the shaman to exclude the stimuli or ordinary reality from entering through the eyes. Then members of the tribe or village come to the shaman, asking for healing or other help. Because shamanic work is so intense, shamans do not usually practice it for more than a couple of hours each night.

Shamans are typically very well grounded in this ordinary reality—so grounded that they can in fact move over into that other dimension with discipline and focus, which is the only way to be effective in helping others. For this reason, those individuals who are commonly hearing voices or seeing things all the time should not enter shamanism but should instead try to do things that will give them a better grounding. They need more ordinary reality, not less of it.

Drumming, Drugs, and the SSC

The idea that all (or even most) shamans rely on psychedelic drugs for their journeys is false. In fact, the areas of the world where shamans use psychedelics to induce their journeys are not nearly as numerous as one might think. The Upper Amazon is one area where shamans depend on psychedelics like ayahuasca to get them into nonordinary reality.[5] In other parts of the Amazon and in the Orinoco basin, they use psychedelic snuff quite extensively. In Siberia the *Amanita muscaria* mushroom has traditionally been considered to be a tool of the shaman, but I found from my investigations in the Soviet Union that the mushroom is normally not used by the real shamans, who use only the drum. It is used by the people who are unable to make the journey with the drum alone.

In fact, the simple, monotonous sound of the drumbeat is the most common vehicle of the shaman's journey, not psychedelics. The drum is well described in the literature of shamanism as being used by shamans all over the world, except for certain places like Australia or Southeast

Asia, where they may use click sticks, or gongs and metal bangles, for percussion sound.

In modern anthropology, the importance of the drum was very much underestimated. Few really thought that the drum had a significant effect in shamanic experience: it was just something that the natives used as an accompaniment to their dancing. However, in doing fieldwork with Northwest Coast Indians, who use only the drum in their shamanic work, I discovered that the drum could in fact take a person to the same place as the psychedelics, just by itself. And, of course, it can do so much more safely and in an integrated way, without the side effects and other hazards associated with drugs. Its effects are much more controllable and precisely predictable than those of strong psychedelics.

A reason the drum is not used in the Upper Amazon for shamanism may be that it is too humid there to keep drum skins taut for a long enough period to complete a journey or a healing without interruption; so it is convenient, from the shamanic point of view, that there are several species of potent psychedelics growing naturally in the region that can induce the shamanic journey without drumming. For the rest of the world, where it is relatively easier to make and use a drum for journeying, this is in fact the shaman's preferred method.

How a Shaman Is Recognized

A shaman is recognized in a variety of different ways. In Siberia, for example, a shaman may inherit the power and knowledge through his or her family. Elsewhere in Siberia, a person may have a serious illness and be expected to die, but then have a miraculous recovery. When that happens, the people of the tribe say that healing power must have come to this person, who would not otherwise have survived the illness, and that maybe the power can be used to overcome the same illness in others. So they go to such a person to see if he or she can help cure the illnesses of others. In this way the shamanic healer can be born.

In other places, such as among the Shuar (Jívaro) in eastern Ecuador, shamans may buy their power from other shamans. In the Conibo tribe of eastern Peru, the shaman may learn primarily from a large tree. There are all sorts of ways that one may become a shaman. It is not true, as some people seem to think, that one must be like Carlos Castaneda and go around asking questions of some guru figure for years and years on end. Actually, this kind of apprenticeship is associated more with tribal priesthoods than with pure or classic shamanism.

Once a person gets in touch with the spirits, there is no need for an ordinary-reality guru, because the spirits supply the answers. The real teachers of the shaman instruct him or her in nonordinary reality. There are no higher authorities.

One of the most interesting things about shamanism is that it is very democratic. All have the potential to get spiritual revelation directly from the highest possible (and nonordinary) sources if they have the methods. It is not necessary to get much secondhand information from ordinary-reality teachers. The human mind, heart, and spirit are lying dormant, waiting for the ancient sound of the drum and for certain basic types of training in order to come alive.

An important aspect of shamanism is that it provides us with an ancient means of solving everyday problems—not just big metaphysical questions or life-and-death issues, but also simple questions. Of course, we do not have exactly the same problems that the ancient shamanic cultures had. For instance, we do not have to learn where the caribou herds are wandering in order to hunt for food successfully. But we might want the answers to questions like "Where should I move?" or "What kind of work should I do as a career?" or "How should I organize my work week?"

We are familiar with inspiration. We have all heard how the great scientists have had revelations, often in daydreams, that gave them the solution to some complicated problem that had them stumped for a long time. There are time-tested techniques whereby you can work on a problem—as you should—in ordinary reality, and then make a journey to your teacher in nonordinary reality to get the answer to your question. In this way you will often get tremendous detail, so that you come back with knowledge for the week, the month, the year . . . whatever you are seeking—perhaps even for a lifetime. There is no need to wait for accidental revelations.

Shamanism is a disciplined way of getting knowledge and help which is based on the premise that we do not have to restrict ourselves to working in one reality, one dimension, when we need assistance. There is a whole other reality to help us in our lives—a reality full of beauty and harmony that is ready to provide us with the same kind of wisdom that we read about in the writings of the great mystics and prophets. We need only to keep an open mind and to make the effort to follow the shaman's path.

NOTES

1. Mircea Eliade, *Shamanism: Archaic Techniques of Ecstasy* (New York: Bollingen Series 76, 1964).
2. Eliade, *Shamanism*, p. 5; e.g., also pp. 347n, 456.

3. See my book *The Way of the Shaman* (New York: Harper & Row, 1980).
4. Eliade, p. 6.
5. See my book *Hallucinogens and Shamanism* (New York: Oxford University Press, 1973).

Ecstasy and Sacrifice

ROWENA PATTEE

Man has no body distinct from his soul.
—WILLIAM BLAKE

M Y HEARTFELT INTEREST is in finding ways whereby the fragmenta-
tion, meaninglessness, uniformity, and blind, conditioned autom-
atization of modern life can be turned around toward a harmonization
of spirit, human and natural. Zen Master Shunryu Suzuki Roshi used to
speak to me about turning civilization around. My conviction is that
the pivot for this turn is found at the source of shamanic ecstasy and
sacrifice. For making this turn, neo-shamanic methods of accessing ecstatic
states of consciousness are needed. I define a neo-shaman as a modern
person whose experiences of dying to the limited self and of the resultant
ecstasy lead to self-empowerment and sacrifice for the benefit of his or her
community.

In a strict sense shamanism has origins in religious experiences of
Siberia and Central Asia, whence the word *shaman* derives. Aboriginal
people use shamanism in psychospiritual healing, in maintaining harmony
with the plant, mineral, and animal kingdoms, and in maintaining cultural
solidarity. In a broader sense, shamanism is the aboriginal heritage of all
of us. Wherever the sources of the universe reach down into the embodi-
ment of the human image in corporeal bodies, the shaman emerges as a
source of ecstatic regenerative powers. Shamanic experience is present in
the lives of those of us in the modern world who are searching for the
whole, the eternal, the ecstatically true embrace of reality amid the
fragmented, chaotic, and false remnants of lost traditions.

Mircea Eliade says that a shaman is a master of ecstasy.[1] Ecstasy is not
only an intrinsic nourishment to the shaman, but a fountain of healing

17

energy to the shaman's whole social order through a connection between spirit and nature. If we take the experience of ecstasy as central to shamanism and see diverse mystical religious traditions as cultural extensions of the ecstatic experience, we can begin to see a common source of religions. I regard shamanism as the aboriginal root of religions. To know our religion in its essence is to empower ourselves with direct ecstatic experiences. Ecstasy and sacrifice I regard as the core of both aboriginal and neo-shamanic empowerment.

The word *ecstasy* comes from the Greek *ekstasis* (to displace, to drive out of one's senses). Out of ecstasy comes sacrifice in the true meaning of the word—that is, "to make sacred." Ecstasy and sacrifice are shamanic experiences needed in the midst of the modern global breakdown of traditions and its resulting disorientation, so that regenerative powers within us can be summoned. Within the shamanic initiation experience, a harmonization of the spiritual, social, and natural worlds takes place. The emergence of new forms of global culture depend upon this harmonization.

I shall now discuss the meaning of ecstasy and sacrifice in the context of cultures that are rooted in shamanism. In this discussion I shall relate how shamanic ecstasy and sacrifice are found in many forms of religious traditions.

Ecstasy

What is shamanic ecstasy? Both shamanism and certain mystical religious traditions use the term *ecstasy*. In a recent interview the Sufi teacher Pir Vilayat Inayat Khan said, "I like to call Sufism the metaphysics of ecstasy."[2] He went on to say that the shifting from our ordinary vantage point to the divine vantage triggers off ecstasy. If ecstasy is human consciousness shifted to the divine vantage, we need to ask: what are the characteristics of this vantage?

The following six questions will help to define ecstasy and also to reveal both what certain religious traditions share with shamanism and how they differ from it. I shall first discuss all six questions and then draw some conclusions.

1. Is ecstasy synonymous with trance or a state using trance methods?
2. Is ecstasy attained through silent, immobile, and solitary practices or through methods using sound, movement, and communal activities?

3. Is ecstasy experienced consciously or unconsciously? Can the shaman remember the trance experience?
4. Is ecstasy experienced as a magical flight or journey, as a union with divinity, or as an experience of voidness?
5. Is ecstasy a clairsentient experience of visions and voices, or an experience devoid of such phenomena?
6. Is ecstasy a state of inspiration or of possession?

The first question is whether ecstasy and trance are synonymous. Before discussing this, I might note that many writers use the word *trance* to mean spirit-possession; I shall discuss possession later when addressing the sixth question.

I. M. Lewis, in an anthropological study of spirit-possession and shamanism, regards *ecstasy* and *trance* as synonymous.[3] Also in Duncan MacDonald's translation of the Sufi poet Ghazzali, he describes the Arabic word *waid* as "ecstasy or trance-like state."[4] When describing the Brazilian *candomblé* in Bahia, Roger Bastide uses the French terms *transe* and *extase* as practically synonymous.[5] Mircea Eliade also uses the terms interchangeably as when he says that among the Samoyeds, great shamans undertake the ecstatic journey in a trance.

The second question is whether ecstasy is attained through what in religious traditions is called prayer and meditation or what in shamanic traditions are excitatory methods. The silence, solitude, and immobility of the practices of prayer and meditation are in direct opposition to the dancing, singing, and drumming of the shaman.

For example, among the Pygmies of Malaysia the shaman obtains trance and the state of ecstasy by dancing. Also, in the American Ghost-Dance religion of the nineteenth century, the members of the fraternity danced continuously for five or six days in which there was singing but no drumming. On the other hand, in Bhakti Yoga, a song is *silently* transmitted from guru to disciple as a way to attain *dhyana*, the fullest state of ecstasy.

According to Gilbert Rouget, Teresa of Ávila uses the word *ecstasy* (Spanish *éxtasis*) but distinguishes ecstasy's two aspects: union and ravishment.[6] Ravishment, she says, "goes far beyond union" and is a state wherein "the whole body is broken and can move neither feet nor arms; if it is standing it collapses as though drawn downward by some great force and can scarcely breathe." The Christian mystic's ravishment is an immobility that goes beyond union with the Godhead, contrary to shamanic ecstasy, where union with a supreme God is not spoken of.

Is religious chanting similar to shamanic drumming and singing with the purpose of invoking a trance state? The Sufi state of *fana* is an annihilation in God sought by the practice called *dhikr*, the chanting of the name of Allah. The Japanese repetition of the *nembutsu* is similar. Louis Gardet associates the Sufi *fana* with *samadhi* (the absolution of all action). Yet the chanting of the Sufis and Japanese Buddhists is more similar to shamanic rhythmic drumming and singing than to the yogic practice leading to *samadhi* wherein all action is abolished.

The purpose of shamanic ecstasy is to obtain insight in order to cure and guide souls. Union with or annihilation of the personal self in God is distinctly a religious, not a shamanic, experience, but both shamanic and certain religious mystical traditions use dance, song, and drumming to induce ecstasy.

The third question is whether ecstasy has the effect of consciously or unconsciously awakening the participant to higher energy states toward ultimate reality. Certain forms of channeling and of possession by spirits are characterized by total amnesia of the experience, whereas other forms of both immobile practices (prayer and meditation) and frenzied practices (shamanic drumming, chanting, dancing) of ecstasy are fully conscious.

Although some writers refer to unconscious states of shamans while in trance, I regard this state as possession rather than ecstasy. In healing through the ecstatic trance, the shaman finds the cause of an illness and the exact method for the cure. Therefore, memory of the ecstatic experience is essential for enacting the treatment, though sometimes shamans are unwilling or unable to actually speak about the ecstatic trance experience. The state of amnesia I regard as a state of possession wherein the will of the participant is set aside, whether in religions or shamanism.

The fourth question is whether ecstasy is an experience of magical flights into a "journey" or one of stabilizing one's faculties in a state of being that abolishes all sense of the personal self. Mircea Eliade used the word *enstasis* as a state of samadhi wherein a state of pure being is attained.[7] He thus distinguishes samadhi from ecstasy. Also, Patanjali (second century B.C.), the renowned authority on yoga in India, speaks of *samadhi* as complete absorption in a oneness that excludes thoughts and sense impressions.

The fourth question has more to do with whether the soul returns and unites with the source as pure being or whether it continues its quest of it. The experiences of the plenitude of being (Teresian ravishment) or the void of nonbeing (Buddhist *shunyata*, Sufi *fana*) may be distinguished from the visionary experiences of shamanic "journeys," which Eliade refers to as the magical flight of the soul.

The Greek term *ekstasis* refers to the experiencing of the action of moving through space and thus is more similar to the shamanic journey or "magical flight" of the soul of the shaman. Eliade cites many cases of both South Amerindians and Altainians in ascending and descending to normally invisible realms to either heal or guide the ill or deceased soul to its proper place in the universe.

Magical flights are also prevalent in the myths and mystical techniques of India. Traveling immense distances in a flash and disappearing or flying like a bird are some of the powers that Hindus attribute to kings, magicians, and *arhats*. Flying through the air is one of the powers *(siddhis)* obtained by yogins, according to Patanjali. Accounts also abound in Chinese literature and art of immortals and beings who can fly through the air. The Bön shamans of Tibet use their drums as vehicles to convey them through the air.

The fifth question is whether ecstasy is a state wherein visions and clairaudient information are experienced or whether it is void of such phenomena. This is similar to the fourth question but concerns more the accompanying clairsentient effects of shamanic journeys as opposed to the experience of annihilation of the self. The initiatory visions of a Siberian shaman include being a witness to the dismemberment and renewal of his own body as well as visions of diverse spirits. Often these experiences appear wholly real, though psychologists may label them hallucinatory.

Many Christian mystics and Sufis also experience supersensible visions and voices that modern psychologists might call hallucinations. I distinguish clarisentient phenomena from hallucinations insofar as true visions and voices may either be verified, as in parapsychological experiments, or give authentic directives in the lives of those experiencing them. The proof of such authentic experiences would be that they reveal an integrating and beneficent effect on the life of the person experiencing them as well as those around them.

Clairsentient reality has a time of its own. In other words, many experiences of clairsentient events may occur within a few seconds or minutes of clock time. Henri Corbin, in discussing the clairvoyant vision of the Angel of the Earth, speaks of a faculty of imagination that is beyond the imaginary (arbitrary and unreal) when he says, "The active imagination thus induced will not produce some arbitrary, even lyrical, construction standing between us and 'reality,' but will, on the contrary, function directly as a faculty and organ of knowledge just as real as—if not more real than—the sense organs."[8] Corbin's statement may account for the authenticity of real visionary experiences as opposed to hallucinatory ones.

The sixth question is whether ecstasy is a state wherein the participant is inspired or possessed. Eliade makes the distinction when he says, "The difference between a person spontaneously and temporarily 'possessed' and a prophet lies in the fact that the latter is always 'inspired' by the same god or the same spirit, and that he can incarnate it at will."[9]

I am using the term *shaman* for one who is inspired rather than possessed. The willingly induced state of the inspired I take to be more the state of both the shaman and religious mystics whom Eliade calls prophets, whereas the involuntary state of possession is more like a psychotic state. Although both the shaman and religious mystics may have been possessed during their "call," their empowerment lies in the fact that they have overcome the involuntary, helpless, victimized state of spirit-possession and are cured. The shaman seeks to cure possession, not be possessed.

In religious traditions only the inspired are truly considered transmitters of the truth. In religions more often than in shamanism, however, there is emphasis on the transmission of the teachings from an original prophet or inspired one (Muhammad, Moses, Buddha, Jesus, Rama, and so forth) rather than on continuing direct revelation and inspiration for subsequent followers. The shaman, like religious prophets and teachers, is an inspired, powerful being.

What I infer about shamanism from this analysis of the different qualities of ecstasy is the following:

1. Shamanism uses trance methods whereas only certain forms of religion use them. I use the term *ecstasy* to mean a state of being attained through trance methods.

2. Shamanism shares with certain forms of religious tradition excitatory methods of inducing ecstasy but differs from those using solitude, silence, and immobility in their methods. Historically, both active and quiet, solitary and communal practices can lead to ecstasy, though sometimes for distinctly different purposes.

3. Shamanism shares the experience of conscious trance states with some forms of religions.

4. Shamanic ecstasy, unlike the ecstasy of certain religious traditions such as the Buddhist *samadhi*, the Sufi *fana*, and the Christian "beatific state," is a state of "journeying" or magical flight.[10] In shamanic ecstasy the emphasis is on mystical journeys to the Upper World or Lower World to see the spirits, gods and demons face to face.

5. Shamanic ecstasy, like some religious traditions but unlike others, includes clairsentient phenomena such as visions and voices wherein directives or information is obtained for a

healing or the spiritual heightening of solidarity in the community.

6. Shamanic ecstasy, like religious ecstasy, is a state of inspiration rather than possession.

Sacrifice

The shaman receives his or her power and clarity from an ecstatic state of being, and the natural expression of ecstasy is sacrifice. Sacrifice, which means "to make sacred," is an exchange between the spiritual and material realms. I shall give some correspondences and differences among shamanic practices and certain religious mystical experiences.

Among aboriginal cultures, sacrifice is an act of substitution wherein something from the animal, plant, or mineral kingdom is offered to the spirits who can effect a cure for one or more human beings. Usually the offering is an animal when a human victim is suffering from an illness caused by spirit-possession. Among the Hausa of Nigeria, the act of sacrificing an animal symbolizes a pact between the animal and sacrificer. The spirit is said to accept the blood of the animal in place of human blood.

Blood is often the mystic substance through which sacrifices are made. The Christian sacrifice of Jesus on the cross is remembered through the holy communion of the offering of the wine and bread of the Eucharist, substituting for the blood and body of Jesus. Both the sacrifice of Jesus for assuaging the sins of humanity and the sacrifice of wine and bread are substitutions of one identity for another.

The Christian sacrifice has older and deeper roots in the Egyptian Osirian religion and in the Greek Orphic and Dionysian mysteries. Osiris is the ancient Egyptian Pharaoh who was slain, dismembered, and then resurrected to conceive a warrior-king son, Horus. Osiris' sacrifice was one of the flesh in order to give birth to the spirit through his son, so that balance should rule in the kingdom.

In Greek myths, Orpheus and Dionysus are noted for their shamanic use of dance and music to induce ecstatic states that dissolve and melt distinctions. The Dionysian and Orphic ecstasy was induced through enthusiastic fullness rather than asceticism, though purification was at the heart of it. Dionysus was torn to pieces by the Titans while his heart was rescued by Athena, goddess of wisdom, suggestive of the wisdom born of the dismemberment experience.

Sacrifice leads to a renewal from the dismembered limbs in these as in many shamanic accounts of initiation. Therefore, I take the meaning of sacrifice to be deeper than the apparent offerings of the blood of animals for spirits and deities. Behind the shamanic animal sacrifice stands the meaning of sacraments in general, wherein a spiritual reality supersedes the apparent distinctions of natural created entities. Those who receive the sacrament of the Christian Eucharist participate in a mystical Body of Christ. The offering of incense to the Buddha on a Zen altar is a participation in the *Bodhi* body, the enlightenment that contains and embraces all sentient beings. An offering remains tangibly the same object but it changes its meaning and form according to spiritual perspectives.

The crucial element to the successful substitution of identities in sacrifice is ecstasy, wherein the limited vantage of one's senses expands into the divine vantage. The person is simultaneously aware of a limited vantage where the identities are separate and an ecstatic, divine vantage where the separate identities are, in essence, identical. The oneness of the ecstatic experience enables the initiate to see and experience from a divine viewpoint, and therefore to see and experience how the spirit world, the human world, and the nature world are wholly one in essence, though different in appearance.

When an imbalance occurs among the human, spiritual, and natural worlds, the spiritual world demands an offering. This demand appears in the form of an illness or a failure of crops or in hunting or some "accident" that causes suffering to those on earth. Eliade says, "Only he [the shaman] 'sees' the spirits and knows how to exorcise them; only he recognizes that the soul has fled, and is able to overtake it, in ecstasy, and return it to its body. Often the cure involves various sacrifices, and it is always the shaman who decides if they are needed and what form they shall take; the recovery of physical health is closely dependent on restoring the balance of spiritual forces."[11]

The balancing of the spirit, human, and nature worlds is the shaman's business in aboriginal cultures. It is also the "business" of religious mystics and priests. Such balancing necessitates both ecstasy and sacrifice. Eliade says that shamanic cure involves ecstasy because illness is regarded as an alienation of the soul. The self-alienated cannot experience ecstasy, for ecstasy is a shining of the spirit through the soul, body, and mind. On the contrary, the self-alienated are divided against themselves.

In the shamanism of Australia and North America, many of the spirits have animal forms that the shaman imitates in his dance and cries during a trance induction, so that the shaman and the spirit-animal can "speak" to one another in "spirit language." This is a shamanic demonstration that the shaman can penetrate veils between the spirit, human, and nature worlds, and can "die" to his limited human viewpoint. This "death" is the key to the sacrificial action that opens the doors between the worlds whereby any imbalance can be rectified. The literal object of sacrifice—whether human, animal, plant, or mineral—is a qualitative symbol that magically opens the doors between worlds for the shaman.

The deeper meaning of sacrifice is to "die" to a fixed, limited viewpoint, and come into a way of experiencing and seeing that envelops the triple worlds of spirit, human, and nature. It naturally follows that rectification of imbalances occurs through the energy generated from the inner shift of viewpoint. The expanded perspective is spontaneously a state of ecstasy, and results in the enactments and offerings that balance the triple worlds. In our modern world this is the empowerment that results from seeing with loving eyes and compassionate heart so that actions in daily life spring from a sense of mutual identity.

In a broad sense, sacrifice is the enactment that comes from the experience of ecstasy. Such sacrifice is not victimization but a conscious and voluntary offering, a reciprocation to the sources of life through giving to others in the universe.

Ecstasy, Sacrifice, and Triple Worlds

We can now see that the modern resurrected interest in shamanism is in linking a spiritual world to nature through human consciousness. In this sense, culture and civilization result from and are maintained by the qualities of the shamanic and mystic experiences of ecstasy and sacrifice. For there is no culture or civilization that has endured without ecstatic and sacrificial enactments that link the spiritual, human, and natural worlds, which the ancient Chinese called "heaven/man/earth." The human realm cannot survive without balanced relations with both spirit and nature. This implies that modern technologies, organizations, and ways of life that are not in accordance with heaven and earth, with spirit and nature, will cause suffering in all three worlds. Ecological concerns are spiritual concerns, and spiritual insight leads to taking care of all life.

Basic universal laws are not different in the modern world from what they have been during the rise and fall of ancient and medieval civilization or during times of aboriginal hunting-and-gathering societies. From my studies of religions, cultures, and shamanism, I see that the interconnection of the triple worlds of spirit, human, and sentient nature is universal. The spirit world becomes infernal when imbalances occur among these realms. In the modern world infernal spirits appear as psychosis, crime, war, and their many apparent causes such as hunger, poverty, territorial conflict, and business competition. Shamanism touches these imbalances between worlds close to their core. There is no domain of human interest that shamanism does not touch, for its world view is of an interconnected whole. Therefore I regard ecstasy as an experiential pivot point and sacrifice as an experiential lever for turning modern civilization around.

What is described as the "magical flight" in shamanism is a journey of the soul through ecstatic experience. The power to turn the world around is in actual experience, in what can be practiced and known, not in what is believed or hoped for. Belief and hope are carrots dangled in front of our noses by many religions as well as businesses, and often prevent the actual plunge into the reality of experience. The ecstatic experience may have many names and methods, but its core is an experience of wholeness of the triple worlds of spirit, human, and nature. I invite you now to take a plunge with me into the River of Life.

The River

I am watching the currents of modern civilization and wondering how it can be cured of the basic self-alienation that creates stress and fragmented lives.

I hear the drumming sound of freeways and factories. The drumming is at first so loud as to be deafening, but as I listen deeply within I hear a drumming that comes from my heart. My vision fades into an all-permeating clear blue light, and within the blue light I see the Clackamas River, where I swam as a child.

I find myself freely swimming in the clear currents and diving into the depths. The colors change as I go deeper, from silver blue to green and dark aqua with flashes of brown and yellow. Fishes abound, darting here and there, playing. Playing. My body is slim and light, moving in the waters like the fish. When I emerge, the water glistens in the sunlight, and I sit on a rock by the river, watching and listening.

Silent and in awe, I watch and see the patterns of change in the river. My body changes from a child to a woman in her fifties. The River speaks to me:

> *You have been by my banks many times in skins of all colors during different times. You are a shaman, and because your heart is a drum that beats for the entire earth you can speak to me and hear me. I go by many names, Yenisey, Loire, Irrawaddy, Mississippi, Yukon. I am not limited to this time or this place. I am the voice of the river, the life-force that carries shamans from the Promethean peaks through the blazing ecstasy of death into caves of remembrance. I am the current that carries bodies through time, that reflects images of history and that dissolves all*

resistance to truth. I reflect everything equally. I am the constancy of change where laws find unequivocal proof in my patterns while matter flows through me. I am time and eternity, the chant that echoes down through history and is silenced in mystery. I am the current that the shaman rides.

I reply to the river: "If I am a shaman, why don't I know it? It is true that the status quo doesn't fit me, but I'm confused about being a shaman."

Again the River speaks:

You have not yet remembered yourself fully. The shaman within you remembers the eternal. Some think that the eternal is in the moment of death when the tide in your life turns to essence and mist and clouds are distilled from my sea-womb. When I rise into the air I become invisible, but that is only the cessation of a form. You call it death. But death does not bring eternity. The eternal is all-intelligent, but death never made anyone more intelligent than he was in life. The eternal is present in both life and death. Eternity is in each living instant of my flow, but it can only be known in ecstasy. Ecstasy is a union of time and eternity through love. Then, when opposites unite, your life covers everything. When you experience this, you will realize you are a shaman.

"What do you mean by your 'sea-womb'? Are you not only the river, but all forms of the water cycle? How do I know where you begin and end?"

The sea is both my womb and my tomb. The sea is the place where shamans die to time and all of history is bathed and purified by waves. In my sea waters the entire world process returns to the primal ground of being and nonbeing. The divide between self and otherness is then dissolved in my Sea and the peaks and valleys of my waves become a travel guide for the shaman's soul.

"How is it that shamans die to time and yet can travel by means of waves?"

In my sea the unessential in the shaman's life is dissolved or else sinks to become the dance of matter. Matter is pure resonance of my sea-waves. When the shaman dies to fixed identities and appearances, she can read the patterns of resonance as a language. Otherwise the dance of matter is terrifying, for it appears a chaos, confusion, hopelessness. To take the plunge into my sea depths is to dare to know the unknown, the deep unconscious and the foundation of your body and all bodies. The authentic of the shaman's life then dawns. The soul longs for ecstasy and freedom, but this is possible only if it dies to attachment to limited self-images. For the ecstatic flight and journey the shaman needs a spirit guide.

"How can a spirit-guide be found?"

By invoking a spirit-guide, by clarifying your intention, and by releasing the last stronghold on your fixed self-images. Open to the great world of spirit. The Sky is the spirit. Yet spirit is in all of nature. There is no place the spirit does not go. When humans abuse nature, it is because shamans have not remembered themselves, it is because spirit has not been listened to or seen.

"Who are the shamans now?"

Anyone who listens to the spirit and lives accordingly.

"How can I know the current shamans?"

You will know shamans by how they take care of nature, how they care for themselves, and how they take care of the creatures and plants on earth. In the modern world shamans are artists, housewives, doctors, students, people of any profession who act out of the ecstasy of love. Shamans know the spirit world directly. Otherwise the spirit world is only a belief. Belief can only hope for truth, love, peace, or beauty, for it cannot perform or enact directly out of the spirit world. You can see spirit anywhere if you have eyes to see. Look into the surface of my back here.

I looked and saw the river become still and clear as a mirror. There I saw a great tree reflected in the still waters. My question was answered: that spirit and nature are mirror aspects of one essence. In awe of the simplicity of this awareness, I asked, "How can you be so still in some places and so turbulent in others?"

It is my way. I move as people and circumstances, as the laws of nature dictate. Where there is resistance I am turbulent. Where there is ease and harmony I am still. Crime, disease, poverty, hatred, war—all are forms of resistance where spirit and nature cannot be known. The shaman connects spirit, human, and nature through ecstasy and sacrifice.

"What is sacrifice?"

Sacrifice is the remembrance of my source in the sky. Sacrifice is a return of my distilled essence as clouds to the earth in rain. Sacrifice is simultaneously a distillation of my deep matter in the sea upward to the sky. Sacrifice is the natural exchange and circulation of spirit and matter, matter and spirit. Sacrifice is seeing the wholeness of my flow as sacred and acting accordingly.

"The modern world is being sacrificed to itself. How is it that the modern world is so distressed and so bound up in a frantic drive for more time and more money?"

The mad rush of modern cities is the hastening toward the shamanic death, the turning point of the long suffering of history. Unless this turning point and limit are seen, people become victimized rather than giving sacrifice. Victimization is annihilation, whereas sacrifice is a flow between the spiritual and material worlds. Rushing faster and faster into time, modern man's time is forever rushing away. When living time as quantity, as lifetimes, years, months, weeks, days, hours, minutes, and seconds forever disappearing into zero, modern people never have enough time for anything. Time is my flow, but no time-saving devices can ever catch up with my flow. Human consciousness is enslaved by the expectation of an ever-vanishing end. Only sacrifice can master time, for sacrifice is the exchange between spirit and matter whereby all things are balanced in the eternal present.

"How can the eternal present be experienced?"

The experience of the eternal present is ecstasy, which naturally leads to sacrifice. Slow down, sit down, lie down, go down to my depths and listen to the sounds of your own soul. Everyone who truly wants to can go deep into my waters and find the eternal present directly. In my depths are slow tides in the utmost darkness where ideals, promises, and hopes cease. Allow your soul to journey with the still tides where the self-created dies to itself. All else is desire where all the mirages of history are reflected on my surface and suffering sustains itself.

Hearing the beating of the drum of my heart, I hesitated at the edge of the river and then I dove down to the river's depths. For a moment I felt my uterus and brain at one with both underground pools and the firmament. Disoriented, I knew that I was dying and yet I felt incorruptible. I saw flashes of images of the entire length of my life. Soon after, I heard a thunderous clap and all images ceased.

Silence, mystery, nothingness.

Vast openness nowhere. I felt my boundaries beyond dimensions break into pure ground. My body was fanning out into a limitless universe. I struck the bottom of the One Sea where mind has no limit. As I drifted upward will-lessly, impalpable, translucent, unearthly colors shimmered within my vast body. The whole extent of my awesome body now focused to a central point at the core of the earth, celestial vermilions, magentas, indigos, ceruleans, viridians, creating an ecstatic song beyond sensation. Was this a dream? The "sound" of color rose like ambrosia up through subterranean channels into continents and nations throughout the earth. I experienced the sound of colors of my soul permeate the mountains and valleys of China, the rivers and deserts of Egypt, and the vast steppes of Russia. My body was bone of the earth, flesh of the creatures, blood of the seas, breath of the skies—broken in a thousand fragments yet shimmering in fields of energy beyond form. My bloodstream was filled with communion. I saw the colors of myself as the soul of China, Greece, Europe, Africa, India, Australia, the Oceanic Islands, and the Americas. The shimmering shades of colors moved in great chants beyond the surface of the whole earth and out into the firmaments and beyond.

When I returned from this journey into the depths I found myself lying in the sand beside the sea. I sat up and was surprised at the continuing feelings of being here and yet nowhere and everywhere at once. I felt immense gratitude and humility. Blinking my eyes I asked the River, who now appeared as the Sea, "Was I asleep? Was it all a dream? How could I experience the whole earth?"

Dream is the brother of death, and sleep is their father. You have bathed in my depths. Ecstasy is conscious sleep. My boundaries are not linear. You have experienced the Celestial Earth, the earth known only to shamans. By following the procession of your own death you can hear the transcendent requiem that is behind death and that can eradicate the conflict of all nations. The many white waves breaking on my shores are the myths of the ages, driven up by deep tides and thundering down their testaments before ceasing and sinking back into my primordial womb. In my womb and your soul are the seeds, the patterns for a global civilization. In my depths are the seeds being prepared for a time when shamans will prepare the ground for a new era, where time and eternity meet in each moment. Already the crimes and sins, the possessions and addictions are being reversed in time, for in the eternal there are great light beings who move unhindered in dissolving the unreal. The gesticulating negative thought-forms springing from human desires have created demons in increasing numbers in recent ages and now are being erased through my upward current. Shamans can see the upward current where time reverses and all wounds are healed. Shamans can transform the limited into the limitless. Be true to your own soul and you will find the Celestial Earth and help bring it to life in manifest form.

"How can such splendor of vision and ecstasy become manifest?"

Through sacrifice, the temporary substitution of the world of matter for the world of the spirit so that a fusion of spirit and matter can be revealed. Then my complete flow will be revealed and humans will move with ease through all the phases of my life. The fusion of opposites comes through the sacrifice of the shaman. The shaman can bring the soul's ecstatic journey and deathless power back into time, back into people's lives, back into the community and world of forms. This, then, will be the Celestial Earth made manifest.

NOTES

1. Mircea Eliade, *Shamanism, Archaic Techniques of Ecstasy* (New York: Bollingen Foundation, 1964).
2. *Meditation Magazine* 2, no. 2.
3. I. M. Lewis, *Ecstatic Religion: An Anthropological Study of Spirit Possession and Shamanism* (New York: Penguin Books, 1971.)
4. Duncan MacDonald, *Journal of the Royal Asiatic Society*, 1901.
5. Roger Bastide, *Le Candomblé de Bahía (Rita Nago)* (Paris: Mouton, 1958); quoted by Gilbert Rouget in *Music and Trance* (Chicago: University of Chicago Press, 1985).
6. Rouget, *Music and Trance*, p. 6.
7. Mircea Eliade, *Techniques of Yoga* (Paris: Gallaimard, 1959), p. 93.
8. Henri Corbin, *Spiritual Body and Celestial Earth* (Princeton, N.J.: Princeton University Press, 1977.)
9. Eliade, *Shamanism*, p. 371.
10. See the chapter by Doore, page 217, for a different view.—Ed.
11. Eliade, *Shamanism*, p. 216.

Shamanism: A Religious Phenomenon?

ÅKE HULTKRANTZ

THE QUESTION POSED in the title of this chapter may on first sight appear superfluous. Who cares if shamanism is religious or profane in nature, if it is just a technique for overcoming nature, or if it is a mysterious phenomenon in the messy bogs of supernaturalism?

Certainly scholars have not been overly concerned with this question. Shamanism was originally known to us through Russian accounts of the ethnography of North Siberian peoples. Contemporary Soviet scholars, however, do not usually involve themselves in discussions about the quality of the shamanic ideological world; instead, they refer to the economic and social background of aboriginal shamanism and to its connection with what they call "ethnogenesis"—the origins of tribes and nations. Western scholars, on the other hand, are mostly interested in the shaman's role in community and in shamanic personalities. There is, however, general agreement that shamanism utilizes methods through which certain "irrational" goals may be realized—or may appear to be realized—without using the instruments of our scientific methodologies. Thus, scholarly interest concentrates more on shamanic methods than on ideology.

Still, the problem is there: is shamanism a religious phenomenon? And if it is not, then what is it? In the long run this issue is important, for it refers to humanity's search for an extended or changed reality.

Shamanism is today a serious subject, for two reasons. First, in the wake of the general crisis in traditional religions, professional anthropologists and students of religion have increased their investigations in the shamanic field and have aligned the ecstatic features of shamanism with

33

similar features in other cultural and religious areas. Even medical investigators are now paying attention to shamanism as an alternative medicine.[1] Second, there is a growing of interest in shamanism among the general public, where it is seen as a path to the unknown, whatever the ideological preferences. The itineraries of popular American Indian and Eastern shamans, and in particular Michael Harner's courses on applied shamanism, testify to the width and intensity of this interest.

But both the theoretical and the practical approaches to shamanism involve the problem of what world view is connected with traditional shamanism, or what different world views may be said to characterize the complex of shamanic practices. Here is indeed a problem we cannot pass over. It is a question of both the unity and meaning of shamanism. In this chapter, therefore, an attempt will be made to answer the question of whether shamanism is a religious phenomenon, and to point out the complexity and ramifications of this question. The basic issue, of course, is the precise nature of the relation between shamanism and religion: is it a relation of identity, similarity, cause/effect, or what?

Shamanism, Magic, and Religion

The shaman became a familiar figure in the world of scholarship during the nineteenth century. Russian descriptions from the seventeenth and eighteenth centuries have paved the way for a greater recognition of this enigmatic North Eurasian figure. Incidentally, the Russian empress Catherine the Great composed a jocular novel about the shaman.[2] The discoveries of the nineteenth century further clarified the import of shamanism, and the evolutionist thinker John Lubbock (Lord Avebury) made it one of the stages in his progressive scale of religious ideas.[3] Later publications by Russian, Polish, Scandinavian, German, and British scholars presented shamans in their ethnographical setting.

During this time, the recognition that shamanism was a rather general complex in the history of mankind was slowly spreading. If we disregard the early American concept of shamanism, formulated by Roland Dixon, according to which there is no difference between a shaman and an ordinary medicine man or woman, shamanism became a catchword for all phenomena centered on a charismatic figure of the Siberian (Tungus) type of mystical specialist.[4] The range of shamanic phenomena was presented in such detail that, with the additional information now available, we may accept it as valid today.

The shaman may accordingly be defined as an inspired visionary who, on behalf of the society he serves, and with the assistance of his guardian spirits, enters into a deep trance in which his dreaming ego establishes relations with spiritual powers.[5]

The first documents on shamanism characterized the shaman as a sheer juggler and imposter, a person who understood how to attain social fame and economic privileges through conjuring tricks. (Certainly, some Soviet ethnologists hold similar judgments today!) Somewhat later, in classical descriptions and subsequent theoretical works, the shaman was described as a magician and shamanism as magic. For example, even in such a late work as Wilhelm Schmidt's treatise on the origins of theism, which discusses the Siberian shamans, the author emphasizes the magical character of shamanism, which he maintains is a late, degenerated religious phenomenon.[6]

If by *magic* we mean the efforts of a human being (the magician) to control the course of events by nonrational means, mostly in the form of enforced ritual actions designed to affect spirits, gods, and the secrets of nature, then the shaman is certainly a magician in this sense. However, it would scarcely be appropriate to reduce shamanism to magical practice. The same authors who emphasize shamanic magic curiously enough often claim that shamanism is a religion, a total religious system. Thus we hear from respected scholars that the religion of the North Siberians is shamanism.[7] As I shall explain shortly, however, this is an exaggeration, because shamanism can only be called a complex of notions and practices within a religion, not religion itself.[8] Nevertheless, the nomenclature discloses that there is something more to shamanism than just magic.

There are indeed many traits in the shamanic complex that have a patently religious character. The shaman's experiences are connected with the appearance of ghosts, spirits, and gods. He visits the realms of the heavenly powers and the land of the dead, and is in his turn visited by spirits, to whom he may conduct sacrifices. It is too strong to say that he always forces the powers to act; but at least he tries to persuade them or implores them to do so—which does not exclude his frequent initiation of actions against them on behalf of his tribesmen. We must not forget that the shaman's foremost task is to mediate between his human associates and the spirit world.

It is in particular the merit of Mircea Eliade to have defined the many ways in which the shamanic complex of beliefs, rituals, and myths is connected with religion.[9] Eliade illuminates such religious features as the calling of the shaman by the spirits, the granting of shamanic powers by spirits or the Supreme Being, the cosmic symbolism of the shaman's dress and drum, and the cosmology of three world tiers (heaven, earth, and underworld) connected by the world tree or world pillar. This cosmology is certainly widespread, but it is essential to refer it to shamanism, for only shamans may induce out-of-body journeys to the three realms. (It is another matter whether shamanism created this cosmology. I do not think so, for the ideas of an underworld are missing in several shamanic hunting societies.)

Another feature connected with shamanism is, as I have tried to show elsewhere, soul dualism, or the belief in two alternating soul formations, one—consisting of one or several souls—representing the vitality of body, breath, and mind, and the other being the person himself in his out-of-body appearance during dream and trance.[10] It is usually the latter that makes the shaman's ecstatic soul flight.

It is thus justifiable to call shamanism a religio-magical cultural complex. But magic, as most students of religion and many anthropologists see it, is a deviation from the general religious orientation, and hence it is basically an ingredient of established religion. Indeed, one and the same rite, such as the holy communion in Christianity, may have both a magical and religious significance for an individual. Thus it is *magical* as it means taking part of the divine presence by direct action, and it is *religious* as it means receiving it as an act of divine grace. It is therefore difficult to decide what is magic and what is religion.

At the same time, it has become more and more clear that magic is not as self-evident and "rude" as most people think. It is a ritual expression of a world view, and as such is a contribution to the cosmic balance, involving also humanity and its closer world. It is not easy to say what is reverential submission and what is wishful anticipation in such a ritual configuration.

The Religious Quality of Shamanism

After these considerations it seems possible to speak about the religious quality of shamanism. The use of the label *religion*, however, needs further elaboration. When some eastern European authors exclude shamanism from the range of religious phenomena, they do so because in their vocabulary *religion* is supposed to mean institutionalized religion with a priesthood and a growing class society. In this light, shamanism is of course a prereligious phenomenon.[11] Such a concept of religion, however, seems rather arbitrary.

From my point of view it appears best to disconnect a definition of religion from such extraneous fetters as sociopolitical structure. The most common definition is: a belief in gods and spirits, and in actions (rituals) and narratives or texts (myths, legends) inspired by such a belief. But while this definition says something about the manifest objects of religious belief, it leaves the *essence* of religion—the underlying meaning—out of perspective.

Anthropologists speak of sacred places here, sacred drama there, supernatural beings somewhere else. But all these places, occurrences, and beings appear in many publications without any palpable justification, or merely as explanations of wrong reasoning and misplaced feelings. This dismembered concept of religion is today welcome among those anthropologists who want to fragmentize religious phenomena into world view, ritual, miscellaneous beliefs, and so forth. It serves their interest to assess such manifestations as epiphenomena of social ideas and actions—fantasies nourished by these ideas and actions—and nothing else.

Against this view of religion as a hotchpotch of diverse spirits and gods, sacred places, and supernatural occurrences, some authors, including myself, have launched the idea of religion as a collective entity of its own. A perusal of North American Indian reflections on the subject guided me to the conclusion that religion should be defined as "faith in the existence of a supernatural world, a faith that is primarily realized in religious conceptions of various kinds and concretely visualized in rites, ritual observations, and epic traditions."[12]

If the term *supernatural* here calls forth negative reactions, the reader may substitute terms like *metaphysical, other dimension,* or *other reality.* (I am less in favor of *transcendental,* a word whose very meaning—something far beyond us that does not form part of our existence and experience—restricts it use.) The important thing is that we describe the existence of another order which is felt or experienced by the believers to be a connected whole. This does not stand in the way of the fact that within a single religious complex, various conceptions and rites may form mental configurations that even exclude each other, as I have shown to be the case among the Wind River Shoshone Indians.[13] Man's possibilities to formalize and integrate religious elements are naturally restricted.

It is within this religious totality that I want to view shamanism. Of course this does not say everything about shamanism: there is also the element of human care, the shamanic personality, profane existence as a part-time shaman, the construction of drums and other auxiliary instruments, the role-playing of the shaman, his social position and sexual life, the poetry of shamanism, and so on.[14] Nevertheless, all these aspects, so well researched by anthropologists and other authors, are only applications and details played off against the determining background, the shaman's intercourse with another world.

Michael Harner has in effect exposed a similar basic view in his well-known book on shamanism. He contrasts the ordinary state of consciousness (osc) with the shamanic state of consciousness (ssc), which is primarily characterized by trance or, as he says, "a transcendent state of awareness."[15] Harner continues, "A perception of two realities is typical of shamanism, even though some Western armchair philosophers have long denied the legitimacy of claiming such a dual division between the ordinary world and a hidden world among primitive peoples, apparently assuming that primitives cannot distinguish between the two." Harner here refers to his own experiences from fieldwork among the Jívaro of Ecuador.[16]

Whoever penetrates shamanic cases from fieldwork or literature will arrive at the same conclusion. The emphasis given in shamanistic seances to the trance state, or ecstasy, is important in this connection. *Trance* and *ecstasy* are actually two words for the same thing, *trance* being the medical term and *ecstasy* the theological and humanistic term. By falling into a trance the shaman enters the other reality, the unseen world. The trance would not have any meaning if it did not open the doors of this different existence.

The beginning of the trance is marked by the appearance of the shaman's helping spirits. They transfer the shaman from one reality to the next: they accompany him, fly with his soul, turn into his soul (or vice versa), supplant his soul on the soul flight, or possess him. Sometimes ritual or dramatic action occurs instead of the deep ecstasy, in which case it is reasonable to deduce that ritual has supplanted ecstasy.

One expression of the other world, common to the Indians of the Northwest Coast as well as Old World groups such as the Saamis (Lapps), is the notion that the beings of that other world walk upside down, or sleep by day and are active during the night. Just as Christian and Buddhist mystics can only characterize the ultimate reality by negations, shamanic peoples do the same thing by describing a reverse existence.

The different character of the other world is also expressed by ritual action. Shamans around Puget Sound describe and visualize the conditions in the other world as well as the perils of the journey there and back. In Swedish folklore, people experience the dead celebrating their Christmas midnight Mass by turning their frocks inside out. Such records demonstrate that the distinction between two realities is a common idea far outside the shamanic circles. They also show the frequency of the upside-down motif to express the other-worldness. We know other examples of the same kind outside shamanism: the inverted world tree (*arbor inversa*), the inverted pyramid (world mountain) as imperial grave in China, and so on. It should thus be obvious that shamanic accounts of an upside-down world do not necessarily mean that that world is actually upside-down. They reveal instead that it has different character which is, a bit awkwardly, expressed through this metaphor.

To summarize: the shaman lives intermittently—at his calling in his seances—in the world of trance, which is the supernatural world. It may occasionally be accessible to other people if they have visions or feverish dreams, but the shaman is the only person who can approach this hidden world at will. Since the supernatural world is the world of religion, shamanism plays a religious role.

Shamanism and the History of Religions

A further question is in what way shamans, as religious mediators, have contributed to the history of religions. It should be obvious from the foregoing that the shaman's main function is to intercede between the supernatural powers and man. This is the sober conclusion we may draw from the assembled ethnographical material. Some authors are convinced that because of their position, shamans gave birth to religion.

Weston La Barre, for instance, thinks that the earliest religions were the creations of "vatic" personalities, ecstatics of various kinds.[17] "The secular fact remains," he asserts, "that all religions begin with either a paranoid shamanic self-impresario or a shaman-priest impresario or his supernatural Spirit-Helper or animal familiar."[18] La Barre tells us that "every single item of religious 'information' comes from the words of some individual vatic personality, shaman, prophet, or visionary, since it is information about himself. Since, in his trance state, the alleged Cosmic Unknown remains totally and studiously unknown to his sleeping senses, the real Unknown (unknown to himself) is the unconscious self of the visionary."[19] This Freudian gospel is further strengthened by references to the use of psychotropic drugs by shamans. Thus La Barre's basic contention is that a world of illusions is built up by shamans.

Nevertheless, La Barre does not submit binding proof for the truth of his theory, providing us merely with hypotheses that generate each other. We might just as well postulate that religion, as the intuitive certainty of another world, existed from the beginning and was secondarily explored by religious specialists, the shamans. On the other hand, we may join with La Barre in his appreciation of the role of the shaman in transmitting religious messages to humanity. Although modern experiences show us that shamans are not always the best keepers of traditions—as for instance Paul Radin thought—the shamans have perpetuated the techniques of communicating with the powers of the unseen world. Thus it does not seem far-fetched to suppose that all later ecstatics who have given rise to religious renewals may be traced back to the shamans of ancient days.

If shamanism has meant so much during the long span of humanity's existence, it is perhaps not so surprising that in an age characterized by a search for religion, shamanism should reappear. People who have recently lost shamanism are trying to revive it, and it is making its entry into Western societies where it was abandoned long ago. Whether in its new expressions the details of the shamanic world picture correspond to the old ones is a different question, to be solved by future investigators.[20] It is, however, interesting to find that in its new manifestations shamanism retains the claim that the trance makes man pass into a world which is the world of spirits and gods, the world of religion.

NOTES

1. For example, at the Seventh International Congress of Arctic Medicine in Umeå, Sweden, in June 1987, a particular section was created for the study of shamanic medicine for the first time.

2. See Vilmos Voigt, "Shaman—Person or Word?" in *Shamanism in Eurasia*, vol. 1, ed. Mihály Hoppál (Göttingen: Edition Herodot, 1984), pp. 13–20; quoted here p. 14.

3. John Lubbock, *The Origin of Civilisation and the Primitive Condition of Man* (London, 1870), p. 119.

4. Roland Dixon, "Some Aspects of the American Shaman," *Journal of American Folklore* 21 (1908): 1–12. This view is represented even today by some American anthropologists.

5. Compare Åke Hultkrantz, "A Definition of Shamanism," *Temenos* 9 (1973): 25–37, and the same, "Ecological and Phenomenological Aspects of Shamanism," in *Shamanism in Siberia*, ed. by V. Diószegi and M. Hoppál (Budapest: Akadémiai Kiadó, 1978), pp. 27–58.

6. Wilhelm Schmidt, *Der Ursprung der Gottesidee*, vol. 12, *Synthese der Religionen der asiatischen und der afrikanischen Hirtenvölker* (Münster in Westfalen: Aschendorffsche Verlagsbuchhandlung, 1955), pp. 615–761.

7. This was the opinion of the well-known shamanologists Wilhelm Radloff, M. A. Czaplicka, and Henn Findeisen.

8. Cf. Hultkrantz, "A Definition of Shamanism," pp. 36 f., Mihály Hoppál, "Shamanism: An Archaic and/or Recent System of Beliefs," *Ural-Altaic Yearbook* 57 (1985): 121–140, quotation from p. 134ff.

9. Mircea Eliade, *Shamanism: Archaic Techniques of Ecstasy* (New York: Bollingen Series 76, 1964).

10. Åke Hultkrantz, "Shamanism and Soul Ideology," pp. 28–36, in *Shamanism in Eurasia*, ed. Mihály Hoppál, vol. 1.

11. See Vilmos Voigt, *Glaube und Inhalt*, Drei Studien zur Volksüberlieferung, Folklore Series of the Eötvös Loránd University (Budapest, 1976), p. 85ff.

12. "The Concept of the Supernatural in Primal Religion," *History of Religions* 22, no. 3 (1983): 231–253, quotation from p. 253.

13. Åke Hultkrantz, *Belief and Worship in Native North America* (Syracuse, N.Y.: Syracuse University Press, 1981), pp. 28–47.
14. The study of the shaman's role-play is a new field of research. See Lauri Honko, "Role-Taking of the Shaman," *Temenos* 4 (1969): 26–55, and A. L. Siikala, *The Rite Technique of the Siberian Shaman* (Helsinki: F. F. Communications 220, 1978).
15. Michael Harner, *The Way of the Shaman: A Guide to Power and Healing* (San Francisco: Harper & Row, 1980), p. 21.
16. Ibid., p. 47
17. Weston La Barre, *The Ghost Dance: The Origins of Religion* (New York: Doubleday, 1970).
18. Weston La Barre, "Hallucinogens and the Shamanic Origins of Religion," pp. 261–294, in *Flesh of the Gods: The Ritual Use of Hallucinogens*, ed. P. T. Furst (New York: Praeger, 1972). Quotation from p. 269ff.
19. Ibid., p. 264ff.
20. Cf. the remarks in Hoppál, "Shamanism: An Archaic and/or Recent System of Beliefs," p. 136.

Seeing Is Believing: The Four Worlds of a Shaman

SERGE KING

ONE of the most confusing things to students of shamanism is the way shamans look at the world. It confuses my students now and it certainly confused me as I was growing up in this tradition. When I was a teenager living on a farm my father would sometimes talk about the crops and the animals around us just like the neighboring farmers would, and sometimes he would talk "to" the same crops and animals as if they were all intelligent beings who could understand and respond to him. Even though I learned to do what he did, it was a good while before I understood the process. There was a time when I found it difficult to concentrate on my work because of all the conversations of trees, flowers, bugs, rocks, and buildings going on around me. Then, somehow, I learned to switch in and out of that kind of awareness without knowing how I was doing it.

From M'Bala, my shaman mentor in Africa, I learned to merge with the animals of the jungle after going into a deep trance state. I thought that the trance state was the means to accomplish the change until I realized that he was able to do the same thing in the blink of an eye without going into trance at all. Obviously, trance was just a tool and not the thing that caused the shift in experience.

My Hawaiian kahuna uncle, Wana Kahili, taught me to go on inner journeys filled with wonder and terror, and to see omens in clouds and leaves and furniture. Yet he also taught me to be very aware of my waking state and how *not* to see omens as well; for there are times when that can be just as important.

My father and M'Bala and Wana Kahili spent very little time in explaining the phenomena that they were teaching me to experience. All felt that experience is the best teacher and that intellectual explanation would get in the way of it. That was a good method for getting me out of my hard head and into my body; but having to deal with the doubts and fears generated by the nonshamanic culture I also lived in slowed down my learning considerably. In my own learning and teaching I have found that satisfying the intellect often lowers the analytical and emotional barriers to learning, allowing for a much faster assimilation of experience. So I spent years in nonjudgmental analyzing of my personal experiences and those of other shamans in order to more fully understand what we were doing when we did what we did, so that it could be shared more easily.

The real starting point was Wana Kahili's teaching that there were four worlds (levels or classes of experience) that everyone moved in and out of spontaneously and usually unconsciously, but which shamans consciously cultivated. These were *ike papakahi* (literally, first-level experience); *ike papalua* (second-level experience); *ike papakolu* (third-level experience); and *ike papaha* (fourth-level experience). His rough explanation was that these represented, respectively, the ordinary world, the psychic world, the dream world, and the world of being. For teaching purposes I have renamed them the objective, subjective, symbolic, and holistic worlds. He also said that all of these worlds were common to everyone, not just shamans, the only difference being that shamans used them knowingly and with purpose. He added that a lot of confusion in people's lives came from mixing worlds in their thought and speech.

It was my aim to teach a lot of people in a short time about shamanic experience, so even with that helpful start I had a lot of filling-in to do. What follows, then, is a brief résumé of that search and research.

The Shamanic Experience

What are we doing when we do shamanic work? We speak with nature and with spirits; we change the weather and create events; we heal minds and bodies and channel strange beings; we fly out of our bodies, travel through other dimensions, and see what others cannot see; and we pay our taxes, wash our cars, and buy our groceries. Is there a common thread connecting all these widely varying activities, or are they all just a bunch of separate skills?

There is a powerful clue in the first and fundamental principle of Huna, the generic term for the Polynesian philosophy of life in which I was trained. This principle says that "the world is what you think it is."

Another, more popular way of stating the same thing is: "We create our own reality." Most people who say this, however, do not really accept it fully, because they think it only means that everything bad that happens to them is their fault. Moreover, many who accept it with better understanding still limit its meaning to the idea that they are responsible for their feelings and experience, and that if they change their negative thoughts to positive ones they will begin to attract positive instead of negative experience.

Shamans, however, go much further than that. We take that idea to mean that we not only attract experience by our thinking, but we actually create realities. By our assumptions, attitudes, and expectations we make things possible or impossible, real or unreal. To put it another way, by shifting mind-sets we can do ordinary and nonordinary things in the same physical dimension that we share with everyone else. I repeat that shamans are not unique in doing this. Any uniqueness comes from how we apply the principle.

The way to change experience and be able to use nonordinary abilities within a given reality is to shift from one set of beliefs (or assumptions, attitudes, and expectations) about that reality to another set. It sounds so very simple, and it is. The most difficult part—and it can be extremely difficult for some—is to accept the simplicity, because that means changing one's idea about what reality is.

The model I am about to present has been specifically designed to enable modern shamans to make clear and conscious distinctions between reality levels or mind-sets. In a society more familiar with and accepting of shamanism this would not be as necessary. The same sort of shifts would be made, but they could be made more intuitively because there would be fewer contradictory mind-sets from other philosophies, both religious and secular. As an example, let's imagine that a modern anthropologist is on an island in the South Pacific studying the native culture. One day the village shaman comes in from weeding his taro patch and tells the villagers that while he was working, the goddess Hina came down on a rainbow and warned him that a hurricane was approaching, whereupon she turned into a bird and flew away.

The shaman moves easily from weeding to talking to the goddess, and the villagers accept it easily because they expect the shaman to be able to weed his taro and also talk to gods. The anthropologist, however, is likely to be stuck in a mind-set that can only allow for drug-induced hallucination, mental aberration, fakery, or dramatization of some ordinary perception. The possibility that the shaman actually communed with a spirit is lost to him, as is the ability to do it himself.

As the different worlds are discussed below, keep in mind that each world can be entered into just a little bit, like dipping your toe into a pond of water, or it can be entered as fully as diving into an ocean's depths.

Ike Papakahi: The Objective World

The first-level world is what most people in modern society would call ordinary reality. Using a meadow in a forest as our example, your purely sensory experience of it—the colors of the plants, soil and sky, the smell of the flowers, the sound of birds, the feel of the breeze on your skin, the perception of movement of a doe and her fawn—would take place in an objective-world framework. It would also seem obvious and unquestionable to you, when viewing the meadow from this level, that it is so many square feet in size, that there are so many trees of certain kinds, that some of them are broad-leafed hardwoods and others are conifers, that so many animals of different sorts inhabit the area, that somebody owns it, and so on. And all of this would of course be true—but only at that level of perception. For this first level, as obvious as it seems, is perceivable in that way only because of one fundamental belief or assumption that serves as the framework for the objective world—the assumption that Everything Is Separate. This is the assumption that allows for direct sensory experience, classical physics, and the various philosophies of cause and effect.

It is often quite difficult for people brought up with that assumption to see it as just an assumption. It is so obvious that it appears to be the only possible truth. But that is the nature of fundamental assumptions. All experience tends to be consistent with one's assumptions about experience. It's like putting on rose-tinted glasses and forgetting you are wearing them. If you never remember that you can take them off, you will always think that rose is the natural and only color the world can be. Inconsistency enters in when one becomes aware, consciously or subconsciously, of other assumptions—as, for example, when the glasses slip, or when you start to remember that you once put them on, or when you have a dream about a green world. Then you may open up to the experience of other levels. Shamans are taught as early as possible that the objective world is only one way of seeing.

The idea that everything is separate is very powerful and very useful. It has encouraged travel, exploration, science, industry, and all the miracles of modern technology, including those that brought about the publishing of this book. However, it has also been used to justify slavery, racism, wars, vivisection, pollution, and overexploitation of the earth's resources. We need to understand that the assumption itself is neither bad nor good.

Human beings must make other assumptions associated with value systems before good and bad enter the picture, and those can operate at any level of reality. Looking at our meadow objectively, for instance, one might see it as good because it provides a food source for various animals. Or it might be seen as bad because it is taking up valuable space that might better be used for housing or feeding humans. The point is that the use or misuse of the environment or its inhabitants is based on the idea that things are separate as well as on personal value systems.

Two secondary assumptions of the objective world are that everything has a beginning and an ending, and that every effect has a cause. Things are caused to be born or come into being by some act or another, and then they die or cease to be. This is a vital concern of objective-world thinking, and therefore great controversies rage over the physical causes of illness and exactly at what moment a cell or group of cells becomes a human being. Huge amounts of money are spent to determine the social and environmental causes of crime and to preserve historic buildings because the end of their existence would be a cultural loss. And people undergo all kinds of emotional and financial burdens to uncover the specific trauma of their childhood that makes them unhappy today and to extend the life of the physical body. All such actions make perfectly good sense when viewed in the light of the assumptions previously mentioned, but viewed from other worlds they make no sense at all.

Some people make the value judgment that the objective world is bad, and so they seek to escape it or diminish it or deny it. In shamanic thinking, however, the objective world is simply one more place in which to operate, and to operate effectively in any world is the shamanic goal. In his or her essential role as healer, therefore, the shaman may use objective-world assumptions to become proficient in such healing methods as massage, chiropractic, herbs and medicines, surgery and exercise, or nutrition and color therapy, without being limited to the assumptions of those methods.

Ike Papalua: The Subjective World

Now assume you are at the meadow again. This time you are aware of the interdependence of the natural world, of the mutually supportive roles played by the elements of light and shade, wind and water, soil and stone, trees, birds, flowers and insects. You feel as if you are part of that interdependence, not just an observer. Perhaps you feel emotions of peace, happiness, love, or awe. Or perhaps you are aware of the season and are reminded of seasons past and yet to come. If you are a shaman or are sensitive psychically, you will probably be able to make a greater internal shift and become aware of the auras, or energy fields, of everything in the scene before you, and the interplay of those forces as well. You may be able to converse with the plants, animals, and stones, or with the wind, sun, and waters, sharing their secrets and stories. Depending on your background, experience, and skill, you may even be aware of and be able to communicate with nature spirits or with the oversoul or *aumakua* of the meadow itself. While standing there you could suddenly witness a scene from a hundred years ago of Indians camping there after a successful hunt, smoking their pipes around the fire and giving thanks to the Great Spirit. You might even feel that you are or were one of them.

The above examples of subjective-world experience are possible because of the basic assumption of this level, that Everything Is Connected, supported by the secondary assumptions that everything is part of a cycle and in transition, and that all events are synchronous. In the framework of this world, telepathy and clairvoyance are natural facts, as unquestionable as the action of a lever in the objective world. Mental communication, regardless of distance and with anything that exists, is possible because everything is connected. Emotions can be experienced because of empathetic connection. Auras can be seen and felt because energy is the connection. Past and future lives can be known because life is cyclic and time is synchronous. Death, at this level, is only a transition, part of a cycle, whereas in the objective world death is a finality. Everything about this level is true, but again, only from the perspective of this level. This is why people primarily oriented in the objective world have such difficulty accepting psychic phenomena and subjective sciences like astrology as facts, and why those primarily oriented in the subjective world find it so hard to explain their experiences to objectively rooted friends.

Neither world makes sense when viewed from the perspective of the other. If you are born and you die and that's that, then past lives are nonsense. If the stars are a zillion miles away and you are here on earth, then any influence is absurd. On the other hand, if everything is interdependently connected, then cutting down every tree in sight to build more cities is suicide, and if you have been a member of a different race in a previous life, to hate that race today is hypocrisy. A shamanic way out of this dilemma is achieved through the seventh principle of Huna, "Effectiveness is the measure of truth." Instead of trying to decide which viewpoint is right, the shaman uses whichever one is effective and appropriate to the healing aim at hand.

Shamanic healing methods at this level make use of telepathic suggestion and thought forms, acupuncture or acupressure, and energy balancing, transfer, and movement, either by hand or with the use of tools such as crystals and special energy shapes and patterns.

Ike Papakolu: The Symbolic World

Here you are in the meadow once more, only this time you let your imagination soar and you see the openness of the meadow as representing your own openness to love and life, the trees become representations of your inner strength and highest aspirations, the birds sing promises of joy, and in the sunlight is the touch of God upon your brow. You are filled with the beauty of the place, so moved that, depending on your inclinations, you immediately write a poem or paint a picture to capture the mood. You have now shifted into a mind-set that has as its basic assumption: Everything Is Symbolic. With a shamanic background you could go further and look for guiding omens in the patterns of clouds, leaves, or bird flights. Or you could do a ritual that would consecrate the meadow and make it an even better healing place for future visitors. A typical shamanic progression of thought at this level is that if everything is symbolic, and if dreams are symbols, then this reality is also a dream. Thus one aspect of shamanic skill is to enter into dreams and change them.

Someone may ask at this point: of what is everything symbolic? And whose dream is it? It would be correct, at this level, to say that everything is symbolic of everything else, but especially of the perceiver, and that the dream is everything's dream, but especially yours. Or we might say, alternatively, that at the symbolic level everything in your personal life experience is a reflection of you, including all the people and things around you. To change experience from this level, you can either change the symbols, change your interpretation of the symbols, or change yourself so that the reflection changes.

The secondary assumptions are that everything is part of a pattern and exists in relationship to something else, and that everything means what you decide it means. Many research scientists and theoretical mathematicians are rooted in this level, seeking meaningful patterns and relationships in the apparent structure of the universe and frequently ignoring the effect on their search of their own decisions about meaningfulness—as well as ignoring any objective applications of their research. For the shaman or other symbolically minded person, it becomes useful to notice how beliefs are reflected in the body and in life experiences, and how easily conditions and relationships are changed when patterns of belief are also changed.

Shamanic healing methods at this level include all faith healings, verbal and visualization therapies (including hypnosis), Neurolinguistic Programming affirmations, guided imagery, placebos, dreamwork, and the use of amulets and talismans.

Ike Papaha: The Holistic World

This time you are not standing in the meadow; you *are* the meadow. You can feel the sunlight being turned into usable energy by the chlorophyll in your leaves as your roots soak up nutrients from the soil, and you gladly give up your nectar to the bee who gathers your pollen to share with other flowers. As the bee you enjoy sucking up the nectar, and you know without thinking that some of the pollen will be shared with other flowers and that plenty will still be there to take back to the extensions of yourself in the hive. You feel the trembling of your throat as you sing your mating song and tip your feathered tail to keep your balance on the pine branch hanging at the meadow's edge, and as the pine you know that you are not at the edge of the meadow but are part of what makes the meadow what it is.

This is a tiny sampling of experience at the holistic level. The basic assumption here is that Everything Is One. In practical terms, it is one's sense of indentity. The deepest experience of it is generally called something like "cosmic consciousness," a woefully inadequate attempt to describe a sense of being one with the universe, which is essentially indescribable because words and language simply cannot contain the experience. The more shallow and common experience of it is one's sense of knowing that one exists. Descartes used a very third-level symbolic approach to justifying this sense of being when he said "I think, therefore I am." An objective approach might be "I sense, therefore I am." The subjective phrase might be "I feel, therefore I am." At the fourth, holistic level, however, we can probably do no better than Popeye, who said, "I am what I am and that's all that I am."

In the holistic world, there is no sense of distinction between oneself and whatever it is that one identifies as also being oneself. To the extent that one is aware of the identification, one is operating in the holistic realm; and to the extent one is aware of "otherness" one is operating in other realms. It will be noticed that in our progression from world to world, the sense of separation—a quite distinct and primary attribute of the objective world—grew less in the subjective world (an increasing sense of connection indicating less separateness), and even less in the symbolic world (although a reflection still implies something else that reflects). A person can also have a holistic awareness of what is considered to be "self" while at the same time having a nonholistic awareness of what is "not-self." Thus a member of a certain tribe in West Africa can have a holistic identification with his own tribe (that is, he may have no sense of personal identity apart from being a tribal member), and have a completely objective, separatist, and hostile view of another tribe.

While holistic identity is a natural human experience—some people normally extend their sense of identity to personal belongings, family, town, or country—it requires considerable skill to enter and operate consciously in this world. Actors and actresses, whose profession developed out of an age-old shamanic tradition, are the best-known practitioners of this skill today. In ancient times, and to a certain extent in modern times, shamans were and are able to take on the identity of animals, nature spirits, and archetypes that pass for gods and goddesses. When in that state of identification, they take on the qualities and powers of those entities. Just as a good actor who is normally shy can play a convincing role as a confident hero by really getting into the part, so can a shaman attain the strength of a bear or the wisdom of a god by contemplation and acting the part so well that the part acts him. This comes from the secondary assumption of this level, that knowing begets being. As Emerson put it, "Do the thing and you shall have the power."

At this level, the shamanic healing modes are primarily of two sorts. First there is "channeling" whereby, to a greater or lesser degree, one takes on the identity of a more powerful healer or becomes one with a greater healing power and then works on someone in a healing way. Second, there is a process that I call "grokking and guiding," whereby one identifies with or becomes the person to be healed and then heals oneself. Needless to say, the latter takes a pretty fair amount of confidence to do successfully. Otherwise one gets so disturbed by the other's condition that one pops out of the holistic level and cannot operate effectively there, or forgets who one really is and takes on the other's symptoms without being able to heal. People who are strongly empathetic may have this experience frequently. Many therapists, for example, identify so much with the problems of their patients or clients that they take on all the ills and problems they are trying to help cure. Therefore, when I train my students in healing at the holistic level, I recommend that they limit any identification process to a maximum of 99 percent, so that the "1 percent shaman" can always return to the core identity.

Moving between Worlds

Shifting mind-sets or moving between worlds in full consciousness is a subtle and delicate process. An approximation of what goes on is the experience of looking at this page of written material. It is possible for you to read the words and absorb the information, then to check it for typographical and spelling errors, then to notice the type size and style and paper quality, and finally to become aware of the page as part of a book which you are holding in a particular location at a particular time. The only thing that has changed is your perception, which you voluntarily changed in order to change your experience. In moving between shamanic worlds, the process is very similar. All that is necessary is to change what one is looking for and then change the assumptions associated with that aim.

The biggest obstacle to this and any other shamanic practice is the interference of critical analysis from other levels. It is quite difficult to practice telepathy, for example, if you keep telling yourself that psychic stuff is nonsense. Similarly, visualization will do you little good if you keep asking, "Am I just making this up?" And it's very hard to make a decent income if you identify yourself as spiritual and identify money as nonspiritual. In order to move easily and effectively between worlds it is necessary to practice dropping the assumptions—and the critical analysis deriving from them—of each world you leave before moving on to the next. With practice (lots of it), this becomes virtually automatic. What helps tremendously is loving yourself without reserve and trusting the God within you. But of course that is good advice whether you are a shaman or not.

Shamanic Trance Postures

FELICITAS D. GOODMAN

M Y INTEREST in the many riddles posed by the religious trance began in the 1960s when, as a graduate student in linguistics and anthropology, I began researching the phenomenon of speaking in tongues, or glossolalia, which is accompanied by this trance. I did extensive fieldwork on this religious behavior and also wrote a book about it,[1] but always felt that it would be valuable if, in additon to observations, I could also do some experimentation. This was not intended to explore speaking in tongues any further, but to gain some understanding of the trance itself. This opportunity presented itself when I began teaching at Denison University and came into contact with students interested in the topic.

For four years, beginning in 1972, I conducted trance experiments with student volunteers, using only a gourd rattle for rhythmic stimulation. But I was not happy with the results. The subjects seemed to have no common experiences. Some felt hot, others cold. Some had stiff muscles, others had relaxed muscles. There were those who had started breathing very fast, but others said that it seemed that they had forgotten to breathe altogether. While for some the sound of the rattle had turned into light, others saw a black hole. On such a basis it was very difficult to draw any significant conclusions from the experiment, and I became more and more disillusioned with what could be accomplished by such means.

Shortly thereafter, however, I came across an article by the Canadian psychologist V. F. Emerson,[2] who pointed out that at least in some meditative disciplines, the belief systems seemed to differ according to what kind of body posture was used during meditation. Could controlled posture have been the missing ingredient in my work with the students? It was worth investigating.

53

With funds supplied by Denison University, I set to work once more. In the summer of 1977 I recruited a group of volunteers from among the graduate students at Ohio State University. From volumes of aboriginal art and other sources I selected body postures where the religious context seemed self-evident. Of course, "religious" needs to be taken here in its widest sense, meaning simply an involvement with the other dimension, the alternate reality. If, for instance, an aboriginal Australian shaman was shown aiming a bone at an unseen, unknown adversary in order to hit him with a magic missile, injury to that enemy could only be thought to happen in the alternate reality.

In fact, this half-kneeling posture, with both arms stretched forward and the line of the right hand prolonged by a stick was one of the first postures I tried with my new volunteers.[3] To my total surprise, even at the first try and working with each person individually, most felt a tremendous current of energy coming from the earth and passing through their bodies. It coursed through the outstretched arm and then radiated out of the stick with such power that in later years we no longer did this posture. Those who experienced its action became afraid that they could possibly do injury to an unintended victim on that other plane of reality.

Thinking back on it now, I feel that perhaps this particular effect could have been predicted, given the general impression and intent of the bone-pointing posture. But working with many other traditional postures in the course of the subsequent years, we found that this Australian one was quite the exception. Usually, it was entirely impossible to predict beforehand what sort of experience a particular way to hold one's hands, a special stance, would mediate. What happened was always surprising and mysterious. As with a radio, where each turn of the dial brings in a different program, so each posture produces its own unmistakable type of vision. Yet there is an endless variety, even with the same posture and the same person.

Take for instance the posture of the Aztec Corn Goddess. The Aztecs, a classical society of ancient Mexico, always represented this goddess as a kneeling young woman sitting on her heels with her outstretched hands placed gracefully, palms down, on her thighs close to her body. What kind of vision might this posture give rise to in trance? As I was demonstrating it to a group of beginners in 1987, I recalled with some amusement my own adventure with this posture a few years back. What I did not realize at the time, and actually could not possibly know, was that this was a posture for changing shape, for metamorphosis. So I was startled when gradually, as if under a master sculptor's hands, my face became elongated into a snout and my buttocks turned into sinewy haunches! Then, as if this were not bad enough, to my utter embarrassment a tail began to grow at the end of my spine! I had the distinct feeling that this was going to be my body form from now on and for as long as I lived, and I was greatly relieved when, at the cessation of the rattle, the offending appendage dissolved. It took a while, however, before my face flattened out to its accustomed shape. Now these twentieth-century teachers, nurses, secretaries, psychologists, and physicians would equally experience how fleeting their human appearance was. If all went well, as if in response to a magic formula, they would slip back into the age of our beginnings, when humans could at will turn into animals and animals could be people. And indeed, when the rattle stopped and they began to tell what had happened, it was clear that the posture had once more worked its wonder.

One subject, for instance, reported that her body dissolved into many particles and that these particles had then all been washed in light of many hues—purples, blue-greens, and yellows—until finally all her normal boundaries were gone. Being laundered in light had taken so long that the fifteen minutes of the experiment were over before this subject could go any further. For others, the animal form may have been too difficult to reach at their first attempt, so they made it only to the world of plants. Thus one subject told of being "jabbed and poked until a tree began growing through me. I was getting very leafy and was beginning to produce blossoms." Or, as a third subject saw it, "There was a corncob suspended on a string, or maybe it was really a heart. A dagger appeared, and it tore open the heart, which curiously was not painful at all. Out of the heart there emerged many different flowers."

Others managed to reach the animal kingdom, although a bit uncertainly, on wobbly legs as it were, as toddlers starting to walk on their own. Thus one subject saw a frog, which kept jumping in and out of the water. He related:

> I joined him and became an alligator. I swam out to sea and turned into a mermaid. I swam for a long time and finally arrived at an island. I wanted to climb ashore, but was worried about how to do that with my fish tail. But as soon as I tried to do it, I discovered that once more I had my legs back, so I actually could also survive on land.

To overcome this initial uncertainty, others resorted to a little "cheating." They met some unsuspecting animal in the other dimension and, not being skilled enough to accomplish a transformation on their own, they slipped into it, like a hermit crab into an empty shell. For instance:

I felt that I was rising up right away and saw some spirits dancing.
I saw a river flowing down toward a mountain, so I entered it,
became a fish, and followed its flow. I arrived in a misty forest, I
left the river and started walking among the trees. Suddenly I
saw a black wolf. It had a white spot. I merged with the wolf and
then became part of the mist.

Actually it is quite rare that in this posture a beginner immediately
accomplishes a perfect metamorphosis such as the one we hear about in
the following account by a female subject:

There was darkness and I felt pain in my face, a kind of suction
on my forehead. Then my forehead turned into the head of a
black bird, and I took off. For a long time, I flew over the
countryside. Finally I landed on a tree. There were Indians
dancing around it, and I watched them dance until the rattle
stopped.

Change, however, is instantaneous, even for novices, in another posture,
namely that of the "Olmec Prince."

The Olmecs were the earliest classical Indian society of Central America. The figurine from which the posture is taken is called the Prince
because the young man wears an unusual, rather ornate headdress. He
sits cross-legged, supporting himself with his fists, which are placed on
the floor in front of him rather close together and bent at the wrist. Even
more remarkably, he has his tongue between his lips and his eyes are
rolled up, a sure sign of a very deep trance.

After using this posture one trance subject reported, "I was very small,
floating along the lips of a sea mammal." Another said, "I was a cat,
maybe a lion, then decided I'd rather be a frog. So I was a frog and had
my own pool." And according to a more detailed report, one subject
found herself in a sort of cave, having no idea what she was:

There was light coming in from the front, and I was expecting
someone. Then somebody came—I did not see the person
clearly—who threw some meat into the cave. I devoured it, I
could taste the raw meat, it was so intense that I felt like I wanted
to throw up. I was a young catlike animal and had a long tail. All
I did was wait. There was a hole in the back of my cave; through
it I could see a village down in the sunshine, and I knew that the
people who lived there belonged to me. Then it was as if a

volcano had erupted and I soared high over a pyramid, which was very steep and tall and made of stone. There were people walking up on the pyramid and I was a cat walking up with them. Then I was in a room inside the pyramid, and I could see the designs on the wall. There was something, I don't know what, in the middle of the room, which I was guarding, and I finally understood that I was a panther. Food was thrown to me once more, but I wasn't hungry. A man appeared—actually I only saw his arm, because I was so low as a cat—and he was putting on an ivory bracelet. We were in a tent, then we went outside and walked among the people. I felt that I was bigger now and was let go to hunt, but there was a sudden noise that made every hair on my body rise up. Then the rattle stopped.

Metamorphosis or transformation, however, is not the only kind of experience made possible by combining a set posture with the religious trance. The more than twenty postures we have unearthed in the past ten years serve a number of different human needs. Since illness in particular is such a prevalent and serious human concern, one of the most popular postures is therefore the one dedicated to healing. Figurines representing it are encountered around the world, some of them several thousand years old. Often the posture is assumed by a power animal, such as the lion in ancient Persia. In Siberia and North America it is usually shown in combination with the bear. Even beginners often see the Bear Spirit in their visions when trancing in this posture. This powerful spirit may tear open their abdomen or work on their back in order to heal it.

The Bear Spirit also pays attention to psychological problems. I recall one trancer who did not have much compassion for the suffering of others. In a vision in this posture he was himself covered by a crusty, tough bark, which was scrubbed off by some energetic young bears, leaving him with a highly sensitive new skin. Physicians are often treated to an impressive initiation in which they are torn apart by the Bear Spirit and then reassembled—a visionary experience also known to the Siberian shamanic healers. The new initiates may then appeal to the Bear for information about medicines. It is told that Eagle Shield, a famous Sioux healer at the beginning of this century, received all his remedies from the Bear Spirit, and one of his songs contained the words, "Bear told me about all these things."

There are also postures for divining, and one to attract game. Using a certain posture the trancer departs on a journey to the Lower World, and using still another one he takes a flight to the Bird Spirits in the Sky. The posture of the "singing shaman" lets the trancer taste the rapture of his voice carrying him away to the high places. Yet another one is for enabling the shaman to accompany the soul of a recently deceased person to the entrance of the realm of the dead in the world below, and so on.

An awareness of the power of the trance postures was apparently widespread among shamans as far back as the dawn of human history. A cave drawing from southern France showing the details of the posture needed for a journey to the Upper World may be as old as fifteen thousand years. On the other hand, in the 1970s an Indian shaman of Peru made a sketch for a Swiss anthropologist of three postures known the world over: the healing posture of the Bear Spirit, the posture of the singing shaman, and an especially precious posture leading to the experience of death and rebirth.

The first question we should naturally ask at this point is: why do the postures structure experience in this manner? Except for the Australian posture, as I mentioned earlier, there is nothing in the way hands and feet are positioned that could be understood the way a gesture might be interpreted. A second question concerns the general agreement in experience. Why, for instance, we might ask, will people on both sides of the Atlantic experience the gathering around of multiple helpful spirit beings or energies when they sit cross-legged and place their hands on their chest with their right hand in upper position? And a third question concerns the fact that we are beginning to discover that myths relating to the postures and unknown both to the experimenter and the workshop participants at the time of the first try have a similar content, as do certain of our visions.

Someone might argue that the surprising agreement in visionary content among participants was due to suggestion on my part. Researchers working in the 1970s with members of various Pentecostal congregations who spoke in tongues reported that persons engaging in trance behavior were easily influenced, that they were remarkably prone to suggestion. However, at the beginning of the experiments I myself had no idea at all about how a particular posture might structure the experience. I even steered my experimental subjects in wrong directions. Misled by ideas in the earlier literature, I instructed them to watch for changes in their mood during the trance: did one posture make them more aggressive, for instance? They asserted unanimously that no such thing ever happened, that instead they experienced important perceptual changes—they had visions. Since then, I have therefore made it a habit never to tell beforehand what experience might be expected with a certain posture. Doing so would be foolish anyway because of the great variety of experiences possible with one posture, as I attempted to show earlier. The power of the posture is so intense that on occasion it even prevails over what a person is sure that he or she is going to experience. This happens sometimes when a person will take part in a workshop for a second time, possibly at an interval of a year or two. For example, there was a participant doing the posture of Calling the Spirits for a second time after a lengthy period who then reported, "I was sure this was the posture of the Bear Spirit, and I couldn't understand why I turned into somethng stiff and upright, like a tree!"

Neither do people pick up on elements of each other's stories when they report after a trance, although sometimes there might be a surprised exclamation: "Oh, I was there too!" What does seem to have some effect on the content of the trance, however, is prior cultural conditioning. Indians appear more frequently in visions in the United States than in Europe, for instance, while dwarfs and fairies are rather rare here. The same is true of animal spirits, with buffalo seen more often in America and wolves and foxes predominating in Central Europe.

Although as we saw, postures decisively affect the content of visions, this fact remains elusive when we try to examine it in the laboratory. In 1983 Ingrid Müller, a German medical student, and I did some research on the religious trance at the Neurophysiological Clinic of the University of Munich. We discovered what dramatic changes the body underwent during this kind of trance. Our four male experimental subjects showed a drop in blood pressure and simultaneously an increase in heartbeat, a process that is ordinarily seen only if a person is about to bleed to death or is otherwise in danger of dying. In the blood serum the stressors—that is, adrenaline, noradrenaline, and cortisol—increased slightly, then dropped below normal levels. At the same time, the brain began to synthesize the famous beta-endorphin, the brain's own painkiller. The presence of this endorphin during the religious trance had been suspected for quite a while, but here for the first time we had actual proof of its occurrence. It remained high even after the conclusion of the trance, accounting for the feeling of great joy, of euphoria, which many people experience as a result of trance.

But no matter how gratifying all this was scientifically, we still knew nothing about why postures affected experience differently. We had used two different postures, but the above results remained the same. The difference did not show up in the EEG (electroencephalogram) either. Uniformly, the electrical activity of the brain indicated the predominance of theta waves (6–7 cycles per second), a curious result, because normal adults usually show these kinds of waves only shortly before going to sleep. Yet having visions is very much an awake experience. Perhaps one of the medical research assistants at the Clinic was right when he remarked that the experiences mediated by the postures probably took place at a level that simply could not be accessed by the relatively crude instruments and techniques of a laboratory.

Observers of trancers agree on the favorable effect of the trance experience. Reporting on trance induced only by sonic driving, the medical anthropologist Barbara Lex speculates that it may be due to a tuning of the nervous system brought about by the rhythmic stimulation of the driving technique. While this may well be true, combining the driving stimuli (such as the rattle) with postures obviously adds a heretofore unrecognized curative dimension. The healing power invested in the posture of the Bear Spirit and venerated around the world is only the most outstanding example. Actually, healing can take place in any posture, but miraculously there seems always to be a perfect match between the type of experience and the problem at hand.

For example, I recall a Swiss teacher who had a pronounced dislike of snakes. During a metamorphosis exercise, however, he turned into a snake himself. "I really didn't realize how delicate and vulnerable they were," he remarked ruefully. "I was continually afraid that someone might step on me and break my spine." In another instance, there was a young engineer in one of my workshops who had lost his mother a few months before. No matter what posture we did, his visions always included an element of deep mourning, as if over and over and again he had to open the door of the mausoleum where his mother had been laid to rest. That it was really a feeling of guilt rather than sorrow that troubled him most did not become obvious until we did a diviner's posture. He saw the face of God framed in a white beard, as he remembered it from a picture in his grandmother's bedroom. He thought that final judgment would now be meted out to him, and he felt terrified. Instead he found himself propelled toward that face with irresistible force. Like a missile he penetrated the left eye of the image and came to rest on the other side. It was then that he realized that he had shot through a cardboard cutout. "For the first time in months I feel peace," he said afterward.

By contrast, one female subject experienced consolation in another case of tragic loss when she used a posture to make a journey to the Lower World. This woman was present when her dog was born, and she had named him Bear as soon as she cuddled the black, woolly little creature. She was divorced and childless, and the dog had been her faithful companion for fourteen years. A week before she came to the workshop, Bear had to be put to sleep because he had developed an incurable degeneration of the spine. For several nights the woman had not been able to sleep, just sitting in bed and staring into space. Every time she spoke of her loss at the workshop, she broke into tears. But after the trip to the Lower World, she beamed. Bear was alive. She had seen him, hale and hardy, happily jumping around on a flowery meadow. When she came to the workshop once more this summer, she had just been to see his grave. The coyotes had gotten to it and had scattered his bones. "No matter," she said. "I know he is well. I saw him cavorting around on the banks of the river in the Lower World."

Psychological benefits experienced by participants in my experiments on the effects of postures are also related to what is usually termed "conversion experience." Thus some participants report changes in themselves that have the well-known form of "Previously I was such-and-such type of person; now I am the opposite." For example, some state that they have been able to overcome problems with personal relations, others remark about an increasing sense of self-reliance, and still others report conquering fears or a sense of alienation, and so forth.

Cases showing the curative and healing value of these shamanic postures could be greatly multiplied. We ought to be truly grateful to the ancient sages and shamanic artists for passing their secrets on through the millennia to us moderns. Practicing what they taught can invest our lives, often so humdrum, with an entirely new dimension of insight and exaltation.

NOTES

1. *Speaking in Tongues: A Cross-Cultural Study of Glossolalia* (Chicago: University of Chicago Press, 1972).
2. V. F. Emerson, "Can Belief Systems Influence Neurophysiology? Some Implications of Research on Meditation," *Newsletter-Review, R. M. Bucke Memorial Society* 5: 20–32.
3. For more details, see my article "Body Posture and the Religious Altered State of Consciousness: An Experimental Investigation," *Journal of Humanistic Psychology* 26 (1986): 81–118.

The Bridge, an Essential Implement of Hmong and Yao Shamanism

JACQUES LEMOINE

A HMONG SHAMAN is a roving medicine man, going from place to place wherever he is called by his patients. Everywhere he carries his shamanic implements, which consist mainly of his veil, his gong, his finger ring-bell, his rattle-sword, and his divinatory blocks. People from the patient's household prepare for him a very simple altar where he can gather his "spirit troops," providing him also with a wooden bench to mount. With these basic accessories he can operate. But these are only the Hmong shaman's minimum field equipment when he operates away from home. In his own house he keeps his basis: a two-storied altar, which is the permanent residence of his spirit troops, as well as a cloth bridge between this altar and the front door, supplemented by a cotton thread network that follows a special course from the front door to the altar.

Both bridge and thread are supported by horizontal bamboo poles tied above the altar and the front door and under the ridgepole of his house between the central and left main posts. These bamboo poles are the girders of the bridge and, more precisely in shamanic terms, the "iron and copper girders of the spirit helpers." The bridge is made of indigo cotton cloth and is unfurled only at special occasions—for example, at New Year's, when the spirit helpers are sent back for vacation to the abode of the first shaman (Nya Yee's cavern), or when a new altar has been erected for a new shaman.

What are the use and the meaning of this bridge? For a Hmong shaman, the bridge is a way of communicating with the outer space of nonordinary reality. It is used by the spirit troops in their movements. For example, when a new shaman, having been successfully trained by his master, decides to erect his own altar, a brand-new bridge is unfurled and set up from the new altar to the front door of the disciple's house. His master—for whom he has prepared a temporary altar and a bench—will go and fetch for him his spirit helpers at Nya Yee's cavern. When the master reaches Nya Yee's cavern he sends his own spirits to inquire on which rock the ancestral spirit is staying who is head of this band of spirit helpers. When they have found him, the master tries to see his disciple's house, in spite of the long distance. Then, very much as a mountain-climber would do, he pulls and gathers his own spirit-thread, throwing his own bridge down to his disciple's house. If the disciple's thread and bridge have been already installed, he puts his own bridge in parallel, thus making a twin-track way on which he leads the new shaman's spirit troops, escorted by his own spirit helpers. Once back in this world, the master shaman takes his own bridge back home. From now on, his disciple's spirit troops are settled in their new altar, and the disciple must manage them by himself.

The bridge is therefore much more than a piece of indigo cloth that is materialized for use in special circumstances. It is made of spiritual matter—the matter of the soul—and there are specific ceremonies for strengthening it. For example, every year when sending away his spirit helpers at the New Year's celebration, the Hmong shaman sacrifices a huge hog from his livestock. The animal's soul will be kept in custody and used by the shaman as "copper and iron beams, sturdy as rocks" to reinforce his bridge. At the same time, the shaman will free the soul of the pig sacrificed at the previous New Year.

In order to prove his bridge's sturdiness, he very often organizes a session of spontaneous trance among his family members and neighbors, which is understood as "trampling the bridge" (tla mua chiao). This takes place under the unfurled cloth bridge in the main room between the altar and the front door. All the spirits helpers are gone except for the most personal ones: the spirit of the trance and the seer-spirit who is in charge of guarding the altar. They provoke a trance among the young and the old who want to participate. The purpose of this recreative (and some-times hilarious) exercise is openly to "strengthen the bridge."

The Yao peoples of the Mien subgroup in Southeast Asia also have a kind of shamanistic activity which they name bow'kwaa, which can be translated as "divination" or "diagnosis," as well as an activity referred to as ts'ang wuen, meaning "recapturing of souls," roughly corresponding to the type of "diagnosis" called ua neng shai and the "treatment" known as ua neng khu of the Hmong shamans. The Yao shamans also receive troops of spirit helpers from their masters. But these spirits are only warriors in human guise, and may include the following:

- The soldiers of the Red Flag and those of the Blue Flag
- The Great Prince with his double-edged sword
- The Dragon General with his sharp saber
- The Copper Thunder's Troops and the Iron Thunder's Troops
- The Great General Flying through the Sky
- The Four Merit Supervisors, messengers from the Heavens, the Underworld Hells, this World, and the Waters
- All the Masters in this World and the Beyond

This point is worth examining and comparing with the Hmong shaman's tradition. He also has what he calls his "Chinese" spirit-helpers—the *neng shua*. They comprise both infantry and cavalry, *peng jeng* and *peng mua*. They are provided by the shaman's masters, who include not only his own direct teacher but also the teachers of his own master and the master-blacksmiths who forged his gong and his swords.

The Chinese spirit-helpers of the Hmong shaman come in fours, whereas his Hmong spirit-helpers form pairs. The "Chinese" spirit-helpers are always eight or nine ranks in a row and are as fierce as they are well disciplined. This is about all we know of them, except that they always seem to be available in large numbers in answer to the shaman's call. But a Hmong shaman quite clearly distinguishes this rather anonymous Chinese reserve from his own troops, which he summons, pair after pair, naming them or describing their precise function in his task force.

These Hmong spirit-helpers usually appear in animal forms: birds, insects, mammals, supplemented by a few supernatural and human spirits. If the latter, they can be culture heroes, such as Miss Njua and Mr. Nang—the mother and father of mankind—who are shown weaving the sky and catching in their weft the disease-threads that the cruel god of death, Nzue Shee Nyong, is spreading down over the earth; or they may be demigods, like Miss Black Cloud and her father, the old Dragon. The former represent the Hmongs' genuine contribution to the craft they may well have received from other peoples.

Among the birds, there are three couples of birds of prey: the hawks, the vultures, and the eagles. The hawks are used to catch the "jutting-out shadow" soul as it moves off, whereas the vultures and eagles use their wide-open large wings in gathering together the flocks of spirit-helpers. In other cases, wild ducks plunge into marshes and ponds in order to rescue souls who have fallen into mud, and woodpeckers will use their sharp beaks and prehensile tongues to remove caterpillars and other worms from the "growing bamboo" soul. Among insects and their relatives, the spiders throw out the network of threads on which the spirit-helpers move and perch; a kind of wasp (sphex) that puts its prey to sleep and takes it back alive to its nest will recapture a "jutting-out shadow" soul on the run and bring it back safely to the patient's body. Among mammals, wolves and dogs are set in pursuit of "running bull" souls and will bring them back; tigers will hunt tiger-witches, and elephants will use their formidable strength to hold up a fainting "shadow soul," and so forth.

Returning to the Yao, when the Yao shaman has summoned the main characters mentioned above and mimed their arrival in trance, and when all his troops have been gathered and he sees them ready to go on their assignment, he says:

> Let the horsemen whip their horses, cross the bridge and set off! I throw the Heaven's bridge, the Earth's bridge. I set up the bridge accross this World to the Beyond. I throw the Three Terraces' bridge and the Seven Stars' bridge. I unfurl these bridges and roads all the way to the patient whose body fever has laid down. . . .

Again the bridge is introduced into the plot to pave the way for the intervention of the shaman's spirit squadron in hot pursuit of the supernatural beings who have caused the patient's illness. The Yao shamans, as well as their Taoist priests, use the same gesture (mudra) as a symbol for the bridge: the open right hand striking on the palm of the open left hand, then both hands raised, pressed together over the head. Then, bowing and stretching both hands together in the same position, they pretend to be pulling the bridge back to themselves, saying, "They are back, footmen and cavalry, soldiers and officers! They return, bridges and roads, horses and saddles . . . all of them . . . and in a hurry!"

This return of the spirits is generally followed by their report to the shaman on their investigations in the other world, which the Yao shaman (still in trance) translates for the houselord, saying:

> I have crossed the bow (the bridge) to investigate thoroughly. I have gone into the Beyond to investigate the spirits, and I have seen that the three spiritual souls above the patient's head were flying apart away from him, that his seven bodily souls were wandering. . . . Deprived of his spiritual souls to protect his body, and of his bodily souls to protect his life, he will succumb to the diseases falling upon him. Houselord! My messengers must carry out the alleviation of his sufferings and obtain its abatement

until his complete recovery. . . . You will have to call for me again on a propitious day so that I will send forth my fierce soldiers to recapture all his souls and bring them back, and also to expel the seven disasters and eight sufferings. Thus the patient will recover his health.

To make a long story short, the Yao shaman, like his Hmong counter-part, first makes a deal with the supernatural powers of the Beyond, which are found to be the cause for the patient's illness. This is not exactly a peace agreement, but rather a kind of ceasefire signaling the nonaggravation of the illness and a certain amount of recovery for the patient. If it should happen that the patient feels no better, however, the shaman's dealings will have failed and a new shaman will be called for another trial. When the patient shows a definite change for the better, and when the houselord feels that the patient's recovery ought to be strengthened, the shaman is called in again for the "curing" session.

A Yao *ts'ang wuen* session is much more elaborate than a simple diagnosis. It comprises no less than twenty-one scenes, from the gathering and departure of the shaman and his spirit troops to the safe reintegration of the patient's souls into his body while restoring his destiny. These scenes are followed by the remuneration of all the spirit-helpers.

Recapturing the runaway souls is a very dramatic feat which involves resorting to the use of several bridges. The most important bridge is represented by a piece of white unbleached linen, about twenty feet long, which the shaman changes into a bridge to bring back the souls from the Beyond to this world. But he will also need five to seven more bridges for his task force to move across the space of nonordinary reality. They are bridges across (1) the Skies, (2) the Earth, (3) the Beyond, (4) this World, (5) the Mountains, (6) the Waters, (7) Men and Spirits. The shaman represents these bridges with sheets of paper placed on the ground. This layout is headed by the bridge of the Three Terraces (or Three Crests), which opens on three directions and is used as a turntable by the shaman and his spirit troops.

The main point here is that the shaman will travel along with his troops. He starts by "walking on the constellation," or more precisely, "walking on the Three Terraces," *heng fam toi kong*. It is a succession of steps and jumps (hopping on one foot, with his feet together, with his feet wide apart, and so on), following the network of bridges he has laid out on the ground. During this elaborate exercise he is holding his own white linen bridge in his hand. When, with the aid of the bridges, he has covered some distance in space and reaches the Beyond, he suddenly has a cataleptic fit, falling on his back on the paper bridges and at the same time unfolding his white linen bridge to cover his body. His assistants then straighten the white cloth, which is stretched on the ground from the front door to a sacrificial table at some distance from the shaman's head. They put a jug full of water on his chest, which they eventually press on in order to help the shaman's spirit take off. His body in trance gradually stops shaking and finally becomes still. One can only hear his voice from beneath the piece of cloth buying his way in the Beyond, bargaining to redeem his patient's souls or to extend his lifespan. When necessary, he himself corrects the number of remaining years under his patient's account in the book of destiny.

The shaman's assistants play here a very important part. When, still in trance, he first collapses and keeps shaking under the white cloth, holding in his right hand a little iron dagger the hilt of which is also a rattle, they place on his chest a small wooden board on which one can read three lines of Chinese characters. In the middle of the board is "Instant execution, by express order from *T'ai Shang Lao Chün*"; on the right column, "To the right, the Young Lord who brings back the corporal souls"; and on the left column, "To the left, the Lad who leads the spiritual souls on their way." These two spirit helpers will actually be put into operation when the recaptured souls are brought back home. When the shaman wants to improve his patient's destiny, the assistants again put in his hands a brush and his seal, whereupon his hands emerge from under the cloth and pretend to write and stamp in the book of destiny.

The most important scene for the assistants, however, is when the shaman undertakes to bring back his patient's souls. He charges his specialists (mentioned above) to get hold of the souls and lead them back home on the white bridge. At the same moment they are supposed to reach the house, his assistants hold a torch and search thoroughly in the doorway to see if there is any living being around. They usually find insects and report each catch to the shaman, who acknowledges them as the returning souls. When they have found three of them, the shaman (still under the bridge) throws his divinatory blocks to confirm the souls' safe return. Again his assistants read for him the results. It only remains for the shaman to resurface in this World, which takes place when he starts shaking again. His assistants then roll up the bridge as the shaman springs to his feet, goes to the doorway, and calls back his spirit troops, ways, and bridges.

At this stage we may leave the Yao shaman, who still has to go through seven more scenes before his patient's complete recovery. We have already attended the most striking part of the session. We have seen the shaman's departure, his take-off followed by his troops through the network of his bridges, his traveling, and his intervention in the Beyond. A special bridge is used by the shaman to lead the patient's souls from the Beyond back to his house and body.

If we compare this to similar performances by Hmong shamans in similar circumstances, we find that a bridge is also used to bring lost souls back to this World. This happens mainly when a runaway soul has gone as far as the city of the dead. In such cases, the soul has crossed the bridge without parapets which leads to the city of the dead. When bringing the soul back at the curing session, a bridge is built with planks and bamboo poles, which is eventually covered by a thatch roof, and the patient is made to cross it to and fro (to the Beyond and back) while the shaman calls for his souls to join his body. In order to emphasize the bridge's function as a link between two worlds, it is very often built on the top of a mountain pass. The Hmong indigo cloth bridge, mentioned above, which is, except for the color, the exact replica of the Yao white cloth bridge, is exclusively used by the spirits as a kind of take-off runway for their departure or landing.

Thus the concept of the bridge is clearly the same for the Hmong and the Yao shamans. They both use a loan word borrowed from Chinese: *ch'iao* in Chinese has become *tsh'ao* in Hmong and *chiou* in Mien Yao. But the use of the bridge seems far more developed by the Yao shamans. The Hmong shamans know of two kinds of bridges: the bridge thrown across this World and the Beyond to the city of the dead, and the bridge they stretch for their spirit helpers' safe landing in their house. They meet the first bridge when, after having explored different ways in the unseen part of this World, which is on the side of life, they finally reach its boundary with the Beyond. Obviously they have borrowed from the Chinese the idea of the Nai Ho bridge thrown over the "no return" foaming stream dividing the Beyond from this World, which all the souls of the dead have to cross.

If the patient's soul is already on the other side, which is the side of death, then death is not far away, sometimes already pronounced. The shaman may then try to cross the bridge and attempt to redeem that soul and take it back on the side of life. This is a very bold action, and many shamans dare not to undertake it. Those who do so have to go alone, leaving their "horse" behind, at the entrance of the bridge. When they have been successful and their patient does not die, the emphasis of the curing session is put on a crossing of the bridge by the patient, who thus regains his soul's entirety.

The bridge-crossing ritual is also used by the Chinese Taoist "red-head" priests in similar circumstances. For the Hmong or the Yao it is no doubt a borrowing from Chinese popular Taoism. The different degree of

Chinese influence is quite obvious in what happens after crossing the bridge. For the Yao, as for the Chinese, the other side is Hades, a large city for prisoners divided into ten tribunals and their jails, where the souls of the dead are tried and sentenced to different punishments according to their deeds in this World, in the tenth tribunal they meet the Wheel of Reincarnation, which sends them back to this World into a new body, which may be of a human being, an animal, or an insect according to their merits.

For the Hmong shaman, once they are in this land of the dead, the souls are bathed in a bitter water that washes away all memories of a previous life, and they are ready for reincarnation. But there is no other reminder of the very colorful Chinese Hades. Instead this land is thought to be the abode of mankind's mother. Hmong shamanism is far less permeated by Chinese concepts. This is even more obvious when looking at the Hmong and Yao spirit bridges.

The Hmong spirit bridge is certainly also a borrowing—not only because it is designated with the same Chinese loan word, but also because it is in fact duplicated by the spirits' thread. This is a single thread going first from the front door to the spirits' altar, then back to the front door, then to the main post on the left side of the house (on the right when facing it from the front door), back to the altar again, then back to the front door and from there to the central post and back once more to the altar, where it ends up tied to a silver coin or a stone ax in the shaman's magic water bowl.

This water is a dragon pool, as neolithic axes and adzes found by the Hmong in their fields are thought to have been thrown by thunder which is traditionally associated with the dragon. The silver coin has been given to the shaman by his master when he erected his two-storied permanent altar. When comparing the different use of the thread and the bridge, we see that the thread is mainly the abode of the Hmong vernacular spirit helpers, especially those who have the shape of a bird or an insect, while the cloth bridge is more or less reserved to the Chinese spirit helpers of the Hmong shaman. And this is consistent with their movement in ranks forming actual companies of footmen or cavalry.

This last detail is much developed by the Yao shaman, who sends off his troops on a network of bridges and roads that stretch as they move forward and is still perceptible when a master shaman goes and fetches his disciple's spirit helpers. The Yao, who otherwise are Taoists and quite often attend a rather elaborate Taoist liturgy performed by their Taoist priests, quite naturally resort to shamanism within an entirely Taoist religious context. The bridges of the Three Crests and the Seven Stars, which they quite often use in their performances, are commonplace Taoist ritual and magic. The "Seven Stars" represent the seven stars of Ursa Major (in the Polar Star constellation), while the "Three Crests" are the three stars that form a kind of canopy above it. The Hmong, on the other hand, while ignoring Taoism, retain some Chinese (or Yao) Taoist features passed on to them by their Chinese (or Yao) instructors.

For example, both Hmong and Yao shamans rely on the support of their masters along the lines of a "transmission of power" from generation to generation. To this the Yao add the ancestors. The trance itself is provoked by a three-generations-above ancestor whom the Yao call "the ancestor who leads the shaman." In the Hmong tradition, when a shaman dies, one of his souls goes along with his spirit helpers back to Nya Yee's cave and becomes the head of his former spirit helpers. He is the one who sends the strange, incurable disease of the shaman, which is a forewarning that a troop of spirit helpers is looking for an heir to take them into custody. If he is not the spirit who provokes the trance, he is actually responsible for the first shakings of the new shaman during his initial shamanic illness. Moreover, in a way very close to the Yao, Hmong shamans include the souls of their family members among their troops.

The Miao-Yao ethnolinguistic group of peoples is spread over most of southern China and the northern part of the Indochinese peninsula. Among the various subgroups in which they can be divided, the Hmong Miao, and the Mien Yao represent the southernmost (and westernmost) fractions of the Miao-Yao peoples. Their shamanism has developed while in contact with the more elaborate religions of their powerful Chinese neighbors, Taoism and Buddhism. For the Yao one could even say they are within a special tradition of Chinese Taoism, adopted by the Yao sometimes at the turn of this millennium. Both Yao and Hmong shamans use a significant amount of Chinese words and concepts, and this induces us to postulate upstream the existence of a Chinese shamanic tradition directly (or indirectly) in contact with them. The concept and technique of the bridge, a typical borrowing, has thus become a central ideological tool in their shamanic performances.

The reason for the importance of the bridge is that, like the rainbow, the bridge concept symbolizes a move across space that can be easily equated with a move between two different worlds. Hmong and Yao shamans are human beings whose distinctive feature is to be able to enter the unseen part of the sensible world and to be told by their spirit helpers what is going on there. They usually operate in the interval between illness and death—that is, they have to rescue their patient's souls while they are still somewhere in this World. Once the Chinese (Buddhist and Taoist) concept of a bridge to the Beyond reached them, a new field of action was offered, and they eventually could defy death. Furthermore, the ritual and magical ecstatic practice of "walking on the stars," developed by the Shang Ch'ing Taoist school since the fourth century, which is still part of the Yao liturgy and shamanism, has popularized the idea of using such magical bridges in the universe as a mean of transport, first across space and then from one world to another.

Since the eleventh-century Taoist renovation movement known as the True Doctrine of the Heart of Heaven, there has been a more recent diffusion of Taoist rituals resorting to spirit troops sent by heavenly agencies, which is probably responsible for Taoist doctrine adopted by the Yao. Yao shamans heavily rely on the support of these celestial and terrestrial spirit armies. For the Hmong shamans, these Chinese spirit troops considerably increased the number and efficacity of their task force. The merging of the use of the spirit troops and of the bridge to move them quickly across space and worlds has shaped actual Yao shamanism and also pervaded the Hmong shaman's relation to his spirit helpers. It is more remarkable in the Yao case because, being used in a Chinese Taoist context, it is much more clearly integrated than with the Hmong, where the need to keep two registrars of both vernacular and Chinese spirits has led to some reduplication of the bridge by the thread network.

Neo-Shamanism and the Modern Mystical Movement

JOAN B. TOWNSEND

Ways of personally contacting an alternate reality or "supernatural" world have been an important part of human culture throughout history. The shaman, a person who had a special personal relationship with a group of spirit helpers, played a significant role in this personal contact, although shamanism existed alongside different beliefs about the other world. Shamanism has persisted in small societies throughout the world, but in areas where civilizations developed, shamans have been replaced by priests who represent more organized religious practices directed toward the problems of the society. Nevertheless, in early civilizations, and even within Western civilization, shamanism and allied beliefs have survived in a variety of guises.

From the thirteenth through the eighteenth century in the West, a positive "witchcraft" was practiced that included shamanic-like activities for the good of the community, involving physical and psychological healing and divination. More recently, spiritualists and some psychics have perpetuated parts of this system. Today there is a major reawakening in Western society of portions of the more traditional forms of shamanism.

This reawakening is occurring primarily among a small but important segment of the North American population, which is experiencing a new spirituality characterized by a turning to non-Western religious systems. It is especially significant because it includes well-educated, upper-middle-class people who are in positions where it is possible to influence the society's ideas and trends. Within this group, several distinct belief systems are being redefined and molded into a new mystical movement.

Neo-shamanism is one major thrust of this movement. It blends portions of specific shamanic traditions of different societies around the world into a new complex of beliefs and practices. Since 1983 I have been working with neo-shamans, psychics, spiritualists, healers, and others seeking transcendence. I have also attended a number of workshops where these systems are taught and perpetuated. In this chapter I will focus primarily on those who are involved directly with neo-shamanism, but will sometimes include the psychics, spiritualists, and others in more general discussions. I want to stress that the parameters of the newly emerging mystical movement are broader than merely the term *neo-shamanism* alone would indicate.

Origins of Neo-Shamanism

Periods of religious enthusiasm are not uncommon in the history of the Western world. This latest trend seems unusual, however, and distinct from earlier religious movements such as the Great Awakening of the 1740s and the Second Great Awakening after 1790 in the United States, because it combines a number of different systems of belief and is fostered by a network of individuals sharing a communication system that is unprecedented. Although growing from the seeds of the nineteenth-century and earlier spiritual revivals, this new mystical movement owes its initial definition to the "hippie" and related movements that began in the 1960s and developed into various genres in the 1970s.

These trends were characterized by the search for a new meaning in life, which began to find its expression in a feeling of kinship among all people, a "back to the land" movement, and the valuing of simple, "natural" lifestyles and conservationist concerns. Significantly, there was also a strong interest in nonorthodox theologies, especially spritualist, mystical, and Eastern religious philosophies, as well as Native American culture, including shamanism.

Emphasis was placed on individual, personal involvement in religious mysticism and direct contact with the transcendent rather than on being merely an observer at rituals conducted by church officials. In the 1970s, the psychologically oriented human potential movement emerged, which emphasized the power within each person to attain more from life. Workshops sprang up in which such techniques and philosophy of self-development were taught. These had special appeal to more highly educated people.

Anthropologists have collected information from many native peoples throughout the world, including Indians and Eskimos (called Inuit in Canada), and have described shamanism and other rituals when possible;

nevertheless, religion and shamanism continued to lose research popularity over time in favor of studies of other aspects of culture. Shamanic studies, by and large, were relegated to comparatively obscure publications; the general public had little knowledge of these rich materials. Some of these studies were "discovered" during the 1970s with the rise of neo-shamanism.

In the 1960s, a few anthropologists initiated new work with native shamans who had retained their traditional systems. Their field methods differed from earlier researchers to the extent that some were willing to apprentice themselves and learn shamanic systems firsthand. Especially important to the development of neo-shamanism in the West were Michael Harner's work with South American Indian shamans and Peter Furst's and Barbara Myerhoff's work with Huichol shamanism in northern Mexico.

One of the most significant events in the rapid rise of interest in shamanism was the publication in 1969 of Carlos Castaneda's doctoral dissertation in anthropology and his subsequent books describing his apprenticeship to a Yaqui shaman-sorcerer, Don Juan, in northern Mexico. Thus by the early 1970s the stage was set for the rise of neo-shamanism.

Shamans, Psychics, and Spiritualists

A shaman is a very special individual with specific, extraordinary abilities. Both men and women may be shamans, and some of the most powerful are women, especially after menopause. I use the masculine pronoun in my descriptions simply for convenience. There are specific characteristics that set shamanism apart from other religious activities, since it revolves around the person of the shaman, an inspired individual who is intimately in touch with the spirit world. Not all ceremonial leaders who conduct religious rites in native societies are shamans, and in fact a society may not have a shaman at all. Even in societies that have a shaman, he may not participate or be the main leader in religious ceremonies.

Fundamental to shamanism, of course, is access to an alternate reality that differs from the day-to-day waking reality in which we all function. The shaman is able to enter this alternate reality *at will*, and what occurs there because of his intercession can directly affect ordinary reality.

In his contact with alternate reality, the shaman has a number of helping spirits—human, animal, or other "entities" that directly assist him in healing, divining, finding lost souls, helping the deceased move easily into the land of the dead, protecting his people, and a variety of other activities. The shaman is able to journey in alternate reality and contact entities there for the benefit of his society as well as himself; and, of special importance, he can remember these experiences afterward. Thus he is clearly an integral member of his community.[1]

An important aspect of shamanism, which sets it in contrast to some types of "deep trance" mediumship and "voodoo" possession states, is that the shaman is, with very rare exceptions, *always in control*. He determines if and when he will move into alternate reality, and when he will return. Usually spirits do not completely "take him over," although in shamanic trance a spirit may occasionally speak through him. Moreover, particularly in healing, he may function in both realities simultaneously, removing the intrusive object causing illness in alternate reality at the same time as he is ministering to the sick person in this reality.

To a large extent, neo-shamans, psychics, spiritualists, and healers (both men and women) are involved in the same activities and hold the same beliefs. Psychics are people who use abilities other than those of the five senses—for example, telepathy, and clairvoyance—but do not necessarily have special beliefs about the source of their abilities. Spiritualists are usually psychics, but they also believe in the ability to communicate with and be assisted by the dead and other spirits. Healing of physical or psychological problems may be undertaken by either psychics or spiritualists.

Like the shaman, psychics and spiritualists also stress the existence of an alternate reality. The individual may move into that reality to contact teachers and guides, who may or may not have once lived in this reality. "Guides," or "spirit helpers," are with the person to assist and protect him in ordinary and alternate reality. Alternate reality is also used to affect healing. The healer may function simultaneously in both realities, taking guidance from his spirits while ministering to the sick person in this reality.

The control of the entry to and exit from alternate reality, as well as the recall of events within that reality, are similar among both shamans, psychics, and spiritualists. Normally, the person retains control. He determines if and when he will move into alternate reality and when he will return. There is some debate as to whether trance mediums should be equated with shamans or neo-shamans because the former do not always recall what transpired while they were in deep trance. Nevertheless, at least some deep-trance mediums may also undertake shamanic-like journeys in alternate reality with the assistance of their guides, and recall the events that took place.

Shamans, psychics, and spiritualists all have their spirit helpers around them more or less continually and can call on them for help at will, even in ordinary reality. If a distinction is to be made between these mystical specialists, we can say that in alternate reality, the *shaman tends to go to the spirits*, while in the case of psychics and spiritualists *the spirits tend to come to them*. Clearly there is a fine line between traditional shamans and contemporary neo-shamans, on the one hand, and psychics and spiritual- ists on the other, so that rigid distinctions of "shaman" or "not-shaman" are dangerous to make.

Neo-Shamanism and the Mystical Movement

The shaman is an integral part of his society, but Achterberg and others suggest that the psychic, the spiritualist, and by implication the neo-shaman are marginal individuals.[2] It is true that none of these mystical specialists conforms to the presumably dominant "scientific, materialist" ideology of contemporary North American society. The society of the traditional shaman is a small, homogeneous one, whereas contemporary North American society is large and heterogeneous, with a number of subgroups. Within that context, the people of the mystical movement represent a distinct and very important group. They hold a set of beliefs that differ from those of the general public. They maintain and reinforce these beliefs through a network of contacts. Within the context of the overall movement, neo-shamans, psychics, and spiritualists are definitely integrated, recognizable, and central to its maintenance and continuation.

In small, traditional "shamanic" societies there are usually only a few people who aspire to become shamans and even fewer who attain that position. Shamans undergo long, rigorous training and are exclusive and limited in numbers. In Western society as a whole, neo-shamans and other mystics are also comparatively few in number; nevertheless, *within* the neo-shamanic network, virtually everyone tries to reach a state of transcendence, deal directly with personal spiritual teachers and power animals, and bring about help and healing for members of the network and for the society and world as a whole. In this sense, modern neo- shamanism differs considerably from traditional shamanism.

Many neo-shamans are individuals in search of transcendence who tend not to affiliate with any clearly defined, long-lasting, organization, either church or "cultlike" group. In fact, their "groups" are actually little more than agglomerations of people who come together in workshops and in local meetings. These groups are amorphous, rarely have a formal struc- tured membership, and are comparatively short-lived. People often partic- ipate in a number of these kinds of groups simultaneously, one of which may emphasize neo-shamanism, one healing, one psychic development, and one spiritual seances.

It is perhaps more informative to think of the associations as interlocking, overlapping networks of people that extend throughout North America and into Europe. These "seekers" develop their personal and very individualized belief systems based on their eclectic experiences, and they tend to remain with those beliefs for long periods—likely through their lifetime.

Like the hippies and other forerunners of neo-shamanism, the people who are drawn to these neo-shamanic associations are often disenchanted with traditional religions and often with much of Western society. Although they tend not to be affiliated with any organized religion, they all continue intensive personal quests for spirituality, meaning, and transcendence. They are searching for new ways to organize their lives in a more satisfying manner and hoping to find more meaning in the religious and philosophical sense. They remain "religious" in the broad meaning of the term and retain their beliefs in some form of supernatural God-like being or Consciousness.

When I attended neo-shamanic workshops I invited participants to fill out questionnaires concerning their beliefs and involvement with neo-shamanism and the mystical movement. The responses illustrated how important the quest was to the people involved.[3] It is not simply a fad or a lark indulged in by the bored affluent. With neo-shamanism they feel they have found guidance.

For example, a sixty-eight-year-old male psychoanalyst summed up the quest of most, saying, "I am on a spiritual journey and will continue on it for the rest of my life." Others elaborated that feeling, such as the fifty-two-year-old female high school science teacher who wrote:

> It seems that the loss of rich tradition within organized religions and their lack of ability to deal with significant problems in a modern complex society has driven many people to seek other "truths." The women's movement has raised the consciousness of both men and women, making "canned" doctrines unpalatable at best and giving people the self-confidence to seek their own way.

Some spoke of a belief "in a collective consciousness and the brotherhood of man." For instance, a woman chiropractor, thirty-two, attending a neo-shamanic workshop observed:

> I don't have religious beliefs except that any route to enlightenment is fine. Spiritually is what counts, not religion. Also I

believe that if a person has knowledge and power, these should be used to help/teach/guide/pleasure others. . . . Shamanism give[s] you some practical guidelines to use spiritual power.

Neo-shamanism and other spiritual systems dealing with transcendence and healing, such as those of psychics and spiritualists, seem to fit the seekers' needs for a system providing meaning, a pattern for living consistent with their new, developing values, and direct contact with the supernatural.

Neo-Shamanic Beliefs

There are several basic premises in neo-shamanism that also hold in the overall mystical movement. The core belief, which I have referred to earlier, is in the existence of more than one reality: there is the "ordinary" reality of conscious, waking, everyday life, and there is also the "alternate" reality where the laws of "nature" as we know them in this reality may not apply. Alternate reality is the abode of spirits of the dead, spirits who have never lived, a multitude of other entities, and, often, a Supreme Being. Like their traditional shamanic predecessors, neo-shamans believe that a person can journey in alternate reality to gain help and direction from the spirits and other entities that dwell there, and also that actions in alternate reality can affect ordinary reality. These assumptions differ markedly from those held by the majority in Western society and as such constitute a new world view, a new understanding or paradigm of reality.

The beliefs of neo-shamans are much more eclectic than those of the classic shaman. Beyond the core beliefs, there are many others that are held by some but not all neo-shamans, such as belief in the existence of and importance of auras and *chakras* (energy or power centers in the body) in healing and power activities. Crystals and other objects in this world are believed to have a spiritual essence and a power that can be used for divination and healing. Spirit guides, spirit teachers, and power animals are critical in dealing with alternate reality. Jesus is seen as an important teacher, spiritual helper, and healer, regardless of whether his divinity as the son of God is accepted.

The interconnectedness of all things is fundamental to traditional shamanism and is at the heart of many contemporary seekers' beliefs, whether they are primarily neo-shamans, psychics, or spiritualists. It is also an assumption in much of the new physics, with which many seekers are familiar. Spiritual balance and the need to be in balance with nature as a whole is critical to the spiritual and physical well-being of the individual and the world.

This fundamental assumption that all things are interconnected leads to a heavily ecological focus in neo-shamanism that reminds one of the earlier hippie beliefs, and a serious concern for the survival of the earth and the environment. These concerns are related not only to a fear of nuclear war, but also of more immediate environmental damage to the earth from contamination, nuclear waste, pollution of land, water, and air, and the destruction of forests, animals, and the ozone layer. The concerns are urgent; as one workshop participant put it, "The earth doesn't have much time." It is felt that neo-shamanic work is one tool to arrest these trends and change the course of human development toward human survival rather than destruction.

Human relationships are seen in neo-shamanism as more important than material gain, and a kinship of all people is felt. The earlier hippie ideals of the value of simple, natural living is perpetuated. Independence of thought and the rights of individuals to explore their spirituality are important to everyone. There is also a shared hope and a faith that as people move more into this spirituality, a change can be brought about in the world that will create a better and safer place to live. The unity of all people can actually come to pass, and peace will become a reality. There needs to be a spiritual awakening, and it is to this end that the entire mystical movement is working.

In classical shamanism, illness is caused, broadly, by the intrusion into the body of a foreign object, by soul loss, or by "power" loss, such as the abandonment of a person by his power spirit helpers. Neo-shamans sometimes use classic shamanic techniques for healing, such as sucking to remove the intrusive object in this reality and alternate reality, or journeying in alternate reality to retrieve a lost soul or power spirit. But their interpretation of illness is broader. Most adhere to the germ theory and other contemporary Western models of disease causation and see value in modern medical techniques. In most cases, shamanic healing (or psychic/spiritualist healing) is seen as an adjunct to Western medicine rather than an alternative.

Nevertheless, a common thread runs throughout the neo-shamanic belief system and that of the whole mystical movement: a general disenchantment with conventional medicine. Western medicine's achievements are respected, but many people feel that it has gone too far. Patients are often harmed rather than helped. Severe and catastrophic diseases such as AIDS, cancers, and coronary problems appear to be on the rise. The constant reporting of them in the press leads the public to believe that a virtual epidemic exists for which there is little help. Compounding the helplessness is the escalating cost of medical treatment, which can destroy a family's resources. The holistic health movement, which stresses preventive medicine, is one response. When prevention fails, neo-shamanism and other transcendent techniques of neo-shamanic/psychic/spiritual healing are employed to augment and enhance the standard medical therapies. (See chapters by Achterberg and Dossey in Part II.)

Techniques such as laying on of hands, aura healing, distance healing though meditation and sending of spirit helpers, or shamanic journeying and extraction of illness, are considered valuable supplements to orthodox therapies. Sometimes these can succeed where conventional medicine has failed and the patient has been given up for dead. Healing is not only physical. Even when physical illness is not healed, the healing of the spirit and bringing the patient to terms with himself and "the universe" are thought to be equally or more important.

The Future of Neo-Shamanism

The popularization of mystical and non-Western belief systems such as shamanism for trendy, "instant" Western consumption has been criticized.[4] It can be argued that such searches for transcendence epitomize the shallowness and superficiality of much of today's supermarket society. Just as there is a demand for capsule versions of classic novels like *Moby Dick* for those unwilling to put forth the effort to read the original, so there is a demand for crash courses and capsule versions of spiritual transcendence. Western society is obsessed with instant expertise and a desire to sample a multitude of things without investing great amounts of time or energy and without becoming really knowledgeable about any of them.

Michael Harner countered criticisms of his teaching "crash courses" in shamanism soon after the nuclear accident at Chernobyl nuclear plant in 1986 in the Soviet Union:

> . . . if the nation-states of the world are working day and night on a crash course of their own for our mutual annihilation, we cannot afford to be any slower in our work in the opposite direction. The leisurely teaching that was possible in ancient tribal cultures is no long appropriate. The forces of nuclear and ecological destruction are in a hurry, and we must be, too. People need to be awakened or they may sleep forever. And they need to be awakened not just through ordinary reality education, however important it is, but also through personal, heartfelt spiritual

realization—deep realization of the connectedness of all things.
May we work together, and as fast as we can.[5]

Harner's response typifies the feelings of many in neo-shamanism and
in the mystical movement in general. A real change in attitudes and
consequently in directions of world history can be brought about through
the mystical work as it spreads throughout the world's population. Without a major about-face, the world is headed toward destruction. With a
change toward the mystical and a realization of the oneness of all things,
a new and better world can be brought about in this reality, as well as a
peace that comes from transcendence.

Shamanism possesses important mystical truths and the potential for
transcendent experiences for which so many people in Western society
are desperately searching. While one could "learn" shamanism on one's
own by extensive research and experimentation, it is not a very practical
alternative. The experience of participating in a shamanic group, even if
only for a few days, provides an orientation and a qualitatively different
experience so important for a true *knowing* rather than merely a detached
intellectualizing.

The new paradigm of reality, although fundamentally an individual
phenomenon, is shared by an increasing number of people. The acceptance by society as a whole of such an alternate world view, with its
awareness of alternate realities, spirits, mystical journeying, and ideas of
the unity of all things, depends on many factors. One may be the positions
in society held by the people who profess the new view. It is instructive,
therefore, that the educational level among these seekers is generally high,
and often they are in professional and social positions that make it possible
to affect social and political attitudes inordinately. Further, half the
workshop attendants had children. A large number of local psychics and
spiritualists are also parents. This puts them in a particularly pivotal
position, because these beliefs and the related attitudes and behaviors can
be passed on to their children. The mystical, shamanic beliefs represent a
wholly different attitude toward life. If these beliefs are held by people in
positions of power and by parents, as I believe they will be in a large
number of cases, the new world view—this new understanding and
comprehending of reality—will have a greater chance to be perpetuated
over generations and to develop and spread throughout society as a whole.

I have talked about a new world view that is basic to neo-shamanism
and the mystical movement as a whole. In 1931 Ernst Troeltsch foresaw
the evolution of a "spiritual and mystical religion" that he called the
"secret religion of the educated classes."[6] It is a nondualistic religion that

is tolerant, sees truth in all religions, and draws on many sources. This spiritual and mystical religion is unlikely to produce any formal church organizations. Religious individualism is essential; each person is his or her own priest.

It seems to me that the mystical movement, with its components of neo-shamanism, psychic healing, spiritualism, and other searches for transcendence and healing in the West, is helping to bring to pass that "secret religion" and its new way of understanding the world, reality, and our relationships with all things. Thus I believe that neo-shamanism and the rest of the mystical movement is not a soon-to-be-forgotten fad of a secular, consumer-oriented society; it represents a major trend with the potential to radically shift the beliefs of Western society.

NOTES

1. Compare Mircea Eliade, *Shamanism: Archaic Techniques of Ecstasy*, trans. Willard R. Trask (Princeton, N.J.: Bollingen Series 76, Princeton University Press, 1964/1972); Michael Harner, *The Way of the Shaman: A Guide to Power and Healing* (New York: Bantam New Age, 1980); Larry G. Peters and Douglass Price-Williams, "Toward an Experiential Analysis of Shamanism," *American Ethnologist* 7, no. 3 (1980): 397–418.

2. Jeanne Achterberg, "The Shaman: Master Healer in the Imaginary Realm," *American Theosophist* 73 (10), Special Issue: "The Ancient Wisdom in Shamanic Cultures," pp. 336–349.

3. I want to thank all the people who helped me. Working with them all has been and continues to be a delight. People in the workshops went out of their way to provide me with detailed information. They suffered through an eight-page questionnaire and expanded on questions so that I gained better insight into their beliefs and this movement. If they did not complete the questionnaire during the workshop, they mailed their responses to me. I am deeply grateful to them all. Local psychics, spiritualists, and others also have gone out of their way to teach me and to provide me with both information and insights. On the more practical side, the research was supported by a Canadian SSHRC leave fellowship and the University of Manitoba Grants Committee–SSHRC funds. Edwin Anderson, Beverly Suderman, and Gary Doore have given major editorial assistance. To all, I owe a deep sense of gratitude.

4. See Brian Wilson, *Religion in a Secular Society* (Baltimore: Penguin, 1969); *Contemporary Transformations in Religion* (London: Oxford, 1976).

5. Michael Harner, letter in *Center for Shamanic Studies Newsletter*, Norwalk, Conn., Summer 1986, p. 1.

6. Ernst Troeltsch, *The Social Teaching of the Christian Churches*, trans. Olive Wyon, vol. 2 (New York: MacMillan, 1931). See also Colin Campbell, "The Secret Religion of the Educated Classes," *Sociological Analysis* 39 (2): 146–156.

2

Shamanism and Healing

WHY ARE patients and physicians alike becoming so interested in the ancient healing techniques of shamanism at this particular time in the West? Do these methods really work with people who are seriously ill, or are the successes of shamanism attributable only to the placebo effect or the power of suggestion? Besides healing of the physical body, can shamanism also help in the treatment of psychopathology or neuroses? These are a few of the many questions dealt with by the authors of this section.

Larry Dossey begins by examining the question of why the medical profession is taking so much notice of shamanic healing models and methods at this time, describing what aspects of shamanism he finds most useful in his work as a physician. He argues for the importance of the attention given in shamanism to the inner life of both the healer and patient, as contrasted with the alienating tendency of Western medicine's clinically impersonal, externalist, and "objective" approach. Modern medical science, he asserts, is based on an outmoded mechanistic view of reality in which the only worthwhile casual explanations are regarded as purely physical ones, whereas shamanism offers a more realistic appreciation of the role of many different levels of reality in the process of illness.

Stanley Krippner points out that shamans were the world's first healers, first diagnosticians, and first psychotherapists, and that they have developed sophisticated medical models over the centuries. He maintains that there are shamanic healing methods that closely parallel contemporary behavior therapy, chemotherapy, dream interpretation, family therapy, hypnotherapy, milieu therapy, and psychodrama, thus indicting that shamans, psychotherapists, and physicians have more in common than is generally suspected. Using observations from field notes of healing ceremonies among native shamans such as María Sabina, Don José Rios, and Rolling Thunder, he shows how the therapeutic models of these practitioners are reflected in their practice.

Jeanne Achterberg sees the process of "wounding"—the shaman's ex-

85

perience of a severe crisis leading to personal transformation or spiritual awakening—as central to the process of becoming a healer. Such wounding in this near-mortal sense is not the result of simply going to school and learning a profession, since the tools and techniques taught in the Western medical professions are based on the philosophy of "clinical objectivity," which serves as a shield to protect one from the necessary wounding. Based on her analysis of the shamanic concepts of *disharmony*, *fear*, and *soul loss*, Achterberg suggests that in contrast to the typically Western way of looking at disease, the shamanic way seems more apt to identify causes. She also emphasizes that shamans have long been aware of the power of the imagination and of symbols in the origin and healing of diseases, an issue that Western medicine has only lately begun to explore.

Implicit in Achterberg's discussion, as well as those of Lewis Mehl and Frank Lawlis, is the view that the effectiveness of shamanic techniques goes far beyond the placebo effect or power of suggestion, since these techniques often produce "miraculous" results with patients clinically certifiable as seriously ill or even dying. As these authors show, the successes of shamanic healing methods are not limited to hypochondriacs or others who were not really ill in the first place, but have been instrumental in recoveries even from life-threatening diseases such as cancer.

Lewis Mehl describes Cherokee healing philosophy and techniques in the context of an "integrated" approach to healing that incorporates the best methods of both shamanic and modern Western biomedicine, defining "good medicine" as "that which works." He refers to case histories of his own patients to illustrate the use of shamanic rituals, prayers and stories in the healing process. According to Mehl, even death can involve healing in shamanism. Moreover, even when recovery occurs, true healing always involves a death and transformation of some aspect of the person.

Frank Lawlis discusses shamanic healing methods from the perspective of the treatment programs he has helped to develop in modern pain clinics. In Lawlis's view, the key shamanic concept in this type of work is that of *spiritual transformation* as contrasted with the materialistic model on which traditional Western medicine has been based. He strives for a shift in the patient's perspective of the world, with emphasis on facilitating a clearer understanding of relationships to nature and the body. Lawlis finds the techniques of imagery, drumming, touch, isolation, music, and chanting to be effective shamanic components of pain treatment programs, and illustrates their use with case histories of patients who have been helped by these methods.

Jim Swan focuses on the role of sacred places or "power spots" in shamanic healing, referring to three examples of healers who use special places as an integral element of their healing practice. In tapping the power of place, Swan suggests that shamans may be taking advantage of naturally occurring concentrations of negative air ions or of strong electro-magnetic energy fields, which they are able to perceive because of greater sensitivity to such phenomena developed through shamanic training. He notes that power spots and sacred places throughout the world are often found near earthquake faults or mountaintops that channel these energies, and that our inner electromagnetic fields may become harmonized with such strong outer fields to produce bioentrainment.

Stanislav Grof reports on a new psychotherapeutic method, holotropic therapy, which he and his wife, Christina, have developed during the past decade. Grof's approach was originally inspired by research on LSD psychotherapy but is now based on nondrug techniques of altering consciousness, and involves working with elements of the "death and rebirth" experience characteristic of shamanic initiations. Grof shows how the integration of such experiences, which he explains in terms of his theory of "perinatal matrices," can help in the treatment of certain neurotic conditions, including hysteria, claustrophobia and other anxiety states, depression, suicidal impulses, and addictive behaviors. His chapter clearly demonstrates how shamanic techniques and reality paradigms are beginning to exert a significant influence on modern psychological theories and practices.

The Inner Life of the Healer: The Importance of Shamanism for Modern Medicine

LARRY DOSSEY

BECOMING A SHAMAN has never been just a matter of cultivating intellectual skills. Rather, it is the entire being that is exercised: body, mind, psyche, spirit. Something of the process is vividly captured in the words of an Iglulik Eskimo shaman:

> I endeavored to become a shaman by the help of others; but in this I did not succeed. I visited many famous shamans, and gave them great gifts. . . . I sought solitude, and here I soon became very melancholy. I would sometimes fall to weeping, and feel unhappy without knowing why. Then, for no reason, all would suddenly be changed, and I felt a great, inexplicable joy, a joy so powerful that I could not restrain it, but had to break into song, a mighty song, with only room for the one word: joy, joy! And I had to use the full strength of my voice. And then in the midst of such a fit of mysterious and overwhelming delight I became a shaman, not knowing myself how it came about. But I was a shaman. I could see and hear in a totally different way. I had gained my qaumanEq, my enlightenment, the shaman-light of brain and body, and this in such a manner that it was not only I who could see through the darkness of life, but the same light also shone out from me, imperceptible to human beings, but visible to all the spirits of earth and sky and sea, and these now came to me and became my helping spirits.[1]

Becoming a modern physician, however, is very different. It consists mainly of learning vast amounts of objective data and facts without which one cannot function as a scientifically oriented doctor. The process of medical education emphasizes an overwhelming *externality* to the world of illness and disease: it is all "out there." Therefore it is not surprising that the physician's gaze always seems to be directed outward. That it might be important to look *inward*, into his own self, to consider his subjective and inner life in the pursuit of healing simply does not occur, for the most part.

This should not be surprising. After all, looking outward into the world is consistent with the mandates of modern science, for science is presumedly made possible by the fact that the world is entirely objective, not subjective. The world, including health and illness, does not depend on our thoughts or feelings about it for what it is. If this were not the case, as Jacques Monod emphasized, science would simply not be possible. (That this view is inconsistent with advances in the science of modern physics has not yet entered medicine or the biological sciences in general.)

Thus the subjective life of the healer is ignored as an important factor in the physician's art. It is something that is a superfluous, frivolous concern. When compared with the "knowing" and the "doing" aspects of the physician's life, the "being" aspects pale into insignificance. This is a radical departure from the shamanic and folk traditions of healing, and is a direction that has enormously negative consequences on the power of healers who have become bewitched by this view.

Yet it has not always been so. There was a time in the West, prior to the extreme objectification of nature that occurred with the advent of modern science, when the cultivation of one's inner life was generally considered to be valuable. Looking inward was not only advised for the common man, it was deemed crucial for the specialist in any area of learning.

Ignoring the importance of cultivating one's inner life has resulted in disastrous consequences for modern doctors. Something has been lost as a result, something vital, something that is crucial to the mission of the healer. The overwhelming external focus on illness, the view that it can be treated as a totally objective, outer event, simply has not worked.

This is hardly a secret. Today it is widely acknowledged by insiders within medical education that something dreadful has gone wrong with the process of becoming a physician. The present deficiencies of the training program for young doctors have been the subject of a dramatic landmark report recently issued by the Association of American Medical Colleges, entitled *Physicians for the Twenty-first Century*.[2] The report acknowledges that we are training physicians today who are less-than-adequate healers. And, although it does not single out the unfortunate neglect of the inner development of the physician, it comes very close to doing so, as do the following recent comments, which also come from within the medical education establishment and which describe the actual predicament:

> . . . the present group of recently trained physicians are, in general, insensitive, have poor patient rapport, are deficient in general medical knowledge and examination skills, and have little concern for medicine's impact upon society. . . . Further, few young people in medicine appear to be either emotionally or intellectually satisfied with their profession. . . . [The] current time-consuming training process often takes bright, creative young adults with a love for helping people, and turns them into cold, distant persons who have lost many of their original ideals regarding the practice of medicine . . . [thereby] producing a physician with qualities 180 degrees opposite of those it states it believes in.[3]

Thus it is no secret that something is wrong. It is not only the patient who is sick, but the healers. The result is that today it is difficult to find anyone who is happy with the state of modern medicine, whether patients or doctors. The commonest complaints are by now well known: high costs; uneven availability of health care; the remote, cold, and dehumanizing quality of much of current medical practice; the failure of scientific medicine to deliver the expected goods in many areas; its preoccupation with technological fixes such as drugs and surgery rather than with preventive and educational approaches; and, as we have seen, the inability of physicians to answer to the needs of the sick person for empathy and caring.

It is the last deficiency which I believe is most fundamental. Even if all the other issues were resolved, the perception of a failed mission for medicine would endure. Unless the healer is healed, there can be no healing of anyone else.

The purpose of this essay is not to debate the particular merits of any of these complaints, for such analyses already abound. Rather, I want to start with the undeniable observation that something is amiss in medicine today; to suggest that the most important reason behind the problem is the failure of physicians to understand the vital importance of their own inner development; that this observation is inescapable when viewed against the backdrop of much current clinical data; and that in shamanism we may develop an appreciation for the importance of the healer's inner life as a crucial element in the healing mission.

One of the most striking characteristics of modern medicine is the way the practitioner has come to view his personal relationship with his craft. Essentially it is a position of remoteness. This way of thinking is embodied in the belief, for example, that one does not select a surgeon on the basis of his personality but solely on the basis of his surgical skills. Or that what is most important in choosing an internist is not his personal warmth but his intellectual acumen—his ability to sort out the various pieces of the diagnostic puzzle, or how intrepidly he designs a treatment program. These attitudes reflect the common belief that a genuine distancing from the patient is not only allowable, but may in fact be desirable: too much closeness may cloud the judgment and might ultimately work to the patient's disadvantage.

I realize this will not be agreed on by many physicians who feel that they really do empathize with their patients, that they do indeed enter into a genuine relationship. But the kind of participation I have in mind is much deeper than what is ordinarily conveyed today by the term "the doctor-patient relationship." It goes further than the offering by the doctor of sympathy, empathy, kindness, closeness, or even caring. I believe that factors are involved when a physician meets a patient that are not described by these psychological-sounding terms—factors that we have forgotten but that were sensed keenly by healers and shamans of the past. It is the actual inner life—the spiritual aliveness, the quality of the physician's being-in-the-world—that I have in mind and to which I want to call attention.

But, again, why? To bring up something as nebulous as the inner life of the physician flies in the face of the bedrock assumptions of modern healers that all disease is external, physical, and concrete in origin; that it is the molecules and the atoms of the physical body that go wrong and that cause disease.

For the shaman, however, this modern approach to the patient's problem is a profanation—not just of the patient but of the world at large. To regard the patient's body as a collection of dead, unthinking stuff, to deny the importance of its intricate connections with the multitude of forces that are everywhere working, to see the world as manipulable only by physical means—all this is an insult to the living spirits and powers that permeate all bodies and the entire earth.

Healing a patient for the shaman is not merely a matter of exercising intellectual ingenuity; it is an exercise in power. And the fate of the patient always depends on the shaman's perception of the powers that are operating in the case at hand, and his skills at intervening, propitiating, wielding, marshaling, banishing, and otherwise plying the spirits and powers involved in the particular illness-event.

The shaman's ability to function in this way depends on much more than technical abilities. He must know a great deal more than, for instance, how to use herbs or potions of various sorts. This is only the exoteric side of his art. The inner or esoteric side involves knowledge that is gained only through following a spiritual path laid out by the previous shamans and guides who have gone before him; by listening to the inner voices that have always spoken to persons who are ready to hear. In the tradition of shamanism it would be as unthinkable for a healer to treat a patient without first achieving a high degree of spiritual understanding as it would be for a beginning medical student to attempt to remove a brain tumor. Being a healer in both cases demands the requisite skills—it is only that we have, through the centuries, come to equate skills primarily with technique and intellectual knowledge.

The very definition of shamanism given by Mircea Eliade—a "technique of ecstasy"—tells us straightaway that we are dealing with more than intellectual skills in shamanic healing.[4] Historically the shaman is the dominating figure in the magico-religious life of his community—the "manipulator of the sacred" and the "great master of ecstasy," as Eliade puts it. These terms clearly convey the importance of the inner life of spiritual experience, which has systematically been excluded in the educational process of today's physicians.

True, the modern healer may pay lip service to the importance of the inner life, but it is almost always the inner life of the patient, not that of the healer, that is considered important. To this end the aid of various "specialists of the interior" may be enlisted—the priest, minister, psychologist, or psychiatrist—in helping the patient get well. Yet most physicians think and function as if all these efforts belong to a secondary category that is set apart from the more substantial forms of intervention.

Of course such efforts may marshal a greater desire on the part of the patient to get well, they may stir up his fighting spirit, but these are mere frills in the long run, because they do not get at the *physical* causes, which is where the premium is. The tumor is either susceptible to the drug or it is not; the bypass operation will either work or it will not; the operation was either done in time or it was not. This is where the real power lies, not in the mind of the priest, the minister, the concerned friends, or even the patient.

We can summarize the differences in the way the shaman and the modern physician view the world thus: the modern healer lives in a dispassionate, mechanical world, the shaman in an enchanted one.

But what of it? What ultimate difference does it make that these two sorts of healers, shaman and modern physician, occupy such vastly different postures in the world? The difference is ultimately spelled out in the "bottom line" for any healer: the clinical outcome, the fate of the patient. But we have to go slowly here, for the criteria for a good outcome may differ radically for the shaman and the modern doctor, and may not hinge on the eradication of disease or even on bodily survival.

When we do consider survival, the modern physician may claim supremacy, since he can do so many things that the shaman cannot. Yet there are skills that the shaman can bring to bear, also, which surpass the skills of so many modern doctors. These hinge on the awareness of the shaman of essential meanings which are contained in the entire cosmic surround, and on the meanings of these patterns as they are perceived by the patient. This requires that he know something of the patient's attitudes, emotions, and spiritual qualities. He needs to know what the illness means to the patient—what the illness is "saying"; what occurred in the life of the patient prior to the onset of illness; how the patterns of many elements of the world (sun, moon, planets, stars, weather, plants, animals, other humans) correlate with happenings in the patient's life. These kinds of questions are almost never a part of the modern doctor's quest for cure; but it is essential that the shaman know something of them before proceeding.

The entire question of the meanings of illness is firmly tied to the physician's inner life. Depending on his own inner understanding, the physician will or will not be able to detect the general sort of information that is so valuable to the shaman. If he has an inner inertia or spiritual blindness, he may not be able to see the patterns contained in the illness-event. And many physicians, I feel, sense this: they find it threatening to entertain that there are meanings or hidden patterns contained in illness which they may not have the capacity to see.

This attitude is understandable; for if the patterns do exist and if the physician cannot detect them, then he must admit that there is something about illness that escapes him. To recognize this is an admission of ignorance about the workings of the world and his own personal place in it. To freely admit this frailty is in effect an admission not only of his own weakness, but of the inadequacy of the modern concept of illness as well, which denies that such patterns exist; it is to doubt the assumption that there is no meaning whatsoever to be found in purely physical processes; it is to question the belief that the only meaningful patterns apply to atoms, molecules, and cellular processes.

If the physician admits that there *is* meaning to be found in the most subtle details of the patient's illness, such as in his relationships with his peers and even with the cosmos at large, he is in effect acknowledging that he has been wrong in rather stunning ways; that his theory and training have left something out; that he may be on thin ice as a healer, having omitted so much; that both his personal and professional philosophy are flawed.

These realizations are always a finger pointing to the self, for the question always becomes: if hidden meanings are contained in the experiences of my patients, what meanings may be contained in my own life, to which I am blind? To admit to a deeply insufficient medical theory is to risk the realization of deep personal inadequacy. This is how the question of meanings of illness are related to the physician's inner life, and why the issue of meanings in illness may be resisted so vigorously in spite of evidence for their importance.

Is there any evidence that the shamans may be right? Do meanings exist in illness that are denied by modern approaches? Using scientific approaches, we do not know how to ascertain the meanings contained in many of the cosmic events that the shaman claims to be able to read. But we can still go far using scientific criteria for determining the importance of meanings. And we *must* use science, for it *is* a powerful tool for healers. And for scientifically trained clinicians the question must be: what is the scientific evidence today that meanings matter in clinical medicine?

The evidence, I believe, is overwhelming. It strikes at the heart of modern medical theory and its insistence on a meaning-free basis of all illness. In one disease category after another the perceived meanings that persons take from the world feed back into the overtly physical processes of illness to affect the illness-event in important ways, which are sometimes a matter of life or death. Taken together, this evidence suggests that we have much to learn from shamanism in listening to meanings in health and illness, and that in order to hear them our own inner lives as physicians must be attuned to the task.

What is the evidence that meaning is important? To begin with, let us consider the leading cause of death in our culture, coronary artery disease. Here the approach to understanding the origins of the illness have involved the classical "risk factors." It is well known that the chance of developing coronary atherosclerosis is increased if one smokes or if one has a high blood cholesterol level, high blood pressure, or diabetes. Yet most persons who develop first heart attacks in this country have *none* of the major risk factors, according to a noted authority on the epidemiology of this problem.[5] Evidence suggests that something is being left out in our physically based approach to understanding the origins of this illness, and that it may have to do with perceived meanings.

Consider the 1972 study in the state of Massachusetts which showed that the best predictor for the development of coronary artery disease was *none* of the classical risk factors, but *job satisfaction*. And the second best predictor was what the study committee termed "overall happiness." Here the key seemed to be the importance of meanings: the meaning of one's job, the meaning of life-events, the happiness one perceives. Here it is not possible to lodge the origins of job satisfaction or "overall happiness" in the atoms and molecules; one must invoke larger issues, albeit less concrete ones: the patterns of relationships, the social surround of the person involved.[6]

Moreover, studies have shown that a third of patients admitted to coronary care units for control of life-threatening arrhythmias (disorders of the heartbeat) have experienced tumultuous, emotionally upsetting events in the period immediately preceding the onset of the arrhythmia.[7] In addition, meditation and quiet repose—methods that allow reinterpretations of old meanings and the surfacing of new ones—have been used in treating malignant, near-fatal arrhythmias[8] as well as elevations of the blood cholesterol level.[9]

In immune disorders, perceived meanings are vividly important. Schleifer and his colleagues examined the function of the T- and B-cells in a group of men, all of whom had wives who had breast cancer. Prior to the death of the wife, the immune cells worked normally. But beginning shortly after the death of the wife, and persisting for many months, the T- and B-cells stopped working and could not even be made to work when extracted from the blood of the men, placed in test tubes, and exposed to chemicals that ordinarily stimulate them into immunoactivity.[10]

Thomas has shown that medical students who are poor externalizers of emotion and who have poor love relationships with parents while growing up are more likely to die from malignant tumors of all types.[11] Depression of immune function has been shown to vary according to many indices of psychological function in a multitude of studies, which have been recently been published in comprehensive surveys.[12]

The list goes on, but the recitation of such findings becomes tiresome. Today the role of perception of meaning as a factor in illness is established beyond question, in my judgment, in a broad variety of illnesses. This evolving body of knowledge is increasing at a dizzying rate, and it is only through defining the effects of perceived meanings out of existence (by saying, for example, that all thought is ultimately physical) that their important status can be denied.

In spite of this data, modern physicians do not feel at home in the land of meanings. Suppose the studies *are* valid: how does one come to terms as a doctor with deranged meanings in a patient's life? One cannot write a prescription for job satisfaction or for better interpersonal relationships, to say nothing of "overall happiness." Thus for many physicians it becomes easier to deny the role of perceived meanings in health than to decide just what it might be one should *do* if they *are* important. And not only that; as long as the wraps are kept on their importance, the physician does not have to question his own overall happiness, his own job satisfaction, or the general richness and adequacy of the meanings he perceives in his own life.

The price that is paid today for ignoring these issues is an inadequate brand of medicine and much dissatisfaction by both physicians and patients, which can be remedied, at least in part, by opening up to the side of illness that is reflected in meanings. Scrutinizing the way healers in other times and in other cultures have dealt with meanings may make it easier for modern physicians to open up to their importance in health and illness. The legacy of shamanic methods extends for at least fifty millennia and has always included the importance of meanings, processes, and patterns in illness. Sensing the connection with these great healing traditions, might not physicians be more inclined to resurrect this facet of their art?

But recognizing the ties with the past is only one possible approach; acknowledging the disclosures of current medical science, such as we have reviewed, is another. It is medical science that is beginning to document the importance of meaning in clear and unambiguous ways. Thus the openness by physicians to the importance of meaning can be facilitated by looking to the past as well as to the present, to tradition as well as to current science. If we can relearn the lessons of meaning, so long a part of the shamanic heritage, perhaps the foundation will be laid for a prolegomenon of healing that will include the physician's inner life as a crucial element.

How did we lose the crucial awareness that the physician's inner life is vitally connected to his ability to heal? I do not believe the answer is obscure. We sent it packing, this awareness, because we thought it interfered with the practice of "good medicine," with untainted clinical judgment, with the exercise of proper skill. We thought we could design a totally objective medicine for humankind. Yes, we thought we were doing the right thing by exorcising the inner-directed ways of being a physician; and our ultimate justification could not be gainsaid: we did it in the name of science. But we were wrong.

There is another lesson to be gained, however, about why the inner life of the healer has always been so important. We can say today that the reason the shamans placed so much emphasis on the spiritual insights and inner visions of the healer were *not* that they lacked science, and *not* that they could not reason as objectively as we, but because *healing, in its highest expression, is impossible to achieve without them.* Without these qualities healers cannot heal: it comes to that. This knowledge was not passed along through the shamanic legacy because it simply could not be jettisoned due to a lack of enlightenment; rather, it was maintained *because of the enlightenment* of the ancient healers. Put another way, the method worked; that is why it persisted, as many scholars of shamanism maintain.

Perhaps the modern healer, like the shaman, can once again begin to explore his inner life as an essential part of his training and with the same rigor with which he learns anatomy, physiology, and biochemistry. In proposing such a thing, however, we are not suggesting that physicians once again embrace the *specific forms* of shamanic belief and practice, such as spirit helpers, power animals, the use of drum and rattle, or the employment of ecstasy-producing drugs or the trance. Such things do not suit us today, and it is foolish to wear what does not fit. What we desperately need from shamanism is far more important than the shaman's trappings: it is the *soul* of the healer we need to recover, for that is what we have lost.

To reintroduce "soul" into the art of healing is not to insert an unbridled religiosity; rather, "soul" is a new mode of awareness that is made possible—an insight into the "ground" dimension of all experience. It is a way of seeing that rescues all of life from the sterile vacuity that has become synonymous with modernity. The ability to ascertain the "ground" dimension of all existence makes it possible once again to know the "verticality" that is inherent in the world, which is the quality which Tillich described as starkly and tragically absent from modern life. Failing the capacity to know the ground of all experience, there is no aliveness to life. And a medicine that is constructed groundlessly no longer satisfies.

This, then, is the great legacy of shamanism for the modern healer: a way to make life alive; a way to discover that the world is enchanted and not dead—a way, in essence, of resurrecting the corpse of modern medicine.

In the Middle Ages the Christian mystic Meister Eckhart (c. 1260–c. 1328) remarked that "it is not what we do which makes us holy, but we ought to make holy what we do."[13] That is what the shaman was adept at doing; that is the ability the modern healer has lost—and not just the ability to *make* holy what he does, but, alas, even the ability to *sense* the quality of holiness in the world.

Can we listen to the shaman's timeless message of the importance of the soul-qualities of the healer, which make possible the recovery of a sense of the holy? If we cannot, further impotence and disarray lie ahead for the modern physician. If we can, then medicine may once again become a path, a spiritual journey, for the physician as it has always been for the shaman—in which case we may recover something which has been missing in medicine of late: the power to heal.

NOTES

1. Knud Rasmussen, *Intellectual Culture of the Iglulik Eskimos*. Report of the Fifth Thule Expedition 1921–24, vol. 7, no. 1 (Copenhagen: Gyldendalske Boghandel, Nordisk Forlag, 1929), pp. 118–119; quoted in Michael Harner, *The Way of the Shaman* (San Francisco: Harper & Row, 1980), pp. 22–23.

2. *Physicians for the Twenty-first Century: Report of the Project Panel on the General Professional Education of the Physician and College Preparation for Medicine*. Association of American Medical Colleges, 1985.

3. T. J. Iberti, "American Medical Education: Has It Created a Frankenstein?" *American Journal of Medicine* 78 (1985): 179–181.

4. Mircea Eliade, *Shamanism: Archaic Techniques of Ecstasy* (Princeton, N.J.: Princeton University Press, 1964), p. 4.

5. C. D. Jenkins, "Psychological and Social Precursors of Coronary Disease," *New England Journal of Medicine* 284 (1971): 244–255.

6. *Work in America: Report of a Special Task Force to the Secretary of Health, Education, and Welfare* (Cambridge: MIT Press, 1973).

7. P. Reich et al., "Acute Psychological Disturbances Preceding Life-Threatening Ventricular Arrhythmias," *Journal of the American Medical Association*, July 17, 1981, pp. 233–235.

8. B. Lown, et al., "Basis for Recurring Ventricular Fibrillation in the Absence of Coronary Heart Disease and Its Management," *New England Journal of Medicine* 294 (1976): 623–629.

9. M. Cooper and M. Aygen, "A Relaxation Technique in the Management of Hypercholesterolemia," *Journal of Human Stress*, December 1979, pp. 24–27.

10. S. J. Schleifer et al., "Suppression of Lymphocyte Stimulation Following Bereavement," *Journal of the American Medical Association* 250 (1983): 374–377.

11. C. B. Thomas, "Precursors of Premature Disease and Death: The Predictive Potential of Habits and Family Attitudes," *Annals of Internal Medicine* 85 (1976): 653–658.

12. S. E. Locke and M. Hornig-Rohan, *Mind and Immunity: Behavioral Immunology* (New York: Institute for the Advancement of Health, 1983).

13. Meister Eckhart, "Counsels on Discernment," in *Meister Eckhart, die deutschen und lateinischen Werke: Deutsche Werke* (V. Stuttgart, 1971), p. 198.

Shamans: The First Healers

STANLEY KRIPPNER

S HAMANS have not been taken seriously by most allopathic physicians, despite the fact that many shamanic traditions have developed sophisticated models of healing over the centuries. Furthermore, the models have been flexible enough to survive their contact with allopathic medicine, and even to incorporate its practices. Few allopathic practitioners have deliberately incorporated shamanic wisdom into their practices, raising the question not only of their open-mindedness but of their flexibility.

With the exception of its herbal knowledge, shamanism generally has been ignored or scorned by the medical and academic world. Nevertheless, shamans were the world's first healers, first diagnosticians, first psychotherapists, first religious functionaries, first magicians, first performing artists, and first storytellers. Shamans can be defined as native practitioners who deliberately alter their consciousness in order to obtain knowledge and power from the "spirit world" which can then be used to help and to heal members of their tribe.

There are shamanic healing methods that closely parallel contemporary behavior therapy, chemotherapy, dream interpretation, family therapy, hypnotherapy, milieu therapy, and psychodrama. It is clear that shamans, psychotherapists, and physicians have more in common than is generally suspected. For the shaman, however, the spiritual dimension of healing is extremely important, whereas contemporary physicians and psychotherapists typically ignore it. Shamans often retrieve lost souls, communicate with spirits, emphasize the interconnectedness of their patients with the community and the earth, facilitate spiritual purification for those who have violated social taboos, explain dreams and visions, and stress the importance of spiritual growth, one's life purpose, and being of service to

101

humanity and to nature. These functions rarely attain importance or even respectability in the world views of Western allopathic physicians and other health care specialists.

María Sabina

I visited Oaxaca, Mexico, in 1980 and was able to arrange a rare interview with María Sabina, the legendary shaman who shared her knowledge of the Mazatec sacred mushroom healing ceremonies with the outside world in 1955.[1] Born in 1894, María Sabina had led a life of severe hardship and personal loss. Her father died when she was very young, and she originally ate the mind-altering psilocybin mushrooms to overcome hunger. On one occasion when María Sabina used the mushrooms, the figure of death appeared to her near her sister's side during an illness. She claimed to receive guidance from "higher spritual beings" as to how to cure her sister and her sister recovered. María Sabina went on to become a well-known *curandera*, or herbalist, and people came from miles around to work with her.

Doña María (as she was called, as a term of respect) became convinced that the mushrooms gave wisdom, that they cured illness, and that they represented the blood and flesh of Jesus Christ. Following the death of her second husband when she was in her forties, doña María began to work exclusively with the sacred mushrooms and became known as *sabia*, or "wise one." She told me that the mushrooms sprout because God wills it. In doña María's model of healing, several acts (e.g., making the diagnosis, identifying the cause of the ailment, determining the treatment) are accomplished when the *sabia* and her clients eat the mushrooms together. Doña María stated that Jesus Christ or some other "higher spiritual being" works through the mushrooms to reveal the origin of the disease as well as the remedy.

Doña María observed that her great-grandfather, grandfather, great-aunt, and great-uncle were all *sabias* who ingested the sacred mushroom during *veladas* or evening ceremonies. Doña María avoided conflict with the local Roman Catholic church by attending Mass and helping to found a society of women, the Sisterhood of the Sacred Heart of Jesus. Indeed, the local priest came to her defense when federal authorities attempted to prevent her from conducting her mushroom *veladas*.

Doña María's ceremonial liturgy contained an overlay of Roman Catholic imagery, but at its core were the same odes and psalms that were uttered by the high priests of Montezuma whom the Spanish invaders dethroned in 1521. The Spanish Inquisition outlawed the *veladas*, which then went underground for more than four centuries. Once it was discovered that the *veladas* were still being conducted, Oaxaca was flooded with young people from North America and Western Europe who wanted to ingest the psilocybin mushrooms themselves. Doña María was sympathetic with their desire for spiritual knowledge but was also critical of these youths because they did not respect Mazatec traditions and ate the mushrooms with neither adequate preparation nor the guidance of a "wise one."[2]

When I asked permission to take photographs, doña María excused herself, returning a few minutes later in her *huipil*, or hand-embroidered ceremonial gown. One of my friends, feeling the full force of doña María's charisma, became visibly moved and began to cry uncontrollably. Instantly, doña María took her aside, prayed for her, and brushed the woman's body with fresh flowers. Within a few minutes, her tears stopped and the afflicted woman reported feelings of peace and happiness that remained with her for several days.[3]

María Sabina retired as an active practitioner as she approached the ninth decade of her life. She remarried and lived peacefully in her small village until her death in 1985. In the meantime, she allowed recordings and transcripts to be made of the songs and chants that accompanied her *veladas*. In one of them, she gave a description of herself and her role:

> I'm a trying woman,
> I'm a crying woman,
> I'm a speech woman,
> I'm a creator woman,
> I'm a doctor woman,
> I'm a wise-in-the-way-of-plants woman.

In another, she related a visionary experience:

> That's the way it looks when I go to heaven.
> They say it's like softness there.
> They say it's like land.
> They say it's like day.
> They say it's like dew.[4]

Fernando Fernandez

On the San Blas Islands off the Atlantic coast of Panama, the Cuna Indians have preserved many of their traditional approaches to healing.

R. L. Van de Castle, a psychologist, conducted field research among the Cuna, finding that they believe that dreams can foretell an impending illness or disaster.[5] Shamans among the Cuna employ a variety of procedures to ensure a calm sleep, among them making sweet-smelling wood carvings that can be placed in the strings of hammocks.

In 1985 I taught a course on the psychology of dreams in Panama City. Among the participants was Fernando Fernandez, a Cuna shaman in his early thirties. Don Fernando explained the Cuna model of healing, pointing out that he was an *abisua*, or "singer." The other types of Cuna shamans include the *inaduledi*, who specializes in herbal cures, and the *nele*, who specializes in diagnosis and purportedly travels through the earth to the Underworld. All three work closely with the healing spirits and power animals who have been venerated by the Cuna for centuries. There are also nonshamanic healers such as the "grandmothers" who provide assistance during childbirth.

Don Fernando stated that there are several types of *abisuas*. The *kantule*, for example, is a ceremonial singer who officiates at special events such as puberty rituals and ceremonies held when a child's hair is cut for the first time. Don Fernando, on the other hand, is asked to sing when a person is physically or mentally ill, when a woman is having difficulty giving birth, or when an excited animal needs to be calmed down. *Abisuas* may also sing for a variety of other reasons—for example, to assist a worker in holding hot metal during construction or to aid a client who desires to attract a romantic partner. All *abisuas* are allowed to sing for enjoyment when they are not engaged in healing.

Like most Cuna shamans, don Fernando is a part-time practitioner. He lives on Ustopo, the most heavily populated of the San Blas Islands, as well as the most traditional. During his studies at the University of Panama, don Fernando was asked questions about Cuna culture by one of his professors. He was embarrassed not to know the answer and realized that his professor knew more about Cuna traditions than he did. This experience motivated don Fernando to become an *abisua* and, with some of his friends, to found the Society for the Preservation of the Cuna Culture. One of his interests is recording and preserving the hundreds of healing songs used by *abisuas*.

Cuna healing songs are complex and difficult to learn. Don Fernando admitted that he had only mastered fifteen of them. The shortest healing song lasts about an hour, the longest—the Song of the Dead—lasts about fourteen hours and took him a year to learn. Don Fernando allowed me to tape record the *akuanusa*, a song used to combat fevers. He also knows such songs as those used to treat headaches, to overcome fear, to ease the difficulties of childbirth, to treat alcoholism, and to rid a house of unwelcome ghosts. The content and style of these songs vary, but all of them call upon the spirit world for assistance.

The Cuna model of healing holds that most diseases are caused by germs and other microorganisms. However, even germs have spirits; epidemics are viewed as nature's punishments when human beings have offended the spirit world. Medicines—stones as well as plants—also are imbued with spirits. Nushu, an important healing spirit, can be contacted by shamans in their dreams and asked for advice.

The Cuna model holds that society has the duty to provide healing services to the community as well as a quiet place to recuperate. Families need to support the advice given clients by the practitioners. The prognosis is favorable if community and family support is given and if the client follows the practitioner's advice. It is believed that people are composed of eight spirits who inhabit various parts of the body—for example, the hands, the heart, and the head. A spiritual practitioner must treat the various spirits differently, as each has its own temperament. If a client dies, one or more of these spirits will go to heaven unless the person committed evil acts while alive.

Considerable attention is paid to the prevention of disease and misfortune. If a *nele* believes that a dream presents a premonition of sickness, he might advise daily medicine baths for his client. Fifty spears carved from black palm trees are placed in a canoe filled with water for this ritual. In addition, powdered wood is placed in the bath to cleanse the dreamer's eyes. If no adverse incidents take place during the month of this regimen, it is concluded that the misfortune has been prevented.

José Rios

The Huichol Indians live in the Mexican Sierras, primarily in the state of Nayarit. El Colorin, a small village, is the home of José Rios, also known as Matsuwa, a Huichole word meaning "pulse of energy." Born in the late 1870s, don José became a successful farmer but lost his right hand in an accident. He regarded this event as a call from the spirit world and began an apprenticeship that lasted for sixty-four years.

I met don José in 1977 when he came to California at the request of people who wanted to "find their lives," as he put it, by learning Huichole wisdom. Don José told me that he had learned many lessons from Tatewari, the "Grandfather Fire," and Tayaupa, the "Father Sun." He related that he frequently had gone into the wilderness alone to take peyote, a cactus bud with mind-altering properties. Through peyote, he gained access to Kauyumari, a power animal identified as the Little Deer

Spirit. This ally helped him travel through a dark tunnel to obtain *nierika* or visions that told don José some of what he needed to learn as he proceeded through his long apprenticeship.

Don José stated, "When you hear me chanting the sacred songs, it is not I who sing but Kauyumari who is singing into my ear. And I transmit these songs to you. It is he who teaches us, and shows us the way. This is how it is."[6] Don José claimed that Kauyumari had taught him how to heal the sick principally through offering prayers to the spirits, by sucking impurities from his client's body, and by using his prayer arrows to balance his client's "energy fields," invisible radiations said to surround such vital body parts as the heart, the sex organs, the stomach, and the brain.

My friends and I once arranged a party for don José, knowing how much he enjoyed music and merriment. When the festivities were at their height, don José's face froze and he became serious. He announced, "One of my Huichole people is ill. I must return to help her immediately." I replied, "But don José, there's no flight to Mexico at this hour; and you are conducting a workshop tomorrow morning!" Don José sighed, "You don't understand. Just leave me alone," and he retreated to a corner of the room where he sat facing the wall for half an hour. When he stood up, the twinkle had returned to his eyes as he announced, "I have been able to help the woman who was sick. Let's get back to the party." I realized that I had been present during a shaman's "magical flight" or out-of-body experience.

Don José has also conducted ceremonies to end drought. During one of his visits to California a torrent of rain followed the Huichole ceremony, ending a dry period. Don José remarked, "You should have told me sooner that you had such problems. I would have come earlier."[7] He has stated that sacred ceremonies are necessary to thank the spirit world for its blessings. Without celebration, the gods may become unhappy and neglect earthly beings.

Don José and other Huichole spiritual practitioners make frequent pilgrimages to Wirikuta, the high desert in central Mexico where peyote can be found. During his peyote ceremonies, don José sometimes chants for several days and nights, seated in his *uweni*, or shaman's chair, so that the power that is manifested will not be dispersed.

For don José, the peyote visions provide a means to diagnose the client's illness and the ensuing treatment may involve herbs, prayers, fasts, or referral to a physician. Clients have the right to obtain care from the Huichole tribe and the duty to cooperate with the practitioner. Not only do don José's clients need to recover from their illnesses but they also need to "find their lives," discovering meaning and joy in their daily activities to prevent the problem from recurring.

Rolling Thunder

In 1982 I spoke at an international conference on shamanism and healing held in the Austrian Alps. The invited shamans and healers met a day before the opening of the conference to discuss the content of their presentations. Because Rolling Thunder was extremely well known in Europe, the conference organizers suggested that he be the first to speak. However, Rolling Thunder, an intertribal medicine man and shamanic healer, retorted, "Don José Rios is my elder; it would not be appropriate for me to speak before him." Because don José was the only person at the conference to have passed his centenary, he was everyone's elder, and at Rolling Thunder's insistence he gave the first presentation.

I had first been introduced to Rolling Thunder in 1970 by a musician, Mickey Hart, a drummer for the Grateful Dead rock band. A year later I introduced Rolling Thunder to Irving Oyle, an osteopathic physician. Following several hours alone in Hart's recording studio, the two practitioners emerged arm in arm. Oyle commented, "We compared our practices. Rolling Thunder said that when a sick person comes to him, he makes a diagnosis, goes through a ritual, and gives that person some medicine that will restore health. I replied that when a patient comes to me, I make a diagnosis and go through the ritual of writing a prescription that will give the patient some medicine to restore health. In both cases a great deal of magic is involved—the type of magic called 'faith in one's doctor.' "

In 1971 I was the program chair for a conference on internal self-regulation sponsored by the Menninger Foundation. During the meeting Rolling Thunder, for the first time, addressed a group of physicians and scientists. He described the "other world" from which he derives much of his healing power and knowledge and remarked, "Many times I don't know what medicine I'm going to use until the 'doctoring' is going on; I sometimes can't remember what I've used. That's because it's not me doing the 'doctoring.' It's the Great Spirit working through me."

Rolling Thunder had a chance to demonstrate his healing ability when a student injured his ankle during a game of touch football. Rolling Thunder asked me to obtain a pail of water and some raw meat. Once this was provided, he prayed to the six sacred directions: "To the East where the sun rises, to the North where the cold comes from, to the South where the light comes from, and to the West where the sun sets. Up to the Father Sun. Down to the Mother Moon." Rolling Thunder drew upon his pipe four times, then handed it to his client. The two men spoke briefly, then Rolling Thunder began to chant.

Lighting a fire in the dining hall fireplace, Rolling Thunder made a sacrifice of the raw hamburger meat and made some passes over the student with an eagle wing. He pressed his mouth to the young man's swollen ankle and held it there for several minutes. Following a series of sniffs, howls, and wails, Rolling Thunder vomited violently, spitting a bilious fluid into the pail. The medicine man repeated this procedure several times, fanned the ankle with the eagle wing, then asked me to bury the contents of the water pail.

What was the outcome of his healing session? Doug Boyd, who observed the proceedings, reported that "the color had returned to normal, the swelling had decreased, and the flesh around the wound was flexible instead of hard. The young man reported that the pain was gone."[8] Andrew Weil, a physician, examined the injury the following morning, claiming that there had been "no objective improvement in appearance, tenderness, or mobility." However, the student told Weil that he had been deeply affected by the ritual because he had never had anyone pay so much attention to him.[9]

Rolling Thunder used ritual, mental imagery, and herbal treatments to "doctor" his clients. Like most shamans, he did not engage in his spiritual practice full time. For many years he worked as a brakeman on the railroads in the state of Nevada. Upon retiring, he organized a small spiritual community called Meta Tantey, or "Go in Peace." Visitors, primarily from western Europe and North America, spent time at Meta Tantey studying Native American medicine and lifestyles. In 1984, after the death of his wife, Spotted Fawn, Rolling Thunder terminated his healing practice but continued to lecture and give counsel.

In Rolling Thunder's model, spritual healing stresses love and respect rather than intellectual understanding. He once said, "It begins with respect for the Great Spirit, and the Great Spirit is the life that is in all things—all the creatures and the plants and even the rocks and the minerals. All things . . . have their own will and their own way and their own purpose. This is what is to be respected."[10]

For Rolling Thunder, the category of "health care personnel" includes allopathic physicians as well as native practitioners; he has been brought into several hospitals to teach patients how to "talk to their bodies" in order to accelerate their recovery. Rolling Thunder observed the behavior of sick people very carefully, often taking three days before deciding on the type of treatment he would offer or even if he should "doctor" them at all. For example, he would send someone with a broken bone or a ruptured appendix to a physician. Prognosis, for Rolling Thunder, depends not only on the client's condition and treatment but on whether or not his "inner healer" has become active.

Some anthropological writers have been harsh critics of Rolling Thunder, arguing that his name does not appear in U.S. governmental registries and suggesting that he is not really an Indian. They also say that he has made a great deal of money by exploiting people he has treated and that his model of healing is not authentic. In response, Rolling Thunder claims that he has kept his name off government rolls because of his dislike of the U.S. Bureau of Indian Affairs. He admits that he has adopted beliefs and practices from several tribal traditions, including Cherokee (the tribe of his birth) and Shoshone (the tribe into which he was adopted). This practice has allowed him to attain intertribal status as a healer. In addition, he has made no secret of the fact that he is part Caucasian. If he had exploited the people he has treated, Rolling Thunder would probably have been sued because he lives in a highly litigious part of the country. Also, his humble lifestyle is not consistent with these charges. Rolling Thunder's political beliefs have made him a controversial figure, and many rumors have been spread over the years to discredit him.

Wallace Black Elk

I first met the Sioux shaman Wallace Black Elk in 1984. Wallace is a great-nephew of Nicholas Black Elk, whose childhood visionary experience is recorded in *Black Elk Speaks*. The vision was one in which Black Elk was given the knowledge of the world tree, the shamanic image that connects Middle Earth (ordinary reality) to the Upper World (extraordinary reality or the "spirit world"). A Sioux grandfather who appeared in the vision told Black Elk that he would save his nation by bringing the world tree to bloom in the center of it.[11] The boy was afraid to discuss his experience for several years, but finally revealed it when he sensed that the traditional rituals were being neglected.

Nicholas Black Elk saw that all things had been created by the Great Spirit for the good of the Earth. Wallace Black Elk's message is the same: "Learn to trust the voice of the spirits."[12] Born in 1921, Wallace received his first vision at the age of nine and now describes his mission as that of a "scout." Most of his colleagues remain close to their people, following the traditional shamanic vow to relieve suffering in any form. But Wallace ventures into new areas to determine if the Sioux idea of spiritual healing will be well received. He is willing to share his model of healing with any group of "Earth People" interested in his message. According to Wallace, it is the present responsibility of human beings to devote each of their acts to the preservation of the endangered Mother Earth. He has been designated as a carrier of the sacred pipe by his tribe, and uses it to conduct rituals when he finds a receptive audience.

Wallace insists that spiritual communication is the greatest need of Earth People today. This can be accomplished through sincere singing and praying, both of which Wallace uses himself to maintain contact with the world of spirit. Referring to one of his powerful experiences, he has remarked, "The power of the Great Spirit is like lightning blasting the senses. My mind is like a color television set; with it I can see all the sacred colors: blue, red, yellow, and white." He has called the sacred pipe his "telephone" because he believes that it provides direct contact with spiritual powers.

Wallace feels that one of his visions may be prophetic. It reflects upon the Western world's laws and regulations, which he believes are based on jealousy and greed rather than the foundation of spiritual communication he espouses.

> There is this huge monster consuming everything with no bottom to its stomach. When the monster gets its mouth halfway around this rock, a fire is going to come out of the center of the rock and blow off the monster's head.

This prophecy seems to be commenting on the exploitative habits of industrialized societies. In the Western world's eagerness to consume, it ingests the rock—that is, the earth—but in so doing, it throws nature out of balance, and volcanoes erupt. Eventually, this power destroys the monster.

Wallace has conducted *inipi*, or sweat lodge, ceremonies for such diverse groups as university students, professional societies, and Indians in prison. In 1985 he conducted one of the first Sun Dances for non-Indians. William Lyon, an anthropologist who has worked with Wallace, observed that he is constantly preparing himself for his next vision quest. To obtain a new vision, Wallace will frequently modify his rituals. For example, Lyon observed that one year the *inipi* ceremony included several new songs as well as a new altar array of ritual paraphernalia.

Inipis are also used by Rolling Thunder, who once invited me to participate in a ceremony. The ritual was organized to facilitate personal cleansing so that my friends and I could help Rolling Thunder conduct a healing session. The structure was built of saplings that had been bent and tied together, and over which animal hides had been draped. A group of nine men sat in a circle as water was ladled over rocks taken from a fire. As the water contacted the rocks, an explosive hiss was followed by a wave of intense heat that enveloped our naked bodies. We took turns adding water, and the heat increased until I thought my skin was on fire. I realized that I could not fight the heat. It was necessary to receive the heat and ride with it. I became one with the heat, one with the hot air, and allowed every breath I took to enhance the feeling. As the sweat poured from my body, I felt purged of anxiety, depression, and all the petty concerns that would prevent me from fully participating in the healing ceremony that was to follow.

Rolling Thunder's invitation is typical of many shamans who invite sincere observers to learn about their traditions. María Sabina felt that the entire world, not only the community of native healers, needed the "old knowledge" to facilitate healing, kindness, and peace throughout the planet. This open attitude is in strong contrast to the secrecy and dogma that characterize some allopathic practitioners who give little attention to spiritual or community aspects of health and healing.

A Model of Shamanic Healing

For several decades, social and behavioral scientists have been collecting data that reflect the wide variety of humankind's healing system. Sickness and injury are universal experiences, but each social group implicitly or explicitly classifies them as to cause and cure. Furthermore, each person has a belief system that provides an explanation of how he or she can maintain health and overcome illness.

Regarding shamanic belief systems, the anthropologist Claude Lévi-Strauss has proposed that the kind of logic developed by tribal people is as rigorous and complete as that of modern science.[13] Similar evaluations have been made by other scientists. For example, in assessing Piman Indian shamanism, the ethnologist B. L. Fontana stated that it is "a nonwestern theory of disease which is as subtle and as sophisticated as any other such theory."[14] The principles of Piman shamanism have been recorded in some detail as a result of a study in which an anthropologist, Donald Bahr, collaborated with a shaman, a Piman translator, and a Piman linguist. In 1986 I met with the Piman Indians who live in the state of Arizona, but the Piman culture also extends throughout parts of northern Mexico.[15]

Among the Pimans, diagnosis is as important as treatment, and it is carried out by the shaman. In the Piman model of healing, a patient's body is seen as the stratified repository of a lifetime's acquisitions of strengths and weaknesses. It is the task of the shaman to make an accurate diagnosis and then to turn the patient over to other practitioners for treatment. In doing this, shamans purportedly are assisted by benevolent spirits; indeed, it is believed that shamans are recruited, trained, and ordered into action by these spirits.

Etiology, or the cause of the illness, depends on the type of disease that is being treated. One type of disease is considered to be untreatable because the body's capacities will deal with it (for example, constipation, indigestion, venomous bites), or because no change is possible (for example, mental retardation, birth defects, and hexes). Another type falls into a category termed "wandering sickness," purportedly caused by impurities such as excessive heat or noxious fluids that "wander" through the body. When Piman shamans heard about the germ theory of illness they neither rejected the idea nor doubted their own system. They merely incorporated the idea of germs into their list of impurities that could cause wandering sickness.

The third category is that of "staying sickness," so named because it "stays" in the body for a considerable length of time. Staying sickness is supposedly caused by improper behavior toward such dangerous objects as buzzard feathers, clouds, coyotes, deer, jimson weed, and roadrunner birds. These objects were endowed with spiritual properties at the time of creation; to transgress against their dignity is an immoral act that brings about sickness. When it was observed that Europeans did not contract staying sickness when they violated power objects, the shamans did not lose faith in their theory. Ingeniously, they concluded that only Pimans could become indisposed from these maladies.

The patient's behavior provides important clues for diagnosis and treatment. Wandering sickness entails such symptoms as fever, hives, piles, or sores. Staying sickness can be identified by compulsive or erratic actions as well as by lethargy or self-destructive activities. The former ailments can be communicable, in contrast to the latter.

The treatment for wandering sickness usually entails herbs. Once allopathic medicines were encountered, they were added to the curative agents for wandering sickness. The treatment for staying sickness involves chanting, singing, oratory, blowing the harmful agencies away from the patient, sucking the harmful agents from the patient's body, eating the flesh of the dangerous object whose violation caused the disease, or placing the patient on a sand painting. Sand-painting treatment is highly recommended for "wind sickness," while a feast is considered useful for "deer sickness" or "rabbit sickness."

In the case of staying sickness, some healing implements (such as crystals, tobacco smoke, and eagle feathers) are used to connect the shaman's power (or "heart") with the patient's self-healing capacities, while others (such as rattles and the shaman's voice) are directed toward the spirits. Herbalists can also appeal to spirits in the course of their treatments. Staying sickness is primarily treated by shamans, while wandering sickness is treated by allopaths or by herbalists. In the Piman system, patients have a right to treatment as well as the duty to cooperate with the practitioner. They also have a duty to refrain from further violation of the dangerous objects that cause staying sickness. Each person has internal capacities or "strengths" located in specific parts of the body. In staying sickness, the strength of each dangerous object interfaces with the victim's strength. Thus the victim's strength can serve as the repository of the disease; once the shaman has located it, such treatments as massaging the muscles or sucking out the impurities can be initiated.

Regarding the question of ethical responsibility—rights and obligations—in the matter of health care, the Pimans believe that the patient's family has the right to obtain treatment for its indisposed family members. Parents have an obligation to avoid violating the dignity of dangerous objects, as this might result not only in their own illness but that of their children. (Parental misdemeanors are considered to be a frequent cause of infant birth defects.) Society as a whole has both the right and an obligation to have healing practitioners available for its members; and society is also obligated to obey traditional spiritual laws so that its people will be protected from plagues and epidemics.

The goal of this healing model is to uphold the "way" or tradition of the Pima, which was given to the tribe at the time of creation. The Piman tradition attempts to be of assistance in the life of individuals and to keep the society "proper." This propriety results in health and joy; failure to follow the traditional commandments results in sickness.

Whether they realize it or not, all healing practitioners operate from a model. The Piman model and shamanic models in general typically differ from the Western allopathic model in that they involve facilitating a closeness to nature, to one's body, and to one's spiritual growth. Moreover, they encourage people to make life decisions in a way that reflects the ideals of harmony and knowledge. These models represent a structured and thoughtful approach to healing, which attempts to mend the torn fabric of a person's connection with the earth as well as the splits that frequently occur between body and mind.

Allopathic medicine, operating from its quite different model, has made great accomplishments since its inception. Yet there are still lessons it can learn from the shamans of the world—lessons that can be of great assistance in its effort to treat human problems, some of which may be more severe now than they were when the ancient shamans received their first visions.

NOTES

1. R. G. Wasson, *The Wondrous Mushroom: Mycolatry in Mesoamerica* (New York: McGraw-Hill, 1980).

2. A. Estrada, *María Sabina: Her Life and Chants* (Santa Barbara, Calif.: Ross-Erickson, 1981).

3. S. Krippner and M. Winkelman, "María Sabina: Wise Lady of the Mushrooms," *Journal of Psychoactive Drugs* 15 (1983): 225–228.

4. Estrada, *María Sabina*.

5. R. L. Van de Castle, *The Psychology of Dreaming* (Morristown, N.J.: General Learning Press, 1971).

6. J. Halifax, *Shamanic Voices: A Survey of Visionary Narratives* (New York: E. P. Dutton, 1979), p. 251.

7. Ibid.

8. D. Boyd, *Rolling Thunder* (New York: Random House, 1974), p. 21.

9. A. Weil, *Health and Healing* (New York: E. P. Dutton, 1983), p. 163.

10. S. Krippner and A. Villoldo, *The Realms of Healing* (Millbrae, Calif.: Celestial Arts, 1976), p. 58.

11. J. G. Neihardt, *Black Elk Speaks: Being the Life Story of a Holy Man of the Ogala Sioux* (New York: Washington Square Press, 1972), p. 182. (Original work published 1932.)

12. W. S. Lyon, "The Dynamics of Change in Contemporary Sioux Shamanism," in R. Heinze (ed.), *Proceedings of the Second International Conference on the Study of Shamanism* (Berkeley, Calif.: Independent Scholars of Asia, 1985), pp. 94–103.

13. C. Lévi Strauss, "The Structural Study of Myth," *Journal of American Folklore* 78 (1955): 428–444.

14. B. L. Fontana, "Foreword," in D. M. Bahr, J. Gregorio, D. I. Lopez, and A. Alvarez, *Piman Shamanism and Staying Sickness* (Tucson: University of Arizona Press, 1974), pp. ix–xi.

15. Bahr et al., *Piman Shamanism and Staying Sickness*.

The Wounded Healer:
Transformational Journeys
in Modern Medicine

JEANNE ACHTERBERG

THE "WOUNDED HEALER" is an ancient descriptor that can be used appropriately in a modern sense for those who have invested their hearts in caring as a profession. It is a concept, though, that challenges the existing model of health care—a model that has spun the last of its web of innovation and lies precariously on the brink of change.

The reader is forewarned that in discussing this topic I must wrestle constantly with the inadequacies of the English language. Information from two vastly different perspectives must be combined—from traditional shamanic cultures, which view everything as whole, alive, and connected; and from the medical/scientific culture, which analyzes, classifies, and names all objects perceived in the external world, treating them as separate entities. For the former culture, the invisible constitutes a level of reality; for the latter, the invisible is nonexistent. The challenge exists in bridging the perceptual gap with words.

A text written by Jaime de Angulo, physician, author, and linguistic expert on seventeen obscure Indian languages, sets the stage for the conceptual differences contained in this chapter.[1] De Angulo was studying the complex and primitive Pit River Indian language structure, and listening to coyote and creation-of-the-world stories.

"All right, Bill," he said to his informant, "but tell me just one thing now: there was a world . . . then there were a lot of animals living on it, but there were no people then. . . ."

"Wha d'you mean there were no people? Ain't animals people?"

115

"Yes, they are . . . but . . ."

"They are not Indians, but they are people, they are alive. . . . Wha d'you mean animal?"

"Well, how do you say 'animal' in Pit River?"

"I dunno . . ."

"But suppose you wanted to say it?"

"Well . . . I guess I would say something like *teeqaade-wade toolol aakaadzi* [world-over, all living]. . . . I guess that means animals, Doc."

"I don't see how, Bill. That means people also. People are living, aren't they?"

"Sure they are! That's what I am telling you. Everything is living, even the rocks, even that bench you are sitting on. Somebody made that bench for a purpose, didn't he? Well, then, it's alive, isn't it? Everything is alive. That's what we Indians believe. White people think everything is dead."

"Listen, Bill, how do you say 'people'?"

"I don't know . . . just *is*, I guess."

"I thought that meant 'Indian.' "

Say . . . ain't we people!"

"So are the whites!"

"Like hell they are! . . . They don't believe anything is alive. They are dead themselves. I don't call that 'people.' They are smart, but they don't know anything. . . ."

So, with that semantic caveat, I will attempt to discuss matters of body, mind, and spirit—the visible and the invisible—with a language base that has been derived for other purposes.

The Modern Interest in Shamanism

The idea of the wounded healer is ubiquitous throughout the more traditional or native health care practices. It implies that some kind of personal transformation or inner work or crisis was encountered. This event then directed a mission and imbued the healer with unusual knowledge about the way of things.

In particular, the notion of the wounded healer has been associated with the shaman. By the term *shaman* I do not necessarily mean the tribal medicine man or woman, nor the herbalist, nor the bone setter, although the shaman might well practice those skills as well as shamanism. Primarily, though, the shamans are those individuals who have the gift of great insight into the human condition, and who have attained wisdom concerning the realms of the spirit. It is with this information that they serve their healing vocation.

The shamans appeared in ancient times as sages who could divine the direction for tribal life, and as physicians during the apex of Greek medicine. They were the wise women or witches during the Middle Ages and Renaissance in Western civilization. The shaman appears in a number of disguises today at the fringes of several fields, including medicine, psychology, and religion.

But of what relevance is the shaman and the related notion of wounded healer to the modern health care practitioner? And why is there such a growing interest in shamanism today—interest that spawned this book, numerous organizations, conferences, and publications?

We must ask ourselves these questions in a serious vein, for there is always the temptation to empower one's work through the identification of ancient and omnipotent personages such as the shaman, even when the connection may be quite dubious. Articles in psychiatry journals, for instance, have frequently likened the work of psychiatrists to that of the shaman. They see both the shaman and themselves as adepts at altering the behavior or mind-set of patients who are experiencing mental imbalance. But although this identification perhaps yields vicarious power, it is far from the truth. These authors would surely be red-faced if they realized the great diversity between the shamanic spiritual path and contemporary psychiatric methodology.

But there are other, more legitimate reasons for the current embrace of the shaman. One is a widespread discontent with the results of modern mental and physical health care. Another is that something is generally felt to be lacking in the training and demeanor of the practitioners—an empathy, an understanding, even a richness of character. Perhaps it is the process of "wounding" or transformation, or the lack thereof, which is the underlying factor for all of the above.

The Wounding

Let us first consider the issue of being wounded, the crisis that leads to personal transformation or spiritual awakening and ultimately to the wisdom to serve the community as a healer.

In cultures that sanction the role of shaman, the potential healer goes through an initiatory period that sharpens sensitivity and insight. Sometimes this is unplanned, such as a grave illness that brings the initiate very close to death. At other times the healers-to-be may go on visionary quests, undergoing supreme deprivation until their minds are unhinged from conventional reality, allowing them to then touch the supernatural. Either way, the mission to heal and the tools for doing so are revealed.

Such events can occur and have occurred in the lives of health professionals in the modern world and have led to vocational choice. Being disabled, or having had a serious disease, or being in recovery from an addiction, or even having a child with a significant handicap has been the wounding or the initiation for many in the health care field. For others of us, the wounding is our own private psychic pain; it is the richness and texture of our own lives, and the emotional ties we establish in our work.

Getting wounded in this near-mortal sense can never occur simply by going to school and learning a trade, whether it be psychology, nursing, doctoring, or whatever. The tools and techniques that are taught in these professions serve as a shield to protect one from the wounding—from the arrow of understanding. "Stay objective, stay away, don't take your patients home" is the standard dogma for the training of all health care professions. And one can do precisely that, enjoying a long and even prosperous life in one's field of choice, yet learning absolutely nothing of value about the human condition, nor facilitating the healing of even a single soul, including one's own.

No, the mission of the wounded healer is difficult, the path treacherous. The shamans know full well that their intense involvement in healing challenges their own lives. They are frequently ill, full of "poison" from their own work. Their journeys to other worlds, other levels of reality, have a dark and threatening side. There is no indication that they are particularly conscious of physical health—attending more to the inner life, no doubt, than the exterior. This forms an interesting contrast with the preachments of the holistic medicine movement, which, like modern medicine, prescribe elaborate rituals for protecting oneself from the energies and emanations of one's patients. It is a difference in healing philosophy to ponder carefully, and one that ultimately has great influence over the lives of both healer and healed.

A woman diagnosed with cancer with whom I was working summarized the concept of the wounded healer very succinctly. She said, "It isn't what therapists do that is of so much importance, but rather who they are." She meant this, not in terms of fame or diplomas, but rather as a reflection of their ability to transcend the mundane and add meaning to their own lives in such a way that it is reflected in the therapeutic relationship.

Healing

Now a few words about healing—a term integral to the sense of this chapter. The word *heal* and all its derivatives are naughty words in modern medicine, where *healer* is synonymous with *quack* or "silver-tongued, slick-haired evangelist." Indeed, from the standpoint of contemporary medical science, even a person's own natural abilities to heal from virtually every trauma of the mind, body, and spirit are given scant recognition in terms of research, nor are they generally credited with bringing about recovery. Spontaneous remission is shrugged off as an anomaly, the placebo effect is viewed as a pest in research, and any disease that does not conform to statistics is rudely classified as a misdiagnosis, a temporary remission, or just plain hysteria. Healing, indeed, is not popular.

What does it mean to heal or be healed, anyway? The "end points" that one accepts as representing healing are highly variant and culture-specific. In the traditional shamanic cultures, healing bears little relationship to the remission of physical symptoms. It refers, rather, to becoming whole or in harmony with the community, the planet, and certainly one's private circumstances. When this happens, physical healing may or may not be observed, and the patient may well die. Obviously, this creates a vast mistrust among observers who come from outside the tradition. After all, what kind of healers could these shamans be if their patients die? From the shaman's point of view, however, the course of life or death is irrelevant, for these are only different experiences along the one continuum of existence.

The shamanic attitude, of course, implies a quite different definition of *healing* from the one that is most familiar to Western civilization—namely, a "return to normal"—where *normal* is culturally defined by some measuring standard created by society's members. A remark made by an Indian medicine man is appropriate here: "With white man's medicine, you only get back to the way you were before; with Indian medicine, you can get even better!"

I would like to note, though, that the human spirit is often triumphant even in the face of atrocious medical treatment. People do creatively move through, learn from, and transcend disease in this culture. And for the therapist, being able to participate in this journey with very exceptional—and often very ill—patients is a great gift and source of enlightenment. Not everyone, of course is able to do this, or even chooses to; and often significant support is required for the efforts.

The Journey of Self-Transformation

The journey of personal growth taken by those undergoing a serious disease process distinctly parallels the initiatory journey of the healer. I now think that for the healer, this voyage means a more or less constant progress on the simultaneously painful and joyful task of self-awareness and self-development, as well as a commitment to a mission of service. In traditional shamanic societies, the transformational passage was taken for granted as a necessary part of the healer's preparation for his or her vocation, whereas in modern medicine it has been all but forgotten. Nevertheless, the traditional path of self-discovery taken by native healers during their initiatory process has a modern prototype which is becoming more and more common. This transformational journey is not only compatible with modern medicine, it is essential. Healing wisdom will only advance as the best aspects of all systems are thoughtfully combined.

To use my experiences as an example, the journey of initiation was not in preparation for my work but because of it. And the process was not usually engaged by conscious choice or even desire. There is a Latin proverb to the effect that "she who goes willingly, the Fates will lead; she who does not go willingly, the Fates will drag along." The latter best describes my participation.

Neither the trusted methods of medical science nor even the tenets of modern religion were of much assistance in guiding my thoughts, my research, or my clinical practice with persons with catastrophic illness. The confusion, uncertainty, anger, and frustration created a need to learn and even to identify with other cultural traditions such as shamanism, which seemed capable of injecting some wisdom into areas of medicine that had been sterilized by objectivity.

It seemed first of all as if, in the interests of technology and dogma, the essence of what it means to be human was being overlooked in medicine. The oversight has been most painfully felt by those with chronic conditions and those who are dying, both of which are conditions beyond the scope of medicine as it is conceptualized today.

During my early years of research, I also saw strange events that could not possibly be accounted for in terms of what is known about the human body, nor what can be expected from medical treatment.[2] For example, patients with certain types of personalities were likely to live longer following diagnosis of a "terminal" disease. Their blood chemistry analyses revealed amazing correlations between changes in hematology and scores on psychological tests. It was possible to statistically predict longevity on the basis of cancer patients' drawings of their disease, their host defense, and treatment.[3] Many folks died when it did not make sense according to accepted theories. Often they were too young or too healthy, or their disease was not serious enough to cause rapid demise, according to the textbooks. The "biological course of the disease"—a phrase used to imply that a disease progresses independently and according to its own nature—came to have little meaning.

On the other hand, I observed people who had been given the last rites recover and go on to lead productive, satisfying lives. I have also witnessed the miracle of lives well lived under the most traumatic physical limitations, and the miracle of those who move with great awareness and clarity to their final stage of this life. In every case, these apparently miraculous cures could be attributed to inner mental and spiritual resources. These events are more rare than not, but the fact that they do happen deserves consideration and study.

The Meaning of Disease in Shamanism and Modern Medicine

There are some exceedingly strange characteristics to disease, whether it is classified as mental or physical in the Western system. For instance, one rarely sees "classic" cases of anything. People are diagnosed based on clusters of symptoms that look something like what other people have had, and a name has been attached to them. The diagnoses are often whimsical but seem to make people happy. The doctor feels pleased that he or she has identified something; the patient is pleased because he or she has something "real" with a name.

In truth, however, each body/mind/spirit seems to respond to inner and outer life in a unique way, wearing thin or flaring up here or there. I would submit that besides the typically Western way, there are other ways of looking at disease that are more apt to identify causes. The shamanic emphasis on seeing disease in terms of the key concepts of *disharmony*, *fear*, and *soul loss* is one such way.

For instance, as shamans have long recognized, disease is inevitable if life loses meaning and one forgets the feeling of belonging and connection (disharmony). Similarly, a chronic sense of fear will cause a person to lose the love, joy, and trust which are basic foundations of health and without which the force of life itself seems to begin withdrawing from the body. The implications of these two shamanic diagnoses have been scattered throughout this chapter. Both, too, manifest in diseases identifiable to Western medicine. Thus the symptoms that we think represent disease may be merely the epiphenomena of far more basic problems.

Soul loss, on the other hand, is regarded as the gravest diagnosis in the shamanic nomenclature, being seen as a major cause of illness and death. Yet it is not referred to at all in our modern Western medical books. Nevertheless, it is becoming increasingly clear that what the shamans refer to as soul loss—that is, injury to the inviolate core which is the essence of a person's being—does manifest as despair, immunological damage, cancer, and a host of other very serious disorders. It seems to follow the demise of relationships with loved ones, with careers, or other significant attachments.

The Wounded Healer and the Imagination

There is an invisible bond of power between the wounded healer and the healee. The bond is the essence of the work of the healer. All else—all ritual, gadgets, medical maneuverings of the body and manipulations of the mind—are merely reminders of the divine process. The shamans know this full well and strengthen the bond with ritual. Some call this bond love. It comes forth from the desire to make and be made well or whole.

As human beings limping along on the road to perfection, we have invested our faith in what our senses tell us is real. In this society surgery is real, drugs are real, vitamins and acupuncture are becoming somewhat real. For the shamanic cultures, on the other hand, drumbeats, sucking out objects, and crystals are real. All of these have some energy—often quite subtle—that is perceived by the senses and does, therefore, induce some physical change. But in addition to the power of the senses, shamans recognize the power of the imagination as well.

The wounded healer, the man or woman who knows the landscape of the spirit realm, facilitates the moment of unity between healer and healee by reaching into the inner dimensions of spirit with her or his own imagination. And, as if to say "See, there it is," the healer gently assists the healee in remembering what has been forgotten.

The shaman who journeys through the spirit world knows well the terrain of the imagination; the imagination creates pain of the direst order and cripples and kills with the surety of a merciless assassin. Untold numbers of people are dying, not from their disease, but from fear. They reach out for support, for answers to guide them on their journey through illness. Too often, no map is forthcoming.

The imagination is also the greatest healing resource. There is nothing in the recorded history of medicine nor in the findings of modern science that contradicts this outstanding fact. Dreams, visions, and the products of the imagination are responsible for more of the world's information on health and disease than any other phenomenon.[4]

The intimate—indeed, inseparable—association between mind and body allows for exquisite diagnosis as well as physiological control. No thought fails to leave a corporeal mark; no neurochemical signal occurs without being registered by the mind.

The tools for using the imagination in a healing and diagnostic capacity are called many things. They might be referred to as hypnosis, trance, meditation, journeying, imagery, or prayer. Regardless, what is required is a shift into another mode of consciousness, one that can listen in an intuitive way to messages coming from one's own body/mind/spirit complex. The shift permits an atonement with a universal mind, a higher power, a collective unconscious, or with whatever dwells within that guides and gives life its meaning and substance.

Research from numerous credible sources suggests that the imagination can influence or direct the activity of bodily processes. This may only happen with great effort and practice, and when the message is sent with precision over and over again. It appears to be of relatively little importance whether the images are true to textbook, common reality. Rather, what is necessary is that the dynamics are accurate in a healthy sense. This requires some appreciation of the facts of biology and physiology, even though the message to the body may be highly symbolic in form.

There is yet another way that the imagination heals, and that is to enter into a moment of sensing the ecstatic truth of being absolutely and totally inseparable from every other aspect of creation. That moment itself is both the definition and purpose of healing. Sometimes physical problems disappear, and sometimes the patient dies. Either way, with the instant of connection, of unity, healing occurs.

The Power of Symbols

The healing power of external symbols—whether of shamanic or Western allopathic origin—will wax and wane. There is an old joke in the medical profession that drugs and surgical techniques should be used often while they are new because they tend quickly to lose their effectiveness after being on the market for a while—which is true. It should surprise no one, then, that dramatic breakthroughs are constantly being announced for AIDS and cancer, and after the first few clinical trials, the results fizzle out, the researchers are embarrassed, and the public is frustrated.

After years of observing people who are receiving the standard treatment protocols in Western medicine, and others who have elected alternative treatments, it appears to be possible to conclude both that everything heals and that nothing heals. I've seen people get well after having cancer chemotherapy that nearly killed them, others who recovered after being "opened and closed" (i.e., after exploratory surgery had disclosed that too much disease was present to warrant further surgery), and still others who got well after nearly starving to death on strange diets that they could barely tolerate.

A doctor's wife of my acquaintance received the best of medical care for her progressively worsening bone cancer, until her oncologist told her that she might as well try anything, since he could no longer help her. She did, including a psychic surgeon, and came back with no evidence of disease. The oncologist was furious!

On the other hand, another woman who came to me for guidance with anticancer imagery had refused to take an estrogen-depleting agent prescribed to her for her tumors, which "fed" on estrogen. Instead, she adopted a regime that included a macrobiotic diet, intense meditation, and study with her guru—a person who healed with colors—as well as a diviner who swung a pendulum over her blood samples. Her tumors continued to grow until she finally submitted to modern medicine, whereupon they began to shrink. Again, everything heals and nothing heals, depending upon how much power is invested in the symbol. It is high time to investigate the mystery of all this, and in all probability both AIDS and cancer will painfully lead us to the truth.

The Role of the Wounded Healer Today

If, as I have been suggesting, healing is a personal decision by the patient and all power comes from within, then what function does the healer serve, and how can a healer evaluate his or her own success?

It is with some regret, I suppose, and no false modesty that I say I cannot force a healing to take place. I cannot even access my own healing mechanisms on a consistent basis. We all have much to learn. In the final analysis, the "miracle" of healing, the solution to the complex problem of both mental and physical disease as we know them, and the point of transcendence, must be personally defined, sought, and achieved.

Shamanism has much to teach us, especially in regard to that most difficult lesson for those of us in the helping professions: learning to honor the uniqueness of each individual's path. It may be that no two diseases or their purpose in a patient's life are exactly the same. Nevertheless, some general guidelines emerge. First of all, there are respectable and effective techniques in every health care profession, whether of the shaman or the Western physician, which are designed to alleviate suffering and facilitate the natural healing process. But whatever the method of treatment, it must be used with compassion and sound professional judgment.

Thus, in the modern healing role, with all its limitations, one can still touch and pray and ease transitions. The knowledge given us by our patients, our colleagues, and our own restless and struggling minds can be shared to facilitate the ongoing journey of self-transformation on which our healing practice must be based.

From my study of both the shamanic and Western healing paradigms I would concur with Twylah Nitsch, a Seneca medicine woman who suggests that in this journey there are four basic guidelines the healer must ask: (1) Am I happy in what I am doing? (2) What am I doing to add to the confusion? (3) What am I doing to bring about peace and contentment? (4) How will I be remembered when I am gone—in absence and in death?

The first question points to the basic appropriateness or inappropriateness of one's vocation or "calling" as a healer: does the role of healer satisfy one's deepest soul-need? As the shamans have recognized, without this kind of satisfaction there will be a gnawing sense of frustration that can only drain one of energy and lead to eventual failure, possibly disaster. Hence it is of primary importance.

The second and third questions address one's competency and effectiveness: can I really help to bring the patient into a state of clearer awareness in which he or she can learn the lessons that must be learned from this illness and attain to wholeness and peace? Or, on the other hand, am I just adding to the patient's confusion and suffering? Obviously, the answer to this question is critically important as well.

The fourth question concerns the judgment of the community: am I making a contribution that is significant enough to be remembered after I am no longer present? For it is, after all, the interest of the community as a whole, as well as its individual members, that the shaman has pledged to serve. Hence, the judgment of one's peers must be taken into account. Moreover, without their support, recognition, and encouragement, one's work as a healer will lack an important source of empowerment.

NOTES

1. J. De Angulo, "Indian in Overalls," in B. Callahan (ed.), *A Jaime de Angulo Reader* (Berkeley: Turtle Island, 1979). De Angulo's firsthand observations of shamanic work in several Indian tribes are of special interest in these materials.
2. J. Achterberg, *Imagery in Healing* (Boston: Shambhala, 1985). The research briefly discussed in this chapter is reviewed in detail in this book.
3. J. Achterberg and G. F. Lawlis, *Imagery and Disease: A Diagnostic Tool* (Champaign, Ill.: Institute for Personality and Ability Testing, 1985).
4. R. Grossinger, *Planet Medicine* (Boulder: Shambhala, 1984).

Modern Shamanism: Integration of Biomedicine with Traditional World Views

LEWIS E. MEHL

THE BACKGROUND of each of us plants seeds from which we create our present reality. My early years were spent in southeastern Kentucky, among a blend of Cherokee people and Kentucky hillbillies. As I grew up I observed both Cherokee and traditional Appalachian folk medicine. Both were trusted and both worked. Later, in medical school, I was amazed to learn that healings which seemed commonplace in my background were viewed as miraculous from the contemporary Western medical perspective. The professors simply would not believe my childhood experiences. I realized then that modern medicine was lacking an adequate concept of healing and the spiritual base from which healing occurs.

Modern biomedicine arose in virtual contempt of traditional medicines. This contempt can be traced at least as far back as the Catholic church of the Roman Empire. Healing was relegated to the church and to priests. Healers who were not part of the church were heretics. In the Middle Ages, persons who appeared to have healed another could be burned as witches. *The Malleus mallificarum*,[1] a text of that time on witchcraft, condemned all women healers. When religion and medicine began to separate during the Renaissance, there was an understandable avoidance of nonmechanical concepts. The prevailing paradigm was to view the body as a mechanical device. This paradigm allowed escape from the disastrous control of the church.

Many writers have traced the development of this mechanistic world view into the present. Michel Foucault, for example, addresses the origins of these changes in *The Birth of the Clinic*,[2] and Fritjof Capra discusses their evolution in *The Turning Point*.[3] Will and Ariel Durant provide further background in their classic work on Western civilization.[4] Other contemporary writers have commented upon the extreme split between science and religion, medicine and healing, and technology and the humanities. Today we have witnessed the pinnacle of separation between medicine and religion. Perhaps this was necessary, given the prejudices and superstitions of our ancestors; but such a split is no longer healthy and must be resolved for medicine to progress.

There are many patients suffering from chronic diseases for whom modern biomedicine can offer little or no help. For them there are no drugs or surgeries to effect miracle cures. For example, many patients suffer as much from the side effects of their medications as from their disease; yet the medications cannot be stopped or the disease will rage out of control. Thus the modern physician often finds himself in a double-bind, knowing that whatever course he follows will provide no real relief for the patient's suffering, let alone recovery.

In my work at the Center for Recovery from Illness in San Francisco we are taking a new approach with such cases, in which we draw from both the ancient and the modern world in attempting to improve the lives of our patients. To date, modern biomedicine has tended to view the world's traditional medicines with the same jaundiced eye it used in its adolescence to rebel against the Roman Catholic church. Oriental medical practitioners are tolerated at best, and native healers, whether they are American Indian, Laotian, Mexican, or African, are dismissed as uneducated and misinformed, even dangerous.

But despite this official condemnation, who has not heard of miracle cures at the hands of these "third-rate" practitioners? Such stories are passed around at parties over hors d'oeuvres. Most physicians scoff, alluding to trickery or misdiagnosis. Documented stories exist, however, such as a study of the Brazilian healer Ariga,[5] or the excellent book on Eduardo, a Peruvian *curandero*,[6] which confirm the reality of such cures. With so much apparent evidence at hand, why doesn't the medical establishment investigate further?

One reason is that proving these stories would have too many disturbing implications. Our entire Western system of health care and insurance reimbursement would have to change. That system and the medical education producing it are based upon a mechanistic world view with no room for the truths of native healers. Our fear of change keeps us comfortably avoiding this other world while our patients suffer.

Most readers of this book will be familiar, at least in general terms, with the broad elements of the shamanic world view. Hence there is no need to give a detailed exposition of them here, and I shall therefore merely note that the elements of that perspective crucial to our clinical approach are as follows:

1. All parts of the world are interconnected, on all levels of reality, so that whatever happens to one individual affects all others and whatever happens to the others affects the individual, at every level from the physical to the spiritual.
2. The objects perceptible to human senses are local manifestations of larger patterns of energy.
3. That which is imperceptible to human senses is as important in illness as that which can be measured and validated through the senses.
4. Consciousness is all-pervasive; or, otherwise stated, "everything is alive."
5. The universe as a whole is sacred and has purpose and meaning.

These concepts of shamanism are remarkably similar to recent concepts of quantum mechanics, modern particle physics, and the mathematics of topology and catastrophe theory. The essence of the natural scientific method is the "experiment in isolation," in which the experimenter isolates a subsystem as separate from the rest of the universe. In practice he creates a "box" (the isolated system) whose geometric characteristics he can specify. He defines instruments and types of measurements to be used to describe what will happen inside the box. Then he defines an initial state of the box, performs an intervention, and redefines the state of the box at some time interval afterward.

For medicine, the "box" is the body. The initial state is the biochemical and physiological description of the organism at the time of treatment. The intervention is usually a pharmaceutical compound. Medical research assumes that all individuals with the same initial measurements of biochemical and physiological markers are in the same initial state and are isolated from the remainder of the universe.

The shaman, however, laughs at the assumption of such locality. The shaman feels the breath of the sun at every moment flowing through the body of the patient. He senses the dance of the stars in the vagaries of the illness. He watches the movements of the animals as clues to the onset of the disease. In his view, the entire universe is involved in the process of pathology. Thus the shaman denies the validity of the major hypothesis of natural science—that of structural stability of isolated scientific processes. Instead, he works with the world's larger energies, sensing the boundaries and forms of the larger shapes or systems that mold our lives. He speaks to these systems as they interface with the client.

For example, Nancy is a forty-year-old woman with the Epstein-Barr virus. Before being referred to our clinic she had been thoroughly evaluated by modern biomedical techniques, which found that nothing could be done for her. In our program, however, Nancy learned that the shaman speaks about the larger energies of the world in a metaphoric language. Thus she discovered that the "ghosts" of her dead mother (a suicide), best friend (also a suicide), first horse, most loved horse, ex-husband, and others lived within her body in the essence of the viruses.

The shamanic treatment involved expelling these "spirits," combined with teaching her that it was not her job to nurture and care for them. In addition, she was taught rituals of prayer, to enable her to give the energy of her ghosts back to the universe (God, the Creator, Brahman, or whatever label one prefers). She was taught to release her responsibility for these entities she carried. The ritual revealed the energies of the larger systems within her body and pulled that energy from her body.

One way of viewing this process is to regard such "spirits" as the shapes of the larger form of the family system. Family therapists and theorists *talk* repeatedly about family systems. The shaman *senses* or feels the form or shape of that family system and works directly with its energies.

Sacredness and Prayer in Shamanic Healing

The term *sacred* refers to a sense of respect and reverence for the larger systems and energies that govern our lives. American individualism has eroded this concept of the sacred, based on the illusion that we are each in control of our lives—absolute masters of our own destiny. In the shamanic tradition, however, respecting the sacred means acknowledging that we are out of control, that we do not govern the entire fabric of our lives, and that larger energy systems move us here and there. The shaman respects these larger systems, acknowledges their consciousness and intentionality, and works with them.

Whatever God or the Creator is, the shaman knows that we are completely surrounded, completely enclosed by that energy. There is no escape. Therefore we must cooperate. We ask to understand our purpose within the larger energy system. We pray for that purpose to be compatible with our body health. Just as the cells in our human body must die and be replaced, so we too must eventually die and be replaced. But the larger energy systems of which we were a part will continue.

Prayer is the language of the shaman; it is the intentions we broadcast each day. The words used in hypnosis or visualization can also be described as a form of prayer, which is the addressing of the larger systems within which we live.

I am frequently asked to explain how visualization works. Within one context I speak of the potential biochemical and physiological mechanisms involved with hypnosis and visualization.[7] From the shamanic standpoint, the explanation differs. From that perspective, visualization or hypnosis works because prayer works; and prayer works because the larger systems are conscious and can respond to our request for healing.

Who or what are these larger systems? The shaman doesn't know. He senses their shapes and their forms, and works with their energies. Only dogmatic people can precisely define these shapes, and it would be unwise to trust their definitions. For we cannot fully define a system that is larger and more encompassing than ourselves. As Heisenberg's uncertainty principle tells us, we may define one aspect of that system at the cost of knowing nothing else about it. Gödel's theorem informs us further that at our level we have no way of testing the truth value of any of our hypotheses about the larger systems which contain us. We are truly limited in our capacity to grasp the nature of our containers.

What we are left with are our shamanic senses and perceptions. We can perceive the traces made by these larger systems in the sands of our lives, just as the particle physicist perceives the tracks of strange and beautiful energies on the walls of his cloud chamber and makes sense of them according to his own symbolic systems.

In my shamanic work I begin with prayer. I pray to the spirits or energies that contain me, asking them to help me and to help the client. Given my absolute uncertainty, I need that help to guide me through these larger worlds in which the healing must occur. My Cherokee ancestry has influenced the form of those prayers, as has the pan-Indian movement.

I often begin by praying to the four directions, which represent all the corners of the world. Having asked for the help of the four directions and given thanks to them for their presence, there is a need to speak to the spirit of the place where we are at this very moment. When I write these words I speak to the spirit of the meadows between the hills and the bay in my home in Palo Alto. As you read these words, you too may address the spirit of your home and land. These are the spirits of place, whose ground is our present. They ask respect and provide support.

When I travel to the southern Arizona desert, contact of a different nature occurs. There I feel at home, as if I have run across this land many times. I am friends with the spirit of that place. A joyous recognition takes place and we communicate. It is therefore a powerful location for me to work. In each place there are different spirits, and therefore what I am able to do at each place differs in accordance with the nature of my contact with these spirits. In my office I similarly nurture and collect the healing energies within the room where I see my clients. The spirit of place is very important.[8]

Integrated Medicine

When we begin our work with a client, we do not know the realm of the possible for that person. Only the universe (God, Great Spirit, etc.) can sense that. Therefore we must begin with each client with the assumption that a total healing can take place, while at the same time recognizing that the possible may be very limited for that client. Only our efforts will unfold what is to happen.

Some patients are dying. Thus the healing may involve relationships with other family members. It may involve dying with a sense of peacefulness. It may mean a miraculous remission of the illness. We do not know whose time it is to die, so no assumptions are made to that effect.

To have a set of spiritual beliefs as a practitioner is essential. If healing is to be the result of a team effort, as it is at our clinic, these beliefs need not be the same for each member of the medical team, but they must involve a sense of respect for each other and for life as a whole. We must share the same beliefs about the possibility of healing being ever present for the individual. We believe in miracles, and know that our hands are not those responsible. As Paracelsus said: God heals; the surgeon applies the bandages.

Cherokee medicine was traditionally organized in teams of seven different kinds of healers. Simple cases were handled by one medicine person. More complicated cases involved three or four practitioners, and the most life-threatening cases involved all seven. We have followed this same format. Practitioners work together using different modalities and a common philosophy. Through our respect for each other and the client, we weave a blanket of treatment as we proceed.

Love is the source that moves and guides the effective healer—a love that springs from a deeper Source than the individual ego and which has been called by many names in different spiritual traditions. Our work involves tapping its power for our and the client's benefit. It is not necessary to engage in theological discussions about the nature of that Source. We need only live its energies to make its presence known through our work. Clients have their own interpretations of what it is. Some attribute it to us, others to science or to a technique such as acupuncture or hypnosis, and others to Buddha, Sai Baba, Jesus, and so forth. The healing phenomena are important, not the labels attached to their origins.

An old Cherokee saying is, "If it's good medicine, it works." This principle guides our efforts. If we listen closely enough, clients tell us how they can be healed. Hypnosis is helpful in providing clients with suggestions enabling them to disclose full details of their intentions regarding their illness and how we can best assist them to meet their goals.

In approaching an integration of traditional medicines and modern biomedicine, the main requirement is to bring a sense of spirituality (awareness of the realm of spirits) into our day-to-day practice. This does not negate the technological aspects of healing, but enhances it. Following the "Good medicine works" concept, there is no problem with, for example, using penicillin and homeopathics together, or using visualization and surgery together. The idea is to combine the good medicines that work so that each can be more effective.

Cancer and Integrated Medicine

Sam, a nineteen-year-old with cancer, provides an excellent example of the integrated approach to working with patients who are seriously ill. His entire chest was full of cancer. It was a very sad situation. The cancer had been present for some time, as we had not been called until things were quite extreme. We were not laboring under delusions of grandeur, and therefore we did not begin treatment with the intention of bringing about a total cure. Statistically that would be very rare. Although we also begin with the assumption of the possibility of a complete cure, that does not deter us from accepting the reality of death.

Thus we first prepared the patient for dying. Even to live would mean that a part of him would have to die. That part might be a major portion of his self, which would have to be transformed in order for him to live. Healing always involves a death and transformation of some part of the person.

We begin by demanding honesty. There will be no lies if we are involved. Denial and dishonesty serves the illness. Miracles can only arise from facing the truth. The truth was that Sam was dying. He needed to know that fact to be able to change it. As practitioners, we needed to accept that he may want to die, or that death may be required for him. That is the aspect of humility necessary in healing—the constant recognition that forces and energies larger than us are at work creating and managing our destiny. Our patient participated at some level in creating his destiny (certainly not consciously). His participation is required to change that destiny—and destiny can always be changed. It is not a predetermined, preordained law. As we work with the larger spirit energies, we learn that an incredible flexibility exists.

In the course of Sam's treatment, shamanic storytelling techniques were used. Shamans have told hypnotic stories for millennia. In Sam's case, I told an old Pima story about the coyote who went to the Land Above. I started out by noting that coyotes are frequently playing tricks and getting into mischief; and sometimes they really get into serious trouble—just like Sam was in now. One evening Coyote came to listen to Buzzard tell a story about the time he flew to the Land Above. I chose this story because of the obvious allusion to Sam's potentially dying and "flying to the Land Above."

Buzzard told about flying up, flying way up into the clouds, higher than he had ever flown, so high that he himself was terrified, until he came to an opening in the sky that looked like the mouth of a cave. With fear and trepidation he went through that entrance and discovered a whole other world. There were people singing and dancing, and there were animals and plants, some of which he had never seen before. It was exciting, but he was afraid that the hole in the sky would close up and he wouldn't be able to get back down to his own kind.

So, with that fear pounding in his heart, Buzzard ran as fast as he could to the opening and jumped through the mouth of the cave and back into the sky of this world, where his wings took a downdraft of wind that carried him down to the animals' camp, where he told his story. Everyone knew that what Buzzard was saying was true, because buzzards do not lie.

After the story ended, Coyote came to Buzzard and begged to go with him the next time he went to the Land Above. Buzzard didn't really want to take Coyote, but Coyote was so insistent that Buzzard could not say no.

Buzzard knew that coyotes love games of chance. They love to gamble with tricks up their sleeves. He demanded that Coyote not play any of his games of chance with the Sky People. Coyote, on the other hand, figured that he could really clean up with the Sky People. They would not be familiar with his particular games, and he would have the expert's advantage. They would be new to the game and wouldn't suspect his sophisticated tricks.

Buzzard and Coyote worked out a compromise on the gaming, and Buzzard prayed to the Wind God, asking the Wind to lift them up and carry them into the Land Above. Wind came and carried them swiftly above the clouds and through the entrance in the sky to the Land Above. Coyote clung tightly to Buzzard's back, shivering with fear at the great heights and trying not to look down.

When they arrived and Coyote climbed off his back, Buzzard admonished him most sincerely to be back at the cave entrance by sunset. Buzzard said this was imperative because he could not stay aloft at that height in the cold. He needed the last bit of the sun's rays to safely carry them down. But Coyote wasn't listening. He was preoccupied with the money he was going to win from the Sky People. He said, "Oh, sure, fine, yes," the way people do when they aren't listening.

Coyote had a wonderful time. He tried to trick all the people in the sky with his games, but they were too sharp for him. Coyote had finally met his match. And the Sky People had their own games of chance, which fascinated him so that he did not notice the time passing—until suddenly he awoke and it was dark. He had fallen asleep and missed the rendezvous! He was terrified, remembering what Buzzard had said about flying home before dark. He was stuck in the sky and didn't know what to do. (This referred to Sam's situation. Sam was stuck and didn't know what to do, and was not yet acknowledging consciously that he was in such a predicament.)

Coyote ran lickety-split to the opening of the cave, but Buzzard had already left. He saw Buzzard's tracks leading to the opening and ending just at the point at which Buzzard would have jumped into the blue. Coyote looked down and couldn't even see the ground because it was so far down. He cried bitter tears at not having paid more attention to Buzzard or to what he was doing. Coyote did not want to live in the Sky. He wanted desperately to go back to the ground. In his frenzy, he figured that his only course was to jump. Terrified as he was, he backed up and ran toward the opening. Three times he ran and three times he stopped short, panting with fear. On the fourth try he jumped, and it was a long, long way down.

Two days later a big bag of bones hit the ground with a thud. It was Coyote finally landing on the ground. He had been so high that without wings the Wind God had taken that many days to return him to earth.

Coyote's burial was prepared and his bones were placed on the hillside in the proper way in a sacred place. Prayers were made. The Great Spirit was asked to pick up Coyote's bones and give him life again somewhere else. When the prayers and songs ended, the animals returned to their homes, sadly humming Coyote's last song. Complaining about Coyote's tricks had been fashionable, but no one wanted to be rid of that trickster. After all, what would life be without coyotes? Someone has to challenge the rules that have no reason or meaning.

Little did the animals know that night would see the Great Spirit answer their prayers. Spirit took every piece of bone and spread it all over the earth. Every fragment of bone became a coyote. So when the animals awoke in the morning, every distant hill had a little coyote howling at the moon, imploring it to stay awake. And the next evening every distant hill had a little coyote howling at the moon to come out and play. And that's why there are so many coyotes out in the desert howling every night. It's all because of Coyote jumping and falling and the Great Spirit hearing the animals' prayers and creating all those little coyotes to challenge us.

Through the story I was able to tell Sam that he will live even if he dies. And he is going to die, one way or another. Even people who experience miraculous recoveries experience a death. Even small cures involve a death of some old way of being that the illness needed to survive. Sick people sometimes have to leave their job, their relationship, their old way of avoiding emotion. Always a small death is required. With a major illness, a major death is required. Hence if one interviews cancer patients who were expected to die but lived miraculously, it will be found that they are changed people. The person who recovered is not the same as the one who came down with the disease. That individual died with the disease, and someone brand-new confronts us in the present with wellness.

This process is the shaman's journey with the person's spirit to the land of the dead. The shaman takes the patient there and brings him back again. This was my work with Sam. As practitioners we must make that same journey. We must walk with death at our right hand. To stay alive we must be prepared to die.

Other Aspects of an Integrated Healing Program

Of course, more than storytelling treatments were prepared for Sam. Nutrition was important. We teach clients to listen to the foods they eat, and to talk to them. The foods will tell them what is needed. This is shamanic nutrition. It means talking to the food and gaining its cooperation in preparing a balanced diet, a healing diet. We learn to listen to our bodies after eating. Was that food in harmony with what was needed? Or did it bring cacophony to the body's song? Herbs are also important and can be addressed in the same way. Medicine people learned about herbs by walking in the forest and talking to the plants. The plants themselves told the medicine people the purposes for which they could be used.

Even drugs and surgery are another way of working with spirit energy. After all, drugs are prepared by people, and surgery is done by people. If those people who prepared the drugs, for example, did so with the conscious intent to heal; if they prayed over the drugs as they were prepared, the medicine would be so much more powerful.

Healing involves returning the clients to the path of their own lives. When we walk too far afield from our own true nature, illness arises as an alarm that we must get back onto our own path of destiny. Healing produces that return. The body is wonderfully wise. It reacts immediately when we stray from our path. It is modern culture that has taught us to ignore our body. Shamanic treatment requires listening to the unique wisdom of each individual body, not blindly following rules made by the mind. For the body is a part of the earth. The body is the earthly home for our soul. It knows more about life on earth than the mind. When in doubt, we ask the body.

For the Cherokee, sickness was not a permanent state. Sickness was a territory to pass through. It was a purifying experience to return us to our path of destiny and of spirit. Death was not the logical result of illness, but occurred when the person was ready to return to the Creator. A goal was to die in a healthy state so as to make the journey to the Spirit World easily and to be able to actively participate on arrival.

My great-grandmother held these beliefs. When she was eighty-eight, she announced to us that is was her time to die. She had previously been very healthy. She told us that she would die that night and thanked us for being part of her earthly family. Many in the family thought she was crazy and ignored her. She was dead the next morning. Her heart had stopped in her sleep. Autopsy would have no doubt led to a particular diagnosis, but she knew that it was time for her spirit to return.

Illness is the body's message that it is time to listen and to make a change in our path. The body begins that message by an illness perhaps as "trivial" as a common cold. Cold symptoms are a sign to listen to the body and ask what is wrong. How am I ignoring my body's needs? How am I not respecting my body? Instead, television and other advertising media in our culture train us to shut off the body's message by taking Contac or Dristan so we can continue life as usual.

By our failure to listen, our body is disappointed. We have not heard the message. Therefore it will perhaps next try to get our attention with a knee injury or a touch of arthritis. That prompts a visit to the doctor, who prescribes aspirin or an anti-inflammatory drug. Again the body has not been heard. The path to illness of so many patients resembles this. There were so many ignored early warnings.

Why is it so frightening for us to consider illness as a sign to examine the way we live? Perhaps because the family, community, and cultural structures in which we exist are so disordered. To be well may require drastic changes in our families, communities, and cultures. This task is beyond many of us. We go to the doctor for a succession of pills instead. When the body is not heard by the knee, perhaps it tries a migraine headache. Again no luck. The person must lie still but is drugged with morphine or Cafergot. Again no awareness. Finally a very serious illness must ensue to get the person to pay any attention to the ignored message.

Medicine needs to change to lead the way for families, cultures, and communities. It needs to emphasize awareness of the body's needs rather than blockage of its messages with drugs. The shaman-physician can treat the physical needs of the body while also responding to the needs of the soul.

NOTES

1. *Malleus mallificarum*, referenced in G. J. Barker-Benfield, *The Horrors of the Half-Known Life* (New York: Random House, 1975).
2. M. Foucault, *The Birth of the Clinic* (New York: Bantam Books, 1976).
3. F. Capra, *The Turning Point* (New York: Random House, 1982).
4. W. and A. Durant, *The History of Civilization* (New York: Simon & Schuster, 1950).
5. L. Mehl, *Mind and Matter: Healing Approaches to Chronic Disease* (San Francisco: Mindbody/Health Resources Press, 1986).
6. E. Calderon, R. Cowan, D. Sharon, F. K. Sharon, *Eduardo el Curandero: The Words of a Peruvian Healer* (Richmond, Calif.: North Atlantic Books, 1982).
7. L. Mehl and G. Peterson, *Hypnosis, Healing, and Physical Illness* (New York: Irvington Press, 1988), and S. Rosen (ed.), *Hypnosis and Healing* (New York: Irvington Press, 1986).
8. See also the chapter by Jim Swan on page 151.—Ed.

Shamanic Approaches in a Hospital Pain Clinic

FRANK LAWLIS

Pᴀɪɴ is a necessary requirement for growth and learning. In the rare event that a child is born without the ability to sense pain, the likelihood of reaching adulthood is very poor. Such a child cannot learn from mistakes, cannot understand danger, and can develop no interpersonal skills, thus becoming a menace to himself or herself and others. Yet, despite the fact that we learn most quickly through physical or mental discomfort, and that our most memorable transitions are typically accompanied by painful processes, pain is still, by definition, an experience that the normal person avoids and resists.

As co-director of four pain clinics in Texas, I have had a chance to observe the pain cycle at firsthand. I have seen how this cycle, through its persistent stress, eliminates many possible avenues for satisfaction and tends to enhance whatever psychopathology may have existed latently in a person. Also aggravating the ongoing frustration is the mental confusion that accompanies the side-effects of pain drugs. Consequently, depression and poor self-concept run throughout the histories of the incoming pain patients at our clinics.

But I have also witnessed very courageous patients as they faced their pains and transcended them into new planes of consciousness and personal renewals. Since the typical response to long-term pain is bitterness and depression, the challenge is to help find meaningfulness in these experiences. In this task we have found shamanic techniques to be extremely valuable and needed for both physical and mental transition.

139

The Shamanic Approach

The crucial shamanic concept we have adopted is that of spiritual transformation. Rather than embracing a mechanical model that sees the function of the pain therapist as merely fixing the human body to perform as before, even to the maximum of potential, our clinic team strives instead for the *person* to be better than before. This is based on the assumption that the physical status, and even the psychological status, is less important than the spiritual.

What is meant by the term *spiritual transformation* is a change in perspective of the world, a shift in understanding of that person's role in nature and his or her relationship within it. For example, many of our patients have physically worked very hard throughout their lives. For such a person, the meaning of existence is often defined by his or her ability to function as a productive worker. Nature, in this case, especially as related to the person's body, merely represents the necessary power for the person to perform the role of task master. This concept of nature involves the assumption that no special nurturance is needed. The body will function, the earth will meet the person's expectations, and there is no need for attention to anything else.

Chronic pain, however, demands a change in this perspective. It means that things have not gone according to expectations, calling into question the assumptions on which those expectations were based. Nurturance and respect for nature are then seen to be required, as well as nurturance of body and mind. Hence one's mission and relationship with the community undergo a quantum leap toward a complete consideration of the whole conception of life and death, and the need to transform old patterns of thought, emotion, and behavior becomes keenly felt.

Transformation can occur in many ways. In reaching for innovative approaches, we have borrowed from the practices of shamans in a variety of settings. In this chapter some of these approaches are described as part of our in-patient protocol. These techniques of imagery, drumming, touch, isolation, music, and chanting are certainly not new to the shamanic literature. And yet, there is no other hospital I know of that incorporates them into an integrated medical program.

Because of the nature of the medical establishment, some care must be taken in utilizing such procedures in order not to offend the traditional professional and his or her beliefs. The following descriptions are examples of our most consistently used techniques. We have developed Western medicine rationales for each, and particularly as they pertain to pain management. We respect the transformative power of these methods and recommend their consideration for others faced with similar issues.

Imagery

In ordinary reality we live between boundaries. For example, we have the ability to see the light waves of the spectrum within a certain range. Although this range varies from one person to another, it is a very narrow band in the total spectrum, and it is even narrow when compared to the range of perceptions possible to other species. But when we utilize the power of imagination there are no borders. No realms are insurmountable except as we limit ourselves.

The use of imagery is probably the oldest method of transformation in recorded history, discovered and employed by ancient shamans millennia ago.[1] Within the modality of imagery we are not only better able to understand our needs and control our physiology, but we can reach deeper wisdom and possibly even reach planes beyond ourselves.

It is not difficult to find some forms of imagery that impact upon our bodies. Patients often begin by finding what images produce higher or lower heartbeats. For some, imaging onself in a sexual act increases the pulse rate; others find a fearful scene more effective, such as falling or being chased by a powerful figure. A high percentage report the effectiveness of imaging the accident that hurt them. On the other hand, slowing the heartbeat tends to be less variable. Lying in one's bed, fishing or boating on a lake, being at the beach, securely observing a scene from a mountaintop, or merely floating in space are very frequently reported as effective. Whether it is a memory image or a fantasy is irrelevant.

From a physical standpoint, it is natural for patients to begin to explore images that affect pain. For most, this phase takes the form of learning to increase blood flow to painful areas and muscles that are tense. The result is less pain and more control of stress-related concerns.

For example, Alice had severe neck and headache pain as a result of an automobile accident. X-rays revealed a bone fragment, part of the spinal process protruding above the spinal cord. She was in no danger of direct impingement to her nerve pathways, but the bone was a pivotal point for muscular support of her head. Although her condition had lasted a year, she resisted surgery because of the low percentage of significant reductions of pain and the hope on the part of the surgeon that the bone would eventually grow together on its own. Also considered was the fact that she was involved in a miserable marriage, and it was thought that her pain may have been functional on some level in that situation.

During the second week of her treatment, as Alice was exploring her own imagery, she discovered an image of her husband separating the bones in her neck and causing her pain. She also had many dreams that showed her confusion and turmoil to be residing in the region of her neck ("a pain in the neck"). By imaging the reduction of stress in that location and moving it to her voice box, she began to "talk her pain out," replacing the pain with love and warmth for herself. The rest of the story is perhaps predictable in terms of her eventual divorce and remarriage; but the bones did knit together within two weeks (verified by X-ray), and she was employed within six weeks of discharge from the pain clinic.

We all have our favorite stories of success, but the one I like best is that of a patient named Bill, who had a very specific pain in the middle of his back on the right side. There was nothing in his medical history that could explain the terrible pain that he was having on a daily basis; there was just a large bump in his back. During the first week, he imaged whatever came into his consciousness as I touched his back in various places.

My objective was to understand the muscular mechanics a little better. By having the patient report images, I can better detect the referral pain pathways. In this case, as I touched the painful bump, he immediately started reporting an automobile accident he had witnessed. He began to cry, not about the pain but about the feeling of guilt at not responding to crying victims in the burning automobile. As he processed the experience, the bump began to diminish, as if someone were letting the air out of a tire. After a matter of thirty minutes, the pain was gone and he could leave that event without the associated emotion. I might add that his pain did not return.

Similar examples of the power of imagery and its connection with traumatic causes of pain are endless. Imagery is part of every activity in the clinic, from physical therapy to counseling. Only after the power of imagery has led the patient to personally encounter a wider perspective from beyond the present boundaries of experience can his or her perception of life patterns change. Then there may be a new perception of family roles, or of the mechanical relation of behavioral responses upon the body, or of the role of the pain experience itself.

Drumming

Some of my most valuable experiences have occurred while listening to the sound of shamanic drumming for hours and feeling a harmony arise within. From a physiological standpoint, we know that constant audio or visual stimuli at certain frequencies will drive brain wave functions toward a harmonic.[2] We also know that the majority of shamans use the drumbeat for their rituals and travels into new realities. Therefore, drumming experiences are helpful to our patients who are in need of new vistas of perception.

We have experimented with the use of a shamanic drumming cassette tape, measuring the relaxation response via biofeedback instrumentation. It is almost taken for granted now that in most patients the regular beat of the drum will facilitate greater peripheral vascular flow, as measured by the temperature probe, and reduced muscular tension, as measured by the EMG. Individuals have also used the drumming tape for control of their headaches and reduction of high blood pressure.

The most important finding concerning drumming, however, is its usefulness in the facilitation of imagery and the resolution of depression. As I explained earlier, depression is a major issue with pain patients, and one of the central features of depression is the type of obsessive rumination that patients experience as they worry about their problems. They become "stuck" with a resentment (especially about their employers or spouses and children) and cannot release it. Counseling often makes the situation worse because of the tendency of most counselors to try to "problem-solve" the depressive element through logical or cathartic avenues, the result of which is to make the patients more depressed and less energetic. Listening to the drumbeat for long periods appears to help such patients get past the cyclical and repetitious thoughts.

For example, a patient named Carl came to us with severe back pain that had cost him a good job with an oil company and had kept him at home for three years. He was bitter about his former employer and his wife, and refused to participate in the clinic activities to a full extent. Instead he would tell the same stories over and over again about how bad the world was. Drumming was introduced to him during a group session in which I actually beat the drum. I instructed the participants to allow themselves to listen to the beats while at the same time allowing all thoughts and images to come and go without worrying about their meaning. I also discussed the idea that any creatures who might appear in images could have symbolic meaning and might present themselves in interesting ways.

Carl experienced the image of a hawk that flew around his head seven times, then flew in patterns of circles and crosses. The hawk landed on his shoulder and told him that it was time to get on with his life and leave his past. During the discussions of everyone's reactions, Carl was baffled. I explained about power animals but refrained from any demands of interpretations. Whether it was the hawk or the transition of brain waves, Carl did begin to view the world in new terms. He used the drumming tape every day for both biofeedback and evening meditations.

Touch

About three years ago, while I was conducting a workshop at Esalen, I met Richard Pavek, who was very excited about what he was learning about a technique of touch therapy called SHEN.[3] I volunteered to be a subject for his procedure. After my session I had to admit that I felt nothing except some relaxation. Nevertheless, I agreed to allow him to come to Texas and try his approach on some of our pain patients. I was convinced that it could do no harm, but I really was not sure I would see Richard again.

The morning he showed up we were being overwhelmed with difficult problems. After clearing with the administration, Richard was ready to work with some patients with problems, some of which appeared to be very serious. One of these patients was David, a patient who had been hit by a huge crane that had crushed six of his vertebrae. By all reports he should have been a paraplegic, but his spinal cord was intact. Through repeated surgeries his pain worsened, and in desperation he had been sent to the pain clinic.

David's pain was located in his back and right leg, and he would not undergo the agony of getting out of bed without provocation. When he did venture into the hall, he had a tremendous limp and used a crutch. Thirty minutes after I sent Richard to work with him, David was literally dancing down the hall, no limp, no pain. To put it mildly, I was impressed. I sent Richard to another patient, Edith, who was in the middle of a migraine headache. Again, thirty minutes later, she was without pain. Two more patients had the same result. Although the pain syndromes of these patients did not permanently dissolve with one session, when Richard's technique was used with adjunctive therapies the results were successful, to which I attribute the major effect to his SHEN therapy.

I asked Richard to teach my staff, including myself, about the application of SHEN in order to separate the technique from the person practicing it. We have enjoyed results similar to those that Richard obtained and have integrated its use with other approaches. A very simplistic explanation of SHEN is based on an energetic flow or "flex" model. As shamans have known for centuries, the body has different currents of energies that influence our health. Emotional and physical events can interrupt and disturb these flows, and it is their chronic disturbance that eventually leads to disease. Richard's method was based on touching the body with the hands in prescribed ways in order to redirect the energy flows into their appropriate channels.

As depicted by Richard, the most obvious flows occur through the arms, surrounding the body, and circling through the spinal cord. One flow generally goes into the left palm to the right palm. Another flow goes from the right foot, up through the right side of the body, over the top of the head and down the left side, out the left foot. Another common flow of energy is up the spinal cord, over the head, and possibly circling back. The *chakra* centers described in yoga are also centers of energy flow, but it is advisable to read Richard's book for a more extensive explanation.

A further example of the effectiveness of SHEN therapy is the case of Frank and María. Frank was brought into the orthopedic ward of the hospital because of intense back pain, and I was asked to consult. When I walked into the room I knew that Frank was a very sick man. In fact, he had been diagnosed with cancer the year before, and the symptoms of back pain had confusing features. I recruited his wife, María, as my co-therapist and taught her some SHEN flows through his back and legs. The medical diagnostics indicated that the cancer had spread into his spine, and part of his vertebrae had deteriorated, thus explaining the back pain. The family was informed that he would probably never return home and that final arrangements should be planned.

I stopped by each day. María would ask questions and share with me how she had become better in facilitating reduction of his pain. A private nurse was hired, and María taught her what she knew. María was never overly optimistic or in a state of denial about the condition of her husband, yet her love for him and her willing role in his pain relief was clear. At the end of three weeks, Frank was discharged from the hospital. The tumor involved with his spine had dissolved and the vertebrae had begun to heal themselves. To say the least, the ward staff was most impressed.

The Isolation Chamber

One of the most common rituals in many cultures involves a time in which an individual is isolated from the community in order to face the essence of his or her self. For instance, isolation might occur in a sweat lodge or on a journey, but the classic shamanic experience is one of facing the unknown in total isolation, alone in the wilderness. The modern version of complete isolation would be a sensory deprivation chamber, or what is termed a flotation tank.

The majority of our patients find the isolation chamber to be an environment that facilitates emotional release and change. Other patients have fears of the darkness, of being closed in, and of loss of control. These fears have to be respected. During most of the time in isolation, a biofeedback sensor is used to record physiological change, but the primary value is for journeys of imagery and self-expansion.

For example, while working as a file clerk, a patient named Virginia had a file cabinet fall on her chest, resulting in rib fractures and sternum separation. A year later, she was still having severe pain in her chest and was referred to the pain clinic for alternative methods to further surgery and medications. She reported her first experience with the isolation chamber as relaxing and insightful with regard to imagery for pain control. One night Virginia spent the entire night in the isolation chamber and was transformed the next morning. She reported that she had held her hands in a prayerful position and had experienced a heat that began to fill her whole body. She had seen visions of her whole life, and suddenly it was morning. Her pain did not go away, but she commented that it was no longer relevant to her life mission. Her pain was simply a minor issue in her greater relationship to the world.

Time is a subjective element that divides two events. Within the isolation chamber, where events cannot be discriminated very easily, time does not have the same reality as before, and seems to stop. It appears that without the usual framework in which to judge the intrusion of mental or physical pain, relationships can be distorted from the subjective order in which we place them. Without the emotional glue to hold them, a more natural and universal order can become clear, yielding a more global perception.

Being in a general hospital, we often have consultations and referrals from other units. One of our consistent sources is the psychiatric unit, and one of the most preferred modalities for depressive and schizophrenic patients is the isolation chamber, probably for different reasons. The isolation permits the depressive to resolve conflicts in another sphere of reality without having to struggle with verbalization and rationalization. The schizophrenic can decrease the overwhelming array of stimuli and find some safe place for relaxation. No one has ever had a negative experience. Thus, in many ways, I have learned that the wisdom of shamanic rituals has relevance in all ages.

Music and Chanting

Music has been medicinal for humankind as long as recorded history. Every culture seems to recognize the impact of its message, whether it be a victory march or a lullaby for a crying baby or a hymn for a church service. Possibly a theory of psychophysical response could be framed in terms of a pathway from the right side of the brain to the left, producing a serotonin release mechanism. Another theory might be based upon early associations to musical configurations, thus producing behavioral learning from an earlier era.

In association with the music therapy program at Southern Methodist University, we have been researching what components of music affect pain parameters, and I have reached a few conclusions. Primarily, the effects of some kinds of music depend on the preferences, expectations, mood, and culture of the individual. For example, in trials of different kinds of music played for children as a pain management technique in the pediatric oncology unit during bone marrow aspirations and lumbar punctures, we found that the music of Michael Jackson was preferred above all the rest, including the meditation music we use in biofeedback. In the pain clinic we find other variations in preferences, and systematically evaluate what kind of music enhances the activity desired for a particular patient. We buy the patients portable cassette recorders so that they can use them during exercise, relaxation, or sleep. The selections are highly individualistic.

What does seem to be consistent is the positive effects of chanting and humming as a group. Adults become very anxious when they chant, but during group "therapy" they are encouraged to hum a note or a tune while focusing upon either an image or a body part. The group energy and cohesiveness are incredible. Often a patient will break out into song; other times a patient will weep with emotion. Unsolicited confessions of love and philosophy are often verbally expressed.

One such case is that of Steve, who was humming with the group one day when suddenly he began to sing an old gospel song. Others joined in, and the rest of the hour was led by Steve and his selection. After the meeting, Steve admitted that he had not been aware of his behavior but had been in his own reality in another time and place. Far from being fearful, he expressed gratitude to the group and the experience because it had taken him into a spiritual realm and closer to God.

Rather than trying to find a song that everyone knows and can sing in common, which has never been very successful, we generally begin by humming different notes and relaxing. It is very effective to spend an entire hour just humming. Everyone feels refreshed, and occasionally there are extremely positive experiences, such as the one described above. Chanting, however, brings the extra dimension of focusing upon a common contextual theme. Examples of chants are:

"Every day I am better and better."
"I am whole."
"I am one with the universe."

Chanting and humming help depression probably more than any other approach. There are many reasons for these beneficial results. First, chanting helps a person begin to breathe in more appropriate cycles, thereby increasing oxygen content throughout the body. Research has demonstrated that exercise is one of the most powerful predictors of depression relief, possibly because of neurotransmitter changes. And chanting is another form of exercise.

On a more subjective level I find that patients recognize within themselves feelings of affection and transcendence, stimulated by memories. Occasionally these "memories" seem to be of another time. Without exception all are of a positive nature and generalize to the group very easily. Friendship bonds are formed and have endured for many years. I have an average of two calls a month from patients who have been out of treatment for ten years and still recall chanting groups as the most meaningful experiences in their lives.

The Relevance of the Shamanic Approach

The problem with using words to describe the results of our shamanic approaches to pain management, such as I have attempted here, is that words are limiting. If two people do not have similar experiences, the words they use to describe events may have different meanings. But it seems quite likely that no two people have the same experiences; consequently, all verbal descriptions have the potential danger of conveying misinformation.

Moreover, the body does not understand words. Language skills come very late in life, when all the other abilities, such as walking and eating, are firmly in place. *Pain*, either physical or psychological, is not a word that means the same from person to person. It is an experience. Words may help to clarify the experiences, but treatment itself has to be on a nonverbal level. We have learned from our teachers, the shamans, and found the wisdom of silence and listening.

Not all patients, of course, are ready to listen. Not all are willing to get well, because there are costs involved in transformation. There may be costs to therapists as well in the form of legal suits and claims. There are often costs in terms of inappropriate roles within a family that must be given up in the process of transformation. And most of all there are the costs of giving up and surrendering a counterproductive relationship to nature that may have been possessed and valued since birth. All of these costs are fraught with fear of loss. The wonder is that the majority of our pain patients do eventually make the choice of transformation, even when, by definition, all of our referrals are considered potential failures.

I believe that many drugs act against transformation. Medications, in my experiences, either confuse the patient about his or her pain, especially the meaningfulness of it, or numb the ability to have spiritual perceptions, with the result that there is no energy for transformation. I find this true for "recreational drugs" as well. Patients with alcohol or other chemical dependencies seem to have greater difficulty with these concepts. It may be that that certain drugs could be helpful if used in a spiritual way, but given their potential dangers and side effects, as well as the fact that I have no experience or resources for exploring this avenue, my approach to spiritual transformation in the context of a pain clinic has been through the shamanic methods discussed above.

These shamanic practices have helped us and the patients on a consistent basis. We have contributed to shamanism in the sense that we are demonstrating to modern medicine the effectiveness of these approaches. Yes, magic can happen even in modern science, even in the controlled sterility of a hospital. More importantly, however, spirituality can once again be considered as a crucial variable in the healing process.

NOTES

1. J. Achterberg and F. Lawlis, *Bridges of the Bodymind* (Champaign, Ill.: Institute of Personality and Ability Testing, 1980).
2. R. Neher, "A Physiological Explanation of Unusual Behavior in Ceremonies Involving Drums," *Human Biology* 34 (1962): 151–160.
3. R. Pavek, *The Health Professional's Handbook of SHEN* (Sausalito: SHEN Therapy Institute, 1987).

Sacred Places in Nature: One Tool in the Shaman's Medicine Bag

JIM SWAN

THE MORNING OCEAN FOG drifted gently among the giant red cedars, creating a soft, nurturing screen to hide our movements. We parked the car on the shoulder as a woodpecker nearby beat out a staccato, announcing our arrival. My friend, Charlie Two-Tails, a Makah, motioned with his hand to be silent and listen. Aside from the acorn woodpecker, no other sounds punctuated the foggy morning air.

Satisfied with the privacy of the moment, he set off across the road like a shadow. I hurried behind, trying to keep up as he threaded his way through the elk clover and hairy manzanita understory while the elders of the cedar and douglas fir tribe silently watched.

Two hundred yards along a faint deer trail, we came to an opening where a giant cedar had fallen in a storm. Its huge body had cut a swath through the forest as it fell in a recent thunderstorm, stripping branches from its brothers and sisters and crushing anything under its path to the ground into a final resting cushion. The tiny leaflets were still bright green, like lace on an old tablecloth. A pungent smell of cedar sap hung heavy in the foggy air.

Charlie knelt down beside the fallen tree and sprinkled some corn meal as he whispered prayers in his native tongue. In the silence, only bird calls answered, affirming our oneness in this act.

"The Great Spirit says this is good wood to take," he said in a voice of gentle authority. "Ask the tree where to get the wood you want."

I wondered how could I talk with the tree. Seeing my hesitation, Charlie added, "Its spirit is still here."

Trying to set aside my modern mind, I placed some corn meal beside the old one. My mind somehow began reeling off its Latin name, *Thuja plicata*, recalling a dendrology class long ago. Words slowly faded from my awareness as I stood in the foggy morning. I suddenly felt myself drawn toward a place where the trunk had been split, leaving a crack that reached to the very heart of the trunk. It felt right to cut here. I looked at Charlie and he nodded his approval. In amazement I began to cut away at the trunk with my ax, mimicking the work of the woodpecker above.

From this chunk of giant cedar I later carved a whale-shaped rattle. The whale design originated from a dream of a whale I had had following a ceremony. In my hand it looks like any rattle you might find in a museum, but it feels special to me. "A good medicine object connects many worlds," Charlie once said. The rattle symbolizes the connection between the whale in my dream and its favored expression in the form of this ceremonially gathered wooden form, donated by spiritual consent. Its nature defies modern rationality, but when I shake it, it feels different, like the difference between just any acoustical guitar and a twenty-year-old Martin Dreadnaught.

The pebbles inside the rattle come from a special stream where Northwest Coast peoples have gone to bathe and purify themselves since before that giant cedar was a seed. Its "power" comes from its sacred unity. Its music sounds simple, but Charlie says that it's a healing rattle, because it creates more harmony with the source of all things. He adds that we get sick often when we lose our harmony with the source. He makes people well in his way, the traditional way of the shaman, by helping them to recover this sense of harmony, driving out the negative, disharmonious energies and allowing new, fresh, strong ones to come in.

According to Charlie's model of health and healing, good medicine objects frequently arise from natural materials that can be found at certain special places, "where the Creator's heart beats more strongly," he says. These are the sacred places, the glens, the groves, the springs, the mountains, the valleys and caves that remain touchstones of ancient power and problems for modern minds.

"The idea of a sacred place, where the walls and laws of the temporal world dissolve to reveal wonder, is apparently as old as the human race," writes Joseph Campbell.[1] The names of many sacred places of the world ring familiar to our ears—Lascaux, Delphi, Lourdes, Mecca, Stonehenge, Nazca, Macchu Picchu, and Denali are just a few of the better-known sites dotting the face of the earth. The cultures that actively worshiped such places of wonder are today often just memories recorded in history books or seen as quaint pockets of primitives by many. Yet despite our official attitude of seeing anything nonscientific as foolish, world tourism research shows that making pilgrimages to sacred sites is one of the most common of all world tourism motives.[2] Perhaps we need to reconsider what our intuitive minds tell us and give it more credit, for our actions often speak to our behavior coming from motives that reach far beyond rationality.

A thing becomes sacred to us when we perceive it as having a quality that inspires us to call it sacred and regard it as somehow capable of linking us more closely to a spiritual dimension of life. Mircea Eliade defines sacred places as "hierophonies," which are places where manifestations of a sacred nature, called "krakophonies," are more likely to occur. Thus visions, voices, vivid dreams, and profound inspirations have tended to come into the minds of many people down through the ages at certain places. Delphi in Greece, for example, was selected as the site to erect a special shrine to the earth goddess Gaia for more than logistical reasons. The ancient Greek minds saw a mysterious earth force, the "plenum," as being more profound at Delphi, and as such favoring prophecy from the famous oracle who subsequently resided there.

People tend to think in terms of visions and voices as being the domain of saints and prophets or the ravings of madmen. Telling which is which isn't always easy, but it seems that the realm of consciousness to which the shaman journeys to derive power is really much the same territory as that visited by the psychotic. There is an old saying in Wales: "If you spend a night on Mount Patrick Coughlin, you'll come down in the morning either a poet or a madman." And around the world there are many places like Mount Patrick Coughlin.

For a number of years I have been fascinated by this strange relationship between place and personal experience, and through talking about it in front of audiences and writing about it, I have been able to collect hundreds of case histories of people who have felt drawn to certain special places where they have undergone transformative experiences.[3] Many, many people have found themselves entering states of grace where visions, voices, and profound realizations come to them while visiting such and such a place. Often they are afraid to talk about their experiences for fear of being judged crazy, but time after time upon seriously examining these experiences it appears clear that they frequently represent important turning points in one's life.

For example, while hiking on the slopes of Mount Subasio in Italy, conservationist Bert Schwarzschild became distraught when he discovered songbirds being shot on this holy mountain where Saint Francis preached his "sermon to the birds." Climbing to the top of the peak, Schwarzschild

tried to sleep but could not. In the midst of his turmoil, he reports that a
nightingale came and lighted at his feet and began to sing. The song was
so sweet and moving that he began to cry, and in that moment he came
to the conclusion that he would start a worldwide organization to make
Mount Subasio a wildlife preserve. Today, due to Schwarzchild's tireless
years of work making his dream come true, the mountain is a regional
park, with happy birds singing with no fear of hunters.[4]

Others have talked about going to places like the Black Hills of South
Dakota, seen as the "Heart of the Earth Mother" by the Lakota, and
bursting into tears of happiness for no apparent reason. One woman
reports hearing "bells" while hiking on Mount Shasta and that night being
deluged with dreams of the bowels of the mountain bubbling up to the
surface. Awakening, she wrote some of her best poetry ever. A professor
of theology talked of how he felt a heavy ambience while visiting an
ancient shrine at Mesa Verde. As he stood in the ruins feeling sad and
almost moved to tears, a flock of vultures suddenly appeared and began
circling around him. Returning back to his hotel room, he found a message
telling him that a close relative had died.

Many more cases could be cited. A close study of the biohistories of
many famous people, including Alexander the Great, Cleopatra, Genghis
Khan, Adolph Hitler, and Theodore Roosevelt, not to mention religious
figures from nearly all faiths, reveals their feelings of the power of place
in their lives. We have no paradigm or even language to talk about such a
power in our lives today, but it still seems to work in our bones.

One way to seek out a new paradigm to better understand the strange
and marvelous power of places is to look at other cultures that actively
revere special places and see them and their power as natural, normal, and
desirable. The following three examples of shamanic healers who use
special places for healing sheds much light on their concepts of mind-
nature interactions.

The Shamanic Value of Places for Healing

1. Working among the Navaho for many years, Franz Newcomb and
Gladys Reichard report that

> locality is of great importance to the Navaho. Names of people,
> of animals, of dangers, names of arrows, of lightnings and plants,
> have power when known and used properly. Even so, the names
> of places are charms. Whenever a protagonist meets someone

who is more powerful, the first question he must answer is where are you from?"[5]

In the primal mind, the world as we see it is really the result of the interplay of many, many invisible forces and flows. Places are unique not just for their landform and geology. They also are the residing sites for spiritual beings who can and do influence our lives. To call out the name of a special place like Mount McKinley in Alaska is to trigger a set of symbolic associations in which the mountain without serves as a symbol for the mountain within. In the shaman's mind, however, it also invites harmonic resonance with the spirit of that place, which carries certain energies. Thus when a Navaho sand painter carefully constructs a ceremonial painting depicting the four sacred mountains that ring the Navaho homeland—Blanca Peak in the east, Mount Taylor in the south, the San Francisco Peaks in the west, and the snowy peaks of the La Plata Range in the north—he invokes recollections of all the mystic associations with those places and invites their energies into the microcosm of the macrocosm which he is creating to make a client whole and well again.[6]

2. Some 300 kilometers from Caracas, Venezuela, lies Sorte, a national park which is also a healing place for members of the María Lionza religion, a syncretism of many traditions, including old Jaguar cults of Amerindian origin, Haitian voodoo, Yoruba and other African traditions, and Christianity. Today there are more than eleven million people in Venezuela, and more than one million are said to be followers of María Lionza, which is inspired by the teachings of the eighteenth-century spiritualist Alan Kardec and is led by a shamaness. The name María Lionza arises from a mythic figure, a young daughter of a chief who helps poor, oppressed people. Her form is a naked young woman with strong thighs, sitting on a tapir and holding aloft the bones of a human female pelvis. The significance of the tapir is that it is an animal of power, which is in part linked with the very long penis of the male tapir.

In a typical healing ritual in the María Lionza tradition, the client is first counseled by a wise person, or *chichaco*, at a streetside altar in Caracas. If the counselor believes the person could benefit from a ritual to María Lionza, a trip is planned, based upon the patient's payment for any services and provisions of objects for sacrifice, which may include food or live chickens. If the readings are positive after consulting a diviner, who typically casts coconut shells to determine the favorableness of the intended mission, the party will begin their drive to Sorte. Along the way, they will typically stop to make sacrifices and say prayers at special shrines, waterfalls, or grottoes. This part of the trip is led by a shaman who serves as a guide for the process. Arriving at Sorte Mountain, the patient will be led into a circle of chanting mediums after being purified by clouds of thick smoke from large black cigars.

The siting of this circle is determined by shamanic appraisal of the "energies" and "spirits" of the mountain. Sorte, it is said, is especially favorable for healing, as it has an abundance of "energies" and "spirits," which are evidenced by strange lights seen near the peak toward sunset. When the local energy field is sufficiently strong, a shaman in an altered state of consciousness enters the circle. This person is called a *santero* and is in a light trance state. Typically the *santero*'s work is akin to psychodrama, with the climax of the healing session being an emotional catharsis by the patient.

Following this climax, the patient is then led to a special place and told to lie on the ground. Lighted candles are placed around him to clean the aura, white talcum powder is traced out on the ground to draw in favorable energies from the earth and ward off evil forces, and jars or glasses of water are placed beside the prone person to absorb negative energies. After the patient has returned to normal feelings and absorbed sufficient quantities of energies from the ground there, additional counseling may take place and certain herbs may be prescribed. Often these herbs may also come from a special place, since it is supposed that herbs which grow in certain places will have more power.[7]

This example describes many of the ways in which shamans typically may use the power of certain places to heal: invoking the spiritual power of a place; aligning one's mind and acts with the place through sympathetic magic; performing certain special acts at certain places; and using special herbs, stones, or other amulets taken from certain places.

3. Waters, too, can have shamanic value, especially springs. In 1884 Captain Jeff Maltby of the Texas Rangers was commissioned to inspect the Rio Grande Valley. Exploring an area along the banks of the Rio Grande in what today is Hudspeth County, just across the river from the Mexican town of Sierra Blanca, Maltby came across a set of artesian hotsprings accessed by many trails showing centuries of heavy Indian usage. Much of the history of these springs has been recorded in a delightful book by Pat Ellis Taylor, *Border Healing Woman*, which relates the healing powers of these springs and their influence on the life of Mrs. Jewell Babb.[8]

Mrs. Babb and her husband came to buy the springs because they felt they could transform the simple buildings they found there in the late 1950s into a health resort. The location proved too remote to be popular for well-paying guests, but the Mexicans, it seemed, still frequented the springs. Thus people with serious illnesses began to show up at the Babbs' doorstep wanting help.

Mrs. Babb had no training but was able to learn from the *curanderas* (folk healers from Mexico) how to use the muds, mosses, and waters of the springs as a naturopathic medicine chest. She found herself having strange visions and hearing voices as she came to feel closer to the springs, and she developed abilities to do healing with her mind and through massage. In time clients, including Howard Hunt, came to her for help. In her late seventies she moved from the springs but says that she still "carries the power of the springs with her in her mind" wherever she goes, enabling her to continue to help others.

Tapping the Power of Place

Some might argue that shamans are able to use places as healing agents because they employ suggestion to invoke symbolic images of healing deep in the mind through making reference to places in ceremonies and ritual. Clearly this is sometimes the case, but it seems that something else may be at work too. At least some of the "energies" that shamans say are at special places may be actual locally strong electromagnetic fields.

For example, most of the stone circles of England lie within a half mile of earthquake fault lines, and many Native American sacred sites like Indian Hot Springs lie on or near fault lines. Due to underground shifting of rock strata, unusually strong electromagnetic discharges can occur along these fissures. Similarly strong fields can and do occur at mountaintops, especially prior to electrical storms. After some time of being in the presence of such strong outer electromagnetic fields, our inner electromagnetic fields harmonize with them. This results in "bioentrainment," a process in which the environmental fields harmonize with our brain waves and move them into frequencies associated with relaxation and creativity.[9] These same states of mind are also known to be associated with mental imagery that is employed in healing.

Negative ions in the air may also be in abundance at some sacred sites. These relatively unstable but beneficial atmospheric particles have been shown to be linked with mental relaxation and alertness. We can buy negative ion generators, but in nature the same conditions result from crashing ocean breakers, evergreen forests, waterfalls, and uranium ore.[10] Combining locally strong fields with an abundance of negative ions results in an optimal environment for healing and creative inspiration. Sensing places that have such ambient conditions is an awareness of the shaman, gleaned from undergoing various ordeals to make one more aware of the many subtle natural powers of nature. We all have such an awareness to some extent, but seldom deliberately train it through diet, meditation, and practice.

In China for centuries a special kind of Wu shaman, the *feng shui*, has divined the spirit of each place to ascertain the right actions to undertake there in order to preserve harmony with the Tao. And in many other traditions, including the Persian Magi, the Freemasons, the Druids, the Hawaiian kahunas, and the African voodoo priests, we find a similar art of divining the nature of each place. Usually this includes reading land forms, assessing local energies and biological features, consulting spirits, and reading the patterns in the heavens overhead.

Modern architecture and design long ago discarded their geomantic origins, but the enduring beauty of so many of the world's archeological treasures at special sites speaks of a knowledge of the earth which inspires beauty, wisdom, and love to manifest in life. Such touchstones of life lie at the core of true health and healing. Perhaps in our failure to better appreciate the perceptual powers of the shamanic mind and its understanding of the earth we are cutting ourselves off from wisdom of health and healing which could solve many pressing social problems.

In the eyes of those who still know how to kindle the ancient fires of the spirit, a light burns that speaks to the vibrancy of their faith. This light often shines most strongly in people who grow very old while remaining healthy and happy. Their living, vital presence, once seen as being the work of the devil, may in reality be a very significant indicator of what human potentiality can and should be and its roots in kinship with nature. We act in ignorance of this light, and we make forward strides often with negative consequences of equal proportion.

Among the Hopi Indians, whose slow-paced agricultural lifestyle speaks of peace, when one Hopi passes another, instead of saying "Don't work too hard" as we do, they say, "Keep the top of your head open." In their sensitive world view, this is an injunction to keep oneself connected to a higher force of spiritually inspired intuition. It is the force that guides a person to places where the spirit is strong, they say. These are the sacred places—the spots of the fawn—places where light, love, and truth all blend into the unity and health that comes from harmony. This is good advice for us, too, as we strive to bring that harmony into a world caught in a materialistic, mechanical model of reality and which seems all too often to be racing along a path of potential catastrophe.

NOTES

1. Joseph Campbell, *The Mystic Image* (Princeton, N.J.: Princeton University Press, 1974), p. 184.

2. Lester Borley, "Plenary Remarks," World Congress on Cultural Parks, Mesa Verde, Colo., September 1984.

3. J. Swan, "Sacred Places: Can Traditional Wisdom and Modern Science Support Each Other?" *Shaman's Drum*, no. 7 (Winter 1986–87): 24–32.

4. B. Schwarzschild, "Earthwatch: No Birds Sing on Saint Francis' Mountain," *Audubon* 85, no. 2 (March 1983).

5. F. Newcomb and G. Reichard, *Sandpaintings of the Navaho Shooting Chant* (New York: Cover, 1975), p. 69.

6. D. Sander, *Navaho Symbols of Healing* (New York: Harcourt Brace Jovanovich, 1979).

7. J. Geller, "The Healers of María Lionza." Paper presented at American Association for Social Psychiatry Convention, Santa Barbara, Calif., 1977.

8. P. E. Taylor, *Border Healing Woman: The Story of Jewell Babb* (Austin: University of Texas Press, 1981).

9. G. L. Playfair and C. Hill, *The Cycles of Heaven* (New York: Avon, 1979).

10. F. Soyka and A. Edmonds, *The Ion Effect* (New York: Bantam Books, 1977).

The Shamanic Journey: Observations from Holotropic Therapy

STANISLAV GROF

THIS CHAPTER is based on observations from almost three decades of systematic exploration of the therapeutic potential of nonordinary states of consciousness induced by psychedelic substances and various nonpharmacological techniques. The first approximately twenty years involved clinical work with psychedelics and the last ten years experimentation with various powerful nondrug alternatives.

A Modern Method of Shamanic Induction

During this last decade, my wife, Christina, and I have developed a psychotherapeutic technique that we call holonomic integration or holotropic therapy. It combines controlled breathing, evocative music and other forms of sound technology, focused body work, and mandala drawing. With the use of this nondrug approach, it is possible to facilitate the entire spectrum of experience that is characteristic of psychedelic sessions and shamanic journeys.

The objective here is not gradual exploration of various levels of the individual unconscious as in "verbal" Western psychotherapies, but facilitation of a powerful transforming experience of a transcendental nature. Our therapeutic aims and methods are therefore closer in many respects to shamanic traditions of psychophysical healing than to most Western verbal psychotherapies, although our approach does coincide with that of

161

Carl Gustav Jung insofar as we aim to facilitate clients' self-healing by helping them become aware of and reintegrate fragmented elements in the mind-body complex.

In our work using holotropic therapy it is possible to induce phenomena that are often indistinguishable from psychedelic states without any pharmacological agents and with such simple means as increased rate of breathing, sound technology, and certain techniques of body work, which I will describe later. When the phenomena described in this chapter can be triggered by something as physiological as hyperventilation, there can be no doubt that they reflect genuine properties of the psyche.

The principles of holotropic therapy are extremely simple. The client is asked to assume a reclining position with the eyes closed, focus attention on breathing and the body sensations, and maintain a respiratory pattern that is faster and more effective than usual. During the psychological preparation that precedes, he or she is encouraged to suspend analytical activity and accept any experiences that emerge, with full trust and without judging. In this context it is recommended to abstain from abreactive techniques or any other attempts to change and influence the experience. The general attitude should be similar to certain methods of Buddhist meditation—simply watching the emerging experiences, registering them, and letting them go.

After an interval that varies from person to person, the individual starts experiencing strong emotions and develops stereotyped patterns of muscular armoring. As the breathing continues, the emotional and physical tension builds up to spontaneous release and resolution. The physical tensions in general correspond to the areas where the Indian system of Kundalini Yoga places the centers of psychic energy, or *chakras*.

These tensions take the form of intense belt pressure or even pain in the forehead or the eyes, constriction of the throat and locking of the jaws, and tight belts in the areas of the chest, the navel, and the lower abdomen. Related tensions in the hands and arms, feet and legs, neck, shoulders, and small of the back are also quite common. This is, of course, a synoptic and statistical description. In actual experiential work, subjects do not manifest the entire picture described above; they show individual patterns of distribution of these tensions in which certain areas are dramatically represented, others not involved at all.

In the context of traditional psychiatry influenced by the medical model, the reaction to hyperventilation, particularly the famous "carpopedal spasms"—contractions of the muscles of the hands and feet—has been considered a mandatory physiological response to fast and intense breathing, referred to as the "hyperventilation syndrome." It has been associated with an aura of alarm, and when it occasionally happens spontaneously in neurotic (particularly hysterical) patients, it is usually treated with tranquilizers, intravenous calcium, and a paper bag placed over the face.

The use of hyperventilation for therapy and self-exploration proves this view to be incorrect. In every group we have ever worked with, there were several people who responded to hyperventilation with progressive relaxation, a sense of expansion, and visions of supernaturally beautiful light. They ended the session in a profound transcendental experience of cosmic unity. In those who develop physical tensions and difficult emotions, continued breathing brings the condition quite typically to a state of resolution, which is also followed by deep relaxation, peace, and serenity. Often the final outcome of the session is a deep mystical state that can be of lasting benefit and personal significance for the subject. Ironically, the routine repressive approach of traditional psychiatry to occasional spontaneous episodes of hyperventilation thus interferes with a potentially therapeutic process in some neurotic patients.

During the hyperventilation, as the physical and emotional tensions are building up and resolving, the individual can have a variety of powerful experiences, which will be described in more detail later. He or she can relive important biographical events from infancy, childhood, or later life, and experience various other types of transpersonal phenomena. In particular, there is often a confrontation with different aspects of the memory of biological birth and a profound encounter with death—phenomena characterized as the "death and rebirth" experiences in shamanic initiation rites.

In the context of holotropic therapy, the already strong effect of hyperventilation is further enhanced by the use of evocative music or sound technology developed by various cultures specifically for the purpose of changing consciousness—for example, shamanic drumming. Another intensification of the effect of this technique is its use in a group setting, where participants alternate in the roles of experiencers and sitters under the supervision of the therapist.

Ideally, the active breathing itself leads to a resolution of everything that was released and surfaced into consciousness. If the subject ends with some residual tensions or unpleasant emotions, it is possible to facilitate resolution by a technique of focused body work that I first developed for the termination periods of psychedelic sessions.

The basic principle here is to encourage the experiencer to surrender fully to the emerging emotions, sensations, and physical energy and find appropriate ways of expressing them through sounds, grimaces, postures, and movements, without judging or analyzing the experience. The function of the facilitators is to follow the energy flow and encourage its full

external expression. This work continues until the experiencer reaches a
state of resolution and relaxation.

The Sensory Barrier and the Recollective-Biographical Level

The techniques that mediate experiential access to the unconscious tend
to activate initially the sensory organs. As a result of this, deep self-
exploration starts for many people with a variety of unspecific sensory
experiences, such as elementary visions of colors and geometrical patterns,
hearing of ringing or buzzing sounds, tactile sensations in various parts of
the body, or the experience of a variety of tastes or smells. These are of a
more or less abstract nature; they do not have any deeper symbolic
meaning and have little significance for self-exploration and self-under-
standing. They seem to represent a sensory barrier that one has to pass
through before the journey into one's psyche can begin.

As the process continues, the next most easily available realm of the
psyche is usually the recollective-biographical level and the individual
unconscious. Although the phenomena belonging to this category are of
considerable theoretical and practical relevance, it is not necessary to
spend much time on their description. The reason for this is the fact that
most of the traditional verbal psychotherapeutic approaches have been
limited to this level of the psyche. There exists abundant professional
literature discussing nuances of psychodynamics in the biographical
realm. Unfortunately, various schools contradict each other, and there is
no unanimity as to what are the significant factors in the psyche, why
psychopathology develops, and how effective psychotherapy should be
conducted.

A major difference between verbal and experiential psychotherapies is
the significance of direct physical traumatization in the history of the
individual. In traditional psychiatry, psychology, and psychotherapy,
there is an exclusive emphasis on psychological traumas. Physical traumas
are not seen as having a direct influence on the psychological development
of the individual and as participating in the psychogenesis of emotional
and psychosomatic disorders. This contrasts sharply with the observations from deep experiential work, where memories of physical traumas
appear to be of paramount importance. In psychedelic work, holotropic
therapy, and other powerful experiential approaches, reliving of life-
threatening diseases, injuries, operations, or situations of near-drowning
are extremely common, and their significance exceeds by far that of the
usual psychotraumas. The residual emotions and physical sensations from
situations that threatened survival or the integrity of the organism appear

to have a significant role in the development of various forms of psycho-pathology, as yet unrecognized by academic science.

The experiences of serious physical traumatization represent a natural transition between the biographical level and the following realm that has as its main constituent the twin phenomena of birth and death. They involve events from the individual's postnatal life and are thus biographical in nature. However, the fact that they brought the person close to death and involved extreme discomfort and pain connects them to the birth trauma. For obvious reasons, memories of diseases and traumas that involved severe interference with breathing, such as pneumonia, diphtheria, whooping cough, or near drowning, are particularly significant in this context.

Encounter with Birth and Death: Dynamics of Basic Perinatal Matrices

The most characteristic aspect of the experiences originating on this level of the psyche is their focus on physical and emotional pain, disease and decrepitude, aging, dying, and death. The awareness of death finds its expression not only in the eschatological content of the ideation and in visions of dying people and animals, putrefying corpses and cadavers, skeletons, cemeteries, and funerals, but also in a profound experiential encounter with death and dying that has very real and convincing biological and emotional concomitants.

Profound confrontation with death characteristic for these experiential sequences tends to be intimately interwoven with a variety of phenomena that are clearly related to the process of biological birth. While facing agony and dying, individuals simultaneously experience themselves as struggling to be born and/or delivering. In addition, many of the physio-logical and behavioral manifestations of these experiences can be naturally explained as derivatives of the birth process.

It is quite common in this context to identify with a fetus and relive various aspects of one's biological birth with quite specific and verifiable details. The element of death can be represented by simultaneous or alternating identification with sick, aging, or dying individuals. Although the entire spectrum of these experiences cannot be reduced just to reliving of biological birth, the birth trauma seems to represent an important core of the experiential process on this level. For this reason, I refer to this level of the unconscious as *perinatal*.

The term *perinatal* is a Greek-Latin composite word in which the prefix *peri-* means "around or near" and the root *natalis* denotes relation to birth. It is commonly used in medicine to describe processes that immediately precede childbirth, are associated with it, or immediately follow it; medical texts thus talk about perinatal hemorrhage, infection, or brain damage. In contrast to the traditional use of this word in obstetrics, the term *perinatal* is used in this chapter in relation to experiences.

The connection between biological birth and perinatal experiences described above is quite deep and specific. This makes it possible to use the clinical stages of delivery in constructing a conceptual model that helps to understand the dynamics of the perinatal level of the unconscious and even make specific predictions in relation to the death-rebirth process in different individuals.

The experiences of death and rebirth reflecting the perinatal level of the unconscious are very rich and complex. Sequences related to various stages and facets of biological birth are typically of a mythological, mystical, archetypal, historical, sociopolitical, anthropological, or phylogenetic nature. These tend to appear in five characteristic experiential patterns or constellations. There seems to exist a deep connection between these thematic clusters and the clinical stages of childbirth, which occur in the following order.

I. THE EXPERIENCE OF COSMIC UNITY: THE AMNIOTIC UNIVERSE

This important perinatal experience seems to be related to the primal union with mother, to the original state of intrauterine existence during which the mother and child form a symbiotic unity. If no noxious stimuli interfere, the conditions for the child can be close to optimal, involving security and continuous satisfaction of all needs. The basic characteristics of this experience are transcendence of the subject-object dichotomy, strong positive affect (peace, serenity, tranquillity, and oceanic ecstasy), feelings of sacredness, transcendence of space and time, and richness of insights of cosmic relevance.

The specific content of these experiences can be drawn from situations that share with it lack of boundaries and obstructions, such as identification with the ocean and aquatic life forms or with interstellar space. Images of nature at its best (Mother Nature) and archetypal visions of heavens and paradise also belong to this category. It is important to emphasize that only episodes of undisturbed embryonal life are accompanied by experiences of this kind. Disturbances of intrauterine existence are associated with images of underwater dangers, pollution, inhospitable nature, and insidious demons from various cultures.

2. THE EXPERIENCE OF COSMIC ENGULFMENT

This experiential pattern seems to be related to the very onset of delivery, where the previous harmony is disturbed. At first, this happens as a result of alarming chemical signals and later by mechanical contractions of the uterine musculature.

This situation is experienced subjectively as an imminent threat of a vital danger. Overwhelming feelings of free-floating anxiety lead to paranoid ideation and perception. Intensification of this state typically results in the experience of a monstrous vortex or whirlpool sucking the subject and his or her world relentlessly to its center.

A frequent experiential variation of this theme is that of being swallowed by an archetypal beast, entagled by an octopus, or ensnared by a gigantic mother spider. A less dramatic form of the same experience is the theme of descent into the underworld and encounter with demonic creatures. Motifs of classical shamanism indicate the shaman's familiarity with this realm.

3. THE EXPERIENCE OF NO EXIT OR HELL

This experience is logically related to the fully developed first clinical stage of delivery. At this time, the fetus is periodically constricted by uterine spasms, while the cervix is closed and the way out is not available. The subject feels stuck, encaged and trapped in a claustrophobic nightmarish world and loses entirely his or her connection with linear time. The situation feels absolutely unbearable, endless, and hopeless. It seems, therefore, quite logical that the individuals involved frequently identify experientially with prisoners in dungeons or concentration camps, victims of the Inquisition, inmates in insane asylums, or sinners in hell and archetypal figures representing eternal damnation. During the deep existential crisis that typically accompanies this state, existence appears as a meaningless farce or theater of the absurd.

4. THE EXPERIENCE OF DEATH-REBIRTH STRUGGLE

Many important aspects of this experiential matrix can be understood from its association with the second clinical stage of childbirth. In this stage, the uterine contractions continue, but the cervix is now dilated and allows a gradual propulsion of the fetus through the birth canal. This involves enormous struggle for survival, crushing mechanical pressures, and often high degrees of anoxia and suffocation. In the terminal phases of the delivery, the fetus can experience intimate contact with biological material such as blood, mucus, urine, and feces.

From the experiential point of view, this pattern is rather rich and ramified. Beside actual realistic reliving of various aspects of the struggle in the birth canal, it involves a wide variety of phenomena that occur in typical thematic sequences. They are related with deep experiential logic to anatomical, physiological, and biochemical aspects of the birth process. The most important of these are elements of titanic fight, sadomasochistic experiences, intense sexual arousal, demonic episodes, scatological involvement, and encounter with fire. All these occur in the context of a determined death-rebirth struggle.

The specific images involve mythological battles of enormous proportions involving angels and demons or gods and Titans, raging elements of nature, sequences from bloody revolutions and wars, images involving pornography and deviant sexuality, violence, satanic orgies and Sabbath of the Witches, crucifixion, and ritual sacrifice.

5. THE DEATH-REBIRTH EXPERIENCE

This perinatal matrix is meaningfully related to the third clinical stage of delivery—to the actual birth of the child. In this final stage, the agonizing process of the birth struggle comes to an end; the propulsion through the birth canal culminates and the extreme build-up of pain, tension, and sexual arousal is followed by a sudden relief and relaxation. After the umbilical cord is cut, the physical separation from the mother has been completed and the child begins its new existence as an anatomically independent individual.

As in the case of the other matrices, some of the experiences belonging here represent an accurate replay of the actual biological events involved in birth, as well as specific obstetric interventions. The symbolic counterpart of the final stage of delivery is the death-rebirth experience.

Paradoxically, while only one step from a phenomenal liberation, the individual has the feeling of impending catastrophe of enormous proportions. This results frequently in a determined struggle to stop the experience. If allowed to proceed, this experience involves a sense of annihilation on all imaginable levels—physical destruction, emotional debacle, intellectual defeat, ultimate moral failure, and absolute damnation of enormous proportions. This experience of "ego death" seems to entail an instant merciless destruction of all previous reference points in the life of the individual. At this stage, shamans may refer to dismemberment by demons or ferocious animals.

The experience of total annihilation and "hitting the cosmic bottom" is immediately followed by visions of blinding white or golden light of supernatural radiance and beauty. It can be associated with astonishing displays of divine archetypal entities, rainbow spectra, or intricate peacock designs. The subject experiences a deep sense of emotional and spiritual liberation, redemption, and salvation. He or she typically feels freed from anxiety, depression, and guilt, purged and unburdened. This is associated with a flood of positive emotions toward oneself, other people, and existence in general. The world appears to be a beautiful and safe place, and the zest for life is distinctly increased. The shaman returns from the initiatory vision quest charged with a new sense of meaning and purpose.

Journeys beyond the Brain: Transpersonal Dimensions of the Psyche

Experiential sequences of death and rebirth typically open the gate to a transbiographical domain in the human psyche that can best be referred to as *transpersonal*. The perinatal level of the unconscious clearly represents an interface between the biographical and the transpersonal realms, or the individual and the collective unconscious. In most instances, transpersonal experiences are preceded by a dramatic encounter with birth and death. However, there exists also an important alternative; occasionally, it is possible to access experientially various transpersonal elements and themes directly, without confronting the perinatal level.

The common denominator of this rich and ramified group of phenomena is the subject's feeling that his or her consciousness has expanded beyond the usual ego boundaries and has transcended the limitations of time and space. In the ordinary or "normal" states of consciousness, we experience ourselves as existing within the boundaries of the physical body (the body image), and our perception of the environment is restricted by the physically and physiologically determined range of our sensory organs.

Both our internal perception (interoception) and external perception (exteroception) are confined by the usual spatial and temporal boundaries. Under ordinary circumstances, we can experience vividly and with all our senses only the events in the present moment and in our immediate environment. We can recall the past and anticipate future events or fantasize about them; however, the past and the future are not available for direct experience.

In transpersonal experiences, as they occur in psychedelic sessions, in self-exploration through nondrug experiential techniques, or spontaneously, one or more of the above limitations appear to be transcended. The experiences of this kind can be divided into three large categories. Some of them involve transcendence of linear time and are interpreted by the subjects as historical regression and exploration of their biological, cultural, and spiritual past, or as historical progression into the future. In the second category are experiences characterized primarily by transcendence of the ordinary spatial boundaries rather than temporal barriers. The third group is then characterized by experiential exploration of domains that in Western culture are not considered part of objective reality. Many ranges of nonordinary realities accessible in such states have been described and catalogued in shamanic traditions.

In nonordinary states of consciousness, many subjects experience quite concrete and realistic episodes that they identify as fetal and embryonal memories. It is not unusual under these circumstances to experience—on the level of cellular consciousness—full identification with the sperm and the ovum at the time of conception. Sometimes the historical regression goes even further and the individual has a convinced feeling of reliving memories from the lives of his or her ancestors, or even drawing on the memory banks of the racial or collective unconscious. On occasion, subjects report experiences in which they identify with various animal ancestors in the evolutionary pedigree, or have a distinct sense of reliving dramatic episodes from a previous incarnation.

Transpersonal experiences that involve transcendence of spatial barriers suggest that the boundaries between the individual and the rest of the universe are not fixed and absolute. Under special circumstances it is possible to identify experientially with anything in the universe, including the entire cosmos itself. Here belong the experiences of merging with another person into a state of dual unity or assuming another person's identity, "tuning in" to the consciousness of a specific group of people, or of expansion of one's consciousness to such an extent that it seems to encompass all of humanity. In a similar way, one can transcend the limits of the specifically human experience and identify with the consciousness of animals, plants, or even inorganic objects and processes. In the extremes, it is possible to experience consciousness of the entire biosphere of our planet or the entire material universe.

In a large group of transpersonal experiences, the extension of consciousness seems to go beyond the phenomenal world and the time-space continuum as we perceive it in our everyday life. Here belong numerous visions of archetypal personages and themes, encounters with deities and demons of various cultures, and complex mythological sequences. Quite common also are reports of appearances of spirits of deceased people, suprahuman entities, and inhabitants of other universes.

Visions of abstract archetypal patterns, intuitive understanding of universal symbols (cross, ankh, yin-yang, swastika, pentacle, or six-pointed star), experience of the meridians and of the flow of *ch'i* energy as described in Chinese philosophy and medicine, or the arousal of the serpent power *(kundalini)* and activation of various centers of psychic energy, or *chakras*, are additional examples of this category of phenomena. In its furthest reaches, individual consciousness can identify with cosmic consciousness or the universal mind. The ultimate of all experiences appears to be identification with the supracosmic and metacosmic void, the mysterious primordial emptiness and nothingness that is conscious of itself and contains all existence in a germinal and potential form.

Transpersonal Experiences and the Shamanic World View

Transpersonal experiences have many strange characteristics that shatter the most fundamental assumptions of materialistic science and of the mechanistic world view, pointing to a paradigm closer to that which characterizes shamanic belief systems and the various branches of mystical or "perennial" philosophy.

Researchers who have seriously studied and/or experienced these fascinating phenomena realize that the attempts of traditional psychiatry to dismiss them as irrelevant products of imagination or as erratic phatasmagoria generated by pathological processes in the brain, are superficial and inadequate. Any unbiased study of the transpersonal domain of the psyche has to come to the conclusion that the observations involved represent a critical challenge for the Newtonian-Cartesian paradigm of Western science.

Although transpersonal experiences occur in the process of deep individual self-exploration, it is not possible to interpret them simply as intrapsychic phenomena in the conventional sense. On the one hand, they form an uninterrupted experiential continuum with biographical-recollective and perinatal experiences. On the other hand, they seem to be tapping directly, without the mediation of the sensory organs, sources of information that are clearly outside of the conventionally defined range of the individual.

The reports of subjects who have experienced episodes of embryonal existence, the moment of conception, and elements of cellular, tissue, and organ consciousness abound in medically accurate insights into the anatomical, physiological and biochemical aspects of the processes involved.

Similarly, ancestral experiences, racial and collective memories in the Jungian sense, and past-incarnation memories frequently bring quite specific details about architecture, costumes, weapons, art, social structure, and religious practices of the culture and period involved, or even concrete historical events.

Subjects who experienced phylogenetic sequences or identification with existing life forms not only found them unusually convincing and authentic, but also acquired in the process extraordinary insights concerning animal psychology, ethology, specific habits, or unusual reproductive cycles. In some instances, this was accompanied by archaic muscular innervations not characteristic for humans, or even such complex performances as enactment of a courtship dance.

Those individuals who experience episodes of conscious identification with plants or parts of plants occasionally report remarkable insights into such botanical processes as germination of seeds, photosynthesis in leaves, the role of auxins in plant growth, exchange of water and minerals in the root system, and pollination. Equally common is a convinced sense of conscious identification with inanimate matter or inorganic processes— water in the ocean, fire, lightning, volcanic activity, tornado, gold, diamond, granite, and even stars, galaxies, atoms, and molecules. From the standpoint of a paradigm that recognizes the existence of a transpersonal realm, references to communication with other species or even "inanimate" objects, such as reported by shamans, can no longer be seen as necessarily symptomatic of psychopathology.

There exists another interesting group of transpersonal phenomena that can be frequently validated and even researched experimentally. Here belongs telepathy, psychic diagnosis, clairvoyance, clairaudience, precognition, psychometry, out-of-body experiences, traveling clairvoyance, and other instances of extrasensory perception. These, of course, have been extensively studied and utilized in shamanic and other mystical or magical traditions. Although they represent the only group of transpersonal phenomena that has been in the past occasionally discussed in Western academic circles, they have unfortunately been approached there with a strong negative bias.

From a broader perspective, there is no reason to sort out the so-called paranormal phenomena as a special category. Since many other types of transpersonal experiences quite typically involve access to new information about the universe through extrasensory channels, the clear boundary between psychology and parapsychology disappears, or at least becomes rather arbitrary, when the existence of the transpersonal domain is recognized and acknowledged.

The philosophical challenge associated with the observations described above—formidable as it may be in itself—is further augmented by the fact that in nonordinary states of consciousness transpersonal experiences correctly reflecting the material world appear on the same continuum as— and intimately interwoven with—others whose content according to the Western world view is not part of objective reality. We can mention in this context the Jungian archetypes—the world of deities, demons, demigods, superheroes, and complex mythological, shamanic, legendary, and fairy-tale sequences. Even these experiences can impart accurate new information about religious symbolism, folklore, and mythical structures of various cultures previously unknown to the subject.

Transpersonal experiences have a very special position in our attempts to construct an accurate map of the territory of the human psyche. The recollective-analytical level and the individual unconscious are clearly biographical in nature. The perinatal dynamics seems to represent an intersection or frontier between the personal and transpersonal; this is reflected in its deep association with birth and death—the beginning and end of individual human existence. The transpersonal phenomena facilitated by holotropic therapy or traditional shamanic methods reveal connections between the individual and the cosmos which are at present beyond comprehension. All we can say is that somewhere in the process of perinatal unfolding, a strange qualitative Möbius-like leap seems to occur in which deep self-exploration of the individual unconscious turns into a process of experiential adventures in the universe-at-large—a process that involves what can best be described as cosmic consciousness or the superconscious mind.

Therapeutic Implications of the Death-Rebirth Process

The expanded cartography described above is of critical importance for any serious approach to such phenomena as psychedelic states, shamanism, religion, mysticism, rites of passage, mythology, parapsychology, thanatology, and psychosis. This is not just a matter of academic interest; it has deep and revolutionary implications for the understanding of psychopathology, and offers new therapeutic possibilities undreamed of by traditional psychiatry.

In general, the architecture of psychopathology manifested in experiential work is infinitely more complex and intricate than current personality theories suggest. According to the new observations, very few if any emotional and psychosomatic syndromes can be explained solely from the dynamics of the individual unconscious. Many clinical problems have deep roots in the perinatal level of the unconscious. They are meaningfully related to the trauma of birth and the fear of death, and their resolution requires experiential confrontation with the death-rebirth process. Thus we have found our theoretical model of the human psyche compatible with ancient shamanic belief systems, which also involve the integration of death and rebirth experiences.

Experiential work reveals that the dynamic structure of psychogenic symptoms involves extremeley powerful emotional and physical energies. In view of this fact, any effort to influence them seriously by verbal means, as in traditional psychotherapies, is of highly problematic value. It requires a therapeutic context that allows and facilitates direct experience to achieve noticeable results within a reasonable time span. In addition, because of the multilevel nature of psychogenic symptoms, the conceptual framework of the therapist has to include the perinatal and transpersonal levels of the psyche for the therapeutic work to be fully effective.

As long as the process of experiential therapy focuses on the biographical level, the therapeutic results are generally rather limited, unless the material that is confronted involves unfinished gestalts of serious physical traumas. The immediate and long-term results become much more dramatic when the self-exploration deepens and involves sequences of birth and death. The importance of these deeper experiences, so well known to our shamanic ancestors, has heretofore largely escaped the notice of Western verbal psychotherapists. We have found, however, that claustrophobia and other types of anxiety states, depression, suicidal tendencies, alcoholism, narcotic addiction, asthma, migraine headaches, sadomasochistic inclinations, and many other problems can be profoundly influenced by experiences of a perinatal nature, whether these be facilitated by holotropic, shamanic, or other means.

In those cases, however, where the deep roots of the problem reach into the transpersonal domain, final resolution will not be reached until the client allows himself or herself to confront the specific type of transpersonal experience with which it is connected. It can be an intense past-incarnation experience, identification with an animal form, an archetypal or mythological sequence, a theme from the racial or collective unconscious, and many others. Open-mindedness and trust in the process on the part of the therapist as well as the client are the most important prerequisites of successful therapy.

As previously noted, the experiences from deep experiential work also support the general strategy of therapy and self-exploration first suggested by Carl Gustav Jung, who recognized that the psyche has a powerful self-healing potential and that the source of the autonomous healing forces is the collective unconscious. From this perspective the task of the therapist is thus not to understand rationally the problem the client is facing in order to use some specific techniques to change the situation according to a preconceived plan, but rather to mediate and facilitate the client's access to the deeper strata of the psyche. Healing then results from a dialectic interplay between the individual and collective unconscious. One might draw parallels here with the shaman's traditional role as mediator between the human and spiritual realms.

A technique of psychotherapy based on the observations from modern consciousness research, such as holotropic therapy, therefore relies primarily on direct experience as the primary transforming tool. Verbal approaches are used only during the preparation period and then again following the session to facilitate integration of the experience. The therapist creates a supportive framework, establishes a good working relationship with the client, and offers a technique that can activate the unconscious, such as breathing, music, shamanic drumming, meditation, or a psychedelic drug.

Under these circumstances, the preexisting symptoms will get reinforced and previously latent ones will emerge into consciousness. The task of the therapist then is to encourage and support the experiential sequences unconditionally and with full trust in the autonomy and spontaneity of the healing process. The symptoms represent blocked energy and ultimately condensed experience. In this context, a symptom represents an opportunity as much as it does a problem.

When the energy is released, the symptom will be transformed into a conscious experience and consumed in this way. It is important that the therapist support the elemental unfolding without interfering and without investment in the nature of the experience, whether it is biographical, perinatal, or transpersonal. The unconditional support has to continue, even if the therapist does not understand the process or if it is taking a form that he or she has never seen before. Instead of trying to interpret all emerging material in terms of a closed theoretical system—as it is in psychoanalysis and related approaches—the therapist becomes a co-adventurer who can learn new things in every session.

3
Shamanism and Personal Empowerment

THE AUTHORS in this section address shamanism as a spiritual path, emphasizing the uses of shamanic methods to facilitate personal growth and self-transformation. In the first chapter, Michael Harner explains the theory and techniques of shamanic counseling, which he has pioneered and taught for the past several years. He describes and contrasts the practice of shamanic counseling with traditional Western "verbal" approaches, noting that the experiential component of shamanic counseling, which involves the whole person and extensively utilizes the imagery and power of the imagination, makes it a more effective transformative method than those depending mainly on the analytical mind.

In his chapter "Shamanic Tales as Ways of Personal Empowerment," Jürgen Kremer shows how shamanic stories can play a significant role in the process of psychological individuation as well as in the rebuilding of our guiding cultural mythos, which is currently the scientific story. Describing a "tale of power" as "the harvest from altered states" which takes the form of a verbal construction around experiences beyond the limits of everyday consensual reality, Kremer argues that such tales can guide and help individuals to integrate the spiritual, mythical, or archetypal aspects of their internal and external experience in unique and meaningful ways.

In "Shaman's Journey, Buddhist Path," Joan Halifax points to some of the shamanic elements in Buddhism, noting areas of overlap and difference that she believes are of importance to contemporary Westerners. In her view, the shamanic and Buddhist emphasis on the importance of "mind transmission," silence as a spiritual technique, stopping the mind, the practice of the "giveaway," and the concepts of impermanence and interdependence are the areas where shamanism and Buddhism are most closely allied.

Brooke Medicine Eagle emphasizes that shamanism regards the body and its connection with the earth as primary points of reference in transformational work. She refers to the Lakota healers' practice of reddening their hands with paint before healing ceremonies to indicate their dedication to the blood of all the people, and suggests that we metaphorically "paint our whole body red" by developing an attitude in which the physical body is honored as the repository of spirit. Drawing from her experience as a teacher and ceremonial leader, she provides many examples of how whole-body physical exercises can be used to facilitate difficult life transitions or overcome blocks to growth and creativity.

In "Shamans, Yogis, and Bodhisattvas," I focus on the common interest shared by shamans, yogis, and Buddhists in the process of *entrainment*, or the induction of altered states of consciousness by attention to repetitive "driving" stimuli. In discussing the shamanic origins of yoga and the overlap between samadhi and the shamanic state of consciousness, I suggest that the spiritual experiences and aims characteristic of shamanism are not fundamentally different from those of the "contemplative" branches of the mystical tradition, and that ultimately the paths of shaman, yogi, and Buddhist blend into one—the "path of compassionate action"—wherein the mastery of entrainment states is utilized for the achievement of altruistic community goals.

Shamanic Counseling

MICHAEL HARNER

IN THIS CHAPTER the term *shamanic counseling* is used to describe the specific methods I have developed to help clients work on life problems. These methods are "experiential" in contrast to the "verbal" or analytical approaches of traditional Western methods of counseling, and they are based on the journey technique of classical shamanism. Shamanic counseling, specifically Harner Method® Shamanic Counseling,[1] is a system for permitting clients to make their own shamanic journeys of divination to nonordinary reality, where they personally obtain direct spiritual wisdom and guidance in answer to the questions most important in their lives. Other persons sometimes use the term *shamanic counseling* to refer to different methods of working with clients, including certain "medicine way" approaches, or they may use it as a cover designation for shamanic healing. For such reasons, the *Harner Method* designation was adopted to avoid confusion.

Although it is based on the methods of classical shamanism, shamanic counseling has certain innovations that set it apart from traditional shamanic systems. For instance, the divination or problem-solving journey to nonordinary reality has traditionally been made by the shaman on behalf of the client. One of the main features of shamanic counseling, however, is to turn this procedure around so that the client is being counseled to become his or her own shaman for this type of journey. The object of this change is to restore spiritual power and authority to the client.

Another innovation is the use of electronic methods rather than the live drum technique for induction of the shamanic state of consciousness (ssc). In this system the client uses a drumming tape on a cassette player to provide the sonic driving necessary to facilitate the journey to nonordinary

179

reality in the ssc. The sound of the drum perceived only through a set of earphones has been found to be an effective method in this regard, and it has the added advantage of not creating the noise-disturbance problems that can arise when one attempts to use live drumming in the crowded urban settings in which most counseling sessions must take place in our culture.

The use of a drumming tape also permits the shamanic counselor to utilize another major innovation of this system—the technique of *simultaneous narration*, wherein the client is asked to narrate out loud the details of his or her journey as it is happening. Simultaneous narration is possible because the sound of the drumming is confined to the client's earphones and therefore does not interfere with the audibility of the narration as live drumming would do. The client's narration consists of a verbatim description of what is happening in the journey, and provides an opportunity for the client to review the answer to his or her question with the help of the counselor. A recording of the narration is also made as a permanent record of the journey, which is then given to the client to use for his or her own purposes.

After some preparatory and exploratory work, in which the client becomes more familiar with the territory of, and resources available in, nonordinary reality, counseling sessions are usually devoted to seeking an answer to a specific question brought by the client—generally concerning a problem whose resolution is of uppermost importance in the client's life at that particular time. The task of the counselor at this point is to help the client become clear about precisely what the question is and whether it is being asked in the most appropriate form. Through dialogue and mutual inquiry, client and counselor clarify the question. The client then makes a journey to nonordinary reality to seek help in answering the question from the great sources of wisdom that can be found there.

The process of receiving an answer to such life questions typically and spontaneously includes many elements of classical shamanic experience—for example, representation of the answer in pantomine or symbolic enactments by power animals; dialogues with mythic personages or spirits through which profound insights are revealed; initiation experiences; "magical flights"; out-of-body phenomena; and so on. Visionary material that emerges is typically of a mythical or transpersonal nature. Encounters with spiritual forms such as a Great Teacher, interaction with power animals or guardian spirits, visits to realms of extraordinary beauty and harmony, visions of otherworldly lights and landscapes, and communication with spirits of the dead are quite prevalent experiences.

As these come forth and are recorded in the client's narration, a rich source of material for later client/counselor analysis and discussion is obtained, at which stage a cooperative effort is made by both individuals to extract the most significant details of the answer received to the client's question during the journey. Because of the powerful nature of these techniques, psychologists and psychotherapists who have studied this system have expressed the view that shamanic counseling has the potential for significantly accelerating the process of personal growth, in many cases requiring far less time to achieve meaningful results than traditional Western counseling methods.

A System of Person Empowerment

The reason for turning the classical shamanic model around and introducing the concept that the client should become the shaman for the divinatory journey is that we are trying to go beyond the idea that people need to seek spiritual authority from someone in ordinary reality outside themselves. We want to allow people to discover that they can directly and personally divine answers quite accurately to the questions that concern them most if they are given permission and the necessary tools. Shamanic counseling can therefore be described as a method of personal empowerment wherein one comes to acquire respect for one's own ability to obtain spiritual wisdom without relying on external mediators. The whole idea is to return to people what was once taken away from them when state religions began perpetuating monopolies on access to spiritual knowledge.

This innovation, although not traditional, is nevertheless quite in keeping with the basic attitude of classical shamanism, where it has been assumed from the beginning that the individual can gain direct access to spiritual insight. Indeed, it is this assumption that has made shamanic training and the unbroken lineage of shamanic teachers possible. Shamanic counseling merely takes the spiritual egalitarianism of shamanism one step further by saying that with modern methods of communication and technology, more individuals than ever before can now be trained to be their own shamans. So actually we are just trying to practice the spiritual democracy implicit in shamanism from the beginning.

For this reason it is counterproductive in shamanic counseling for the client to "take a back seat," so to speak, by allowing someone else to do the divinatory journey on his or her behalf, which would be contrary to the whole idea of restoring authority to the individual. Instead, every effort is made by the counselor to make the client capable of operating independently in nonordinary reality for the purpose of the divination journey.

Thus the concept of empowerment is crucial in this system—a concept which, it is interesting to note, is filtering into other areas as well with the growth of this so-called "information age." Microcomputers, for example, are now making knowledge in a variety of fields widely available that was once the privileged monopoly of a few specialists. Likewise, in shamanism we are talking about opening up new channels of communication— channels that were once open to our ancestors but that disappeared with the growth of civilization.

Requirements of Clients and Counselors

The most obvious requirement of clients of shamanic counselors is that they be able to visualize, at least to some extent, since if a person is one of the small minority of nonvisualizers, the shamanic journey is unlikely to have enough clarity to be of use in the counseling situation. Probably about 90 percent of the population, however, can visualize well enough for this purpose.

Other than this, shamanic counseling is appropriate for anyone who is seriously interested in bringing all the available resources to bear on the important questions in his or her life. Just as a matter of practical fact, however, the people who come to study these methods are typically well educated and intelligent individuals who are also curious and open-minded. Usually they are not "followers" or advocates of blind faith in any particular teaching or dogma, but are inquiring individuals who would like to find some spiritual method that is workable and that they can trust in their own lives. Combined with these qualities they frequently also have a desire to recover their own authority and autonomy, and are often highly individualistic while at the same time wishing to find a deeper sense of community.

The counselor's basic job in this system is simply to help the client become effective in the methods of shamanic counseling, but not actually to advise the client as to the meaning of symbols or other information that may be encountered in the divinatory journey. These meanings are often discussed in counseling sessions, but the counselor's constant job is to turn back the authority for interpretation to the client. The principle here is that no one is better qualified to understand the messages of the journey than the person who is undertaking it, and also that the messages are perfectly formed for the journeyer in question.

The most important requirement of a shamanic counselor is the strong desire to help others, without which one cannot establish a firm connection to the source of the great power, harmony, and compassion necessary for shamanic work. Besides this crucial prerequisite, an effective shamanic counselor clearly needs to know shamanism thoroughly. Once a person has a deep knowledge of shamanism, most of the other useful qualities of a counselor will follow naturally.

One of these that deserves to be emphasized is the development of an attitude of noninterference, which means that one is able to leave clients alone and affirm their right (and indeed obligation) not to depend on people in ordinary reality for answers to their questions, but to take the responsibility of going directly to the same revelatory sources of deep wisdom that have always been available to the seers, mystics, and shamans throughout history.

In this process the counselor encourages the client in every way possible to develop self-reliance and independence. Genuine concern for the client's welfare (the true basis of professional ethics) demands that counselors resist any temptation to create dependence, requiring instead that they strive to develop an attitude of nonattachment to particular clients— an attitude that does not, however, imply coldness or indifference. This clearly requires the counselors to work on any personal problems (security hangups, fears, greed, and so forth) that may be influencing their relationship with clients. Hence competence in this system presupposes an ongoing effort by counselors to know themselves more and more thoroughly. To this end they are expected to use shamanic counseling for themselves as well as their clients. Counseling can thereby become a true spiritual path involving a continuous process of growth for both client and counselor.

Although the counselor's whole purpose is to enable the client to work independently, it is also important to note that even people who have worked with these techniques for many years often find that they prefer to have someone else present listening to the journey as it unfolds, because this heightens the discipline of having to communicate what is going on, and also tends to intensify the experience for many people. Moreover, it should be kept in mind that this communication process is not just for the other person who is listening, because when one plays back the tape of the narration of the journey, one is in fact communicating to oneself. In this way, details frequently come to one's attention that would have otherwise been forgotten or unnoticed. Hence there is a great value in working with someone else.

Another factor that must be considered is that in reviewing and discussing a journey with a client, an experienced counselor is often able to point out and focus the client's attention on important material that might otherwise have been "edited" out of consideration in a situation of working alone. Many people will tend to block out important symbolic material or other significant aspects of the journey simply because they find it threatening or painful and choose not to deal with it; whereas it is often obvious to the counselor when such editing is occurring, and it is then possible to bring the client's attention gently back to the material in question by asking the right questions.

Finally, shamanic counselors should not make claims to be doing psychotherapy or dealing with psychopathology, nor should they claim to be practicing healing. This needs to be made quite explicit at the outset of the counselor's relationship with a client. The counselor is not giving advice about the problems brought by the client, but is merely a facilitator who puts clients in touch with the sources of guidance in nonordinary reality, from which the answers received are typically wise, benevolent, compassionate, ethical, and harmonious.

Problems Dealt with in Shamanic Counseling

Shamanic counseling works with all kinds of problems that may be brought by clients. Usually the main emphasis is placed on working with personal questions, but through these methods one can obtain incredible wisdom on any major question, whether it concerns oneself or others. In a sense, the great scientists of history who have had revelations (often visual in nature) on scientific problems have been using the same practices unconsciously and without discipline. With these techniques, however, ordinary people can have access to profound insight and even to information about small details concerning how to operationalize and utilize this insight in a practical way.

For example, in response to a question about a health problem, a client may receive extremely detailed instructions about what foods to eat, what herbs to prepare, how much and what kind of exercise is required, and so forth. Or there may be an unexpected and spontaneous healing, perhaps brought about by the intermediacy of one or more entities of various kinds in nonordinary reality. In all cases such as this, the counselor does not claim credit for any benefits received by the client but refers these benefits to their true sources in nonordinary reality.

It is important to emphasize here that although advice on health matters or spontaneous healing may occur in shamanic counseling, this method does not train the counselor in shamanic methods of diagnosis or healing, nor in aspects of shamanism other than the divinatory journey. It has been developed solely for the purpose of allowing clients to get their own answers to important life questions by moving into nonordinary reality and contacting the incredible wisdom that is available there to those willing to spend the time and effort to acquire the appropriate tools and techniques.

This, of course, does not mean that there is no place in contemporary society for the type of classical shamanism in which the shaman makes a journey on behalf of the client for purposes other than divination. Indeed, a person who trains in shamanic counseling is well equipped to turn around and help other people in more traditional shamanic ways once his or her own personal problems have been solved. After all, helping oneself is only the first step in classical shamanism, and these counseling techniques are designed mainly to enable people to take that necessary first step. Later, however, one may wish to help others as it becomes more and more apparent that by helping others one is helping oneself.

Thus many clients find that in the course of working on their own problems they are receiving teachings in nonordinary reality which can be used for wider purposes. For example, by being first counseled as a client, one can gradually learn the techniques of being a counselor. Some people who train in shamanic counseling are already psychotherapists or in the counseling professions and wish to find some other system they can use to benefit their clients; others have not yet entered a helping profession but would like to do so directly as shamanic counselors; and still others wish to use these methods just to help solve the problems in their own lives. The purpose for which one uses shamanic counseling is a highly personal choice.

Autonomy of the Shamanic Counseling System

I am often asked whether it is necessary or useful to have training in traditional Western psychotherapeutic or counseling methods in order to become a shamanic counselor. Of course, many people who use the traditional Western methods have great compassion and concern about others, and they have also learned techniques for establishing rapport and maintaining a client-counselor relationship; but often it takes some "de-programming," so to speak, for such professionals to learn the methods of shamanic counseling. This does not mean that they must abandon the other procedures in which they have been trained—at least not in an absolute way—but only that while doing shamanic counseling they must adopt a methodology that may be new to them and that requires them to have extra discipline in using it compared with someone who is not already involved in another approach. In other words, it is sometimes an advantage not to be burdened with terminologies and models that are not part of and not necessary for the practice of shamanic counseling. There is no particular benefit in already having been trained in Western methods of counseling; what really matters is one's understanding of shamanism—and, of course, what kind of person one is.

It is necessary to emphasize again that the shamanic counselor does not attempt to enter the area of treating psychopathology or even neurosis. This is first of all because we are using a shamanic system, and shamanism does not deal with personal problems in terms of those particular concepts, which have developed specifically within the recent Western paradigm. This does not mean that the phenomena referred to by such concepts do not exist; it just means that shamanism does not work with such models. The shamanic counselor is not attempting in any way to enter into the modern Western systems of psychotherapy where those concepts and definitions are taken for granted. Rather, he or she has a different system that is quite venerable and time-tested yet still very applicable to our problems today.

Nevertheless, if someone has a problem in life—whatever it may be—it is normally possible to get help in solving it through the methods of shamanic counseling. The task of the shamanic counselor is simply to help the client narrow down the definition of the problem so that it is clear in the client's mind. Then, after the problem can be precisely formulated, the client uses shamanic methods to seek help in solving it. But, again, this help does not come from the counselor in ordinary reality; rather, it comes from the client's own divinatory journey to nonordinary reality, *where the real counselors are.*

The life problems addressed in shamanic counseling may belong to people who are not neurotic, who are slightly neurotic, or who are very neurotic. But whether a particular problem emanates from neurotic sources is a whole question that need not concern a shamanic counselor, who simply does not operate within a framework where such a question is relevant. For example, whether a question about how to deal with, say, a certain fear stems from an unresolved mother complex or an early childhood trauma is a consideration that does not enter into the shamanic counseling process. The experience of shamans is that whatever answer or advice may be received in the divinatory journey, it is perfectly formed to benefit its receiver in the most appropriate way, whether this involves processes described in other systems as "resolution of neurotic complexes" or not. In fact, as noted before, many psychotherapists have expressed the view that they see great therapeutic value in shamanic counseling, so the benefits of this system in that respect are not really in question. The question merely concerns which model and terminology one wishes to use in helping clients deal with their problems.

For this reason I am hesitant to use Western psychoanalytic terms, or terms from other systems of working with the mind, to describe what is going on in shamanic counseling. For example, some people may be tempted to describe the shamanic journey in terms of "free association" based on the use of imagery or visualization. I am always uncomfortable, however, in trying to hastily translate what is happening in a little-known field like shamanism into terms that pigeon-hole it neatly into a known system. It is dangerous to use psychological phrases *a priori* to describe these phenomena because it might give people the erroneous idea that we know scientifically exactly what is happening in shamanism, whereas in fact we do not.

This is not to say that shamanic counseling is necessarily incompatible with other approaches. My advice to would-be shamanic counselors, however, is to give shamanism a chance to stand by itself. After all, it has stood by itself for tens of thousands of years, and therefore to make it work successfully it is not necessary to "improve" it by mixing it with concepts and techniques from other systems—for example, by bringing in reference to archetypes of the unconscious, to the *chakra* concept, and so forth. Shamanism deserves to be respected for what it is, and it would seem presumptuous to start innovating before one thoroughly and experientially understands the system by itself and knows what its power is.

Again and again I have seen people begin with very little understanding of shamanism, who gain respect for it as they continue to work with it, and who are finally awed by the power and integrity of the shamanic counseling system in itself when they fully understand what it can do. Shamanism is a fully autonomous system that works on its own; it is not necessary to "help" it. It has been time-tested by humankind longer than any other mental-spiritual system and should be honored as such. Hence, a shamanic counseling method which is based on these proven, ancient ways of working with the human mind and spirit does not need to offer any apology for being independent of other systems. Indeed, because of the experiential nature of this approach, which involves the whole person and extensively utilizes the power of both the mind's visionary and analytical faculties, shamanic counseling often appears to be at least as fully effective a transformative method as those which depend mainly on the analytical mind alone.[2]

NOTES

1. *Shamanic counseling*, as used in this article, is an abbreviation for the system known formally as *Harner Method Shamanic Counseling*, copyright © 1985 by Michael Harner.
2. Information on training in shamanic counseling can be obtained by writing The Foundation for Shamanic Studies, Box 670—Belden Station, Norwalk, Connecticut 06852.

Shamanic Tales as Ways of
Personal Empowerment

JÜRGEN W. KREMER

T HE DOMINANT STORY pervading Western technological societies has been the story of science. The scientific story, however, has led to well-known consequences which are highly problematic—for example, the threat of nuclear holocaust and the possibility of ecological catastrophes such as the destruction of rain forests and the ozone layer, the pollution of air and water, nuclear accidents, and so forth. For this reason, many people today are seeking a more flexible and appropriate paradigm that will allow for solutions to these difficulties. Nevertheless, this search implies no disrespect to science but is, in fact, part of the scientific enterprise itself. Indeed, it would be self-contradictory for science to put its own current scientific narrative on a pedestal as the only true and legitimate story, for this would amount to the creation of a dogma and a state religion that are philosophically founded on belief and faith rather than on the reason and argument claimed by science to be its guiding principle.

The surge of interest in shamanism at a time when the limitations of the traditional scientific story are becoming more and more apparent can hardly be seen as a mere coincidence, nor should it be seen as a mere fad, although a number of its contemporary aspects have that feature. It is thus interesting to note that out of the rich spectrum of spiritual traditions, shamanism seems to capture the attention of an increasing number of people as a possible response to a situation that many regard as a severe crisis.

Reasons for this may be found in the earthiness and groundedness of shamanism, as well as the fact that shamanic stories seem to further the

189

balance between humans and nature, thus appearing as an antidote to the potentially catastrophic ecological consequences of the scientific world view. Further reasons may be found in the openness of shamanism to direct experience of realities and alternate realities, as contrasted with the once-removed and never-quite-cohesive sets of explanations found in science, and also in the fact that the shamanic world view seems to have a more holistic perspective on the human being, paying equal respect to body, sexuality, emotions, imagination, intellect, and spirit rather than relying solely on the analytical mind. Thus shamanism may provide a model of how we may develop stories that allow for ambiguity, intuitive insight, direct experience, and empowerment of the individual. And it may help us to stay connected with the fact that a paradigm, regardless of what nature, is just a paradigm—a model and nothing more.

It is this role of shamanism as a possible model for the rebuilding of the stories in our societies that I wish to consider in this chapter. If we are indeed living in what I have termed a "narrative universe," then the question of how we create our stories and what their qualities are, is of utmost importance.[1] My suggestion here is that shamanism provides us with an important model of how to create a multiplicity of narratives that are experientially based, nondogmatic, empowering, and aligned with the different aspects of internal and external realities rather than dominating and controlling them.

Most contemporary people, at least in Western technological societies, seem to be in a position that Terry Williams describes well in her beautiful book *Pieces of White Shell* vis-à-vis her experience with the Navajo Indians:

> I am not suggesting we emulate Native Peoples—in this case, the Navajo. We can't. We are not Navajo. Besides, their traditional stories don't work for us. It's like drinking another man's medicine. Their stories hold meaning for us only as example. They can teach us what is possible. We must create and find our own stories, our own myths, with symbols that will bind us to the world as we see it today. In so doing, we will better know how to live our lives in the midst of change.[2]

Shamanism may just provide us with the necessary avenues, techniques, and examples to create our own stories and to use those stories and symbols from other people(s) and traditions that we can experientially appropriate. It is my contention that shamanic tales, because of their special nature, may provide a very good starting point for the rebuilding of narratives in Western societies.

Tales of Power

Borrowing the title from Carlos Castaneda's fourth book, I have used the term *tales of power* as a label for shamanic tales.[3] My preference for this term stems from the connotations it has with empowerment of the individual. Tales of power are those stories which reflect individuals' distinctive paths along the particular trajectories of their life histories. They are about the unfolding of the individuals' uniqueness. Power comes from the development of all the aspects of an individual. Tales of power are the harvest from altered states, the means by which the shaman mediates and transfers power from the spiritual to the mundane world. These stories thus have the potential of guiding individuals along on their own unique paths of growth.

The end of Castaneda's *Tales of Power* provides a good example of a tale of power. This particular one gives a good idealized model for what tales of power can potentially do for an individual. The book *Tales of Power* ends with Carlos Castaneda, together with his fellow apprentices, being taken to the rim of an abyss after he has been given the "sorcerer's explanation," which marks the end of his formal apprenticeship. He then reports a leap into the canyon, which he later describes as a number of elastic bounces between ordinary and nonordinary reality—or, to put it differently, between the numinous, intuitive, right-hemisphere reality of the *nagual*, on the one hand, and the mundane, rational, left-hemisphere reality of the *tonal* on the other. He gives us a tale of an act of power that he himself obviously does not understand at the time of its occurrence, and that continues to baffle him for many years.

Castaneda preserves this extraordinary experience as a story that haunts him and guides him toward subsequent learning experiences, which lead to an increasing understanding of his act of power. Not only does his desire on that occasion to understand his movements between the nagual and tonal lead him to return to the area of this learning experience, but, as subsequent volumes and interviews indicate, it leads to new learning experiences, which allow the uncovering of new facets of the original act of power.[4]

For example, in the last chapter of *The Eagle's Gift*, Castaneda describes memories of this experience to which he did not have access before.[5] His descriptions increase in detail and provide an understanding of the event that is embedded in the other teachings provided in the books. And again in his latest book, *The Fire from Within*, the jump into the abyss is mentioned in the foreword and further described in the epilogue.[6] We can observe a concern with the final event mentioned in *Tales of Power* for another ten years. Thus Castaneda's continued work, as published in his books, and his continued struggle with this particular tale of power centering on the leap into the abyss, allowed him to progress in his path, to individuate further, and to understand this particular event better, as described in the subsequent tales.

We can therefore say that tales of power are conscious verbal constructions around numinous experiences outside of everyday consensual reality, which guide individuals and help them to integrate the spiritual, mythical, or archetypal aspects of their internal and external experience in unique, meaningful, and fulfilling ways. Let us examine the crucial elements of this descriptive definition, which can easily be recognized in Castaneda's tale of his jump into the canyon.

Creating an Opening to the Numinous

The nature of the experiences that can lead to the creation of tales of power is, in principle, unlimited. These experiences may be consciously sought, as in a vision quest, past-life regression, or controlled lucid dreaming; they may be spontaneous outside of the framework of direct seeking, as in ordinary dreams; or they may be consciously sought in an effort to explain the meaning of a found (power) object. The decision to preserve such experiences in a tale is, however, conscious and intentional.

Prime examples of such events are visions received in ceremonies or during ceremonial drug experiences and dreams; but they can also be experiences induced by anything from movies and books to personal encounters. The important thing is whether a shift in awareness is entailed. It is not the stimuli of the experiences that are crucial, but the nature of the experiences they induce in conjunction with the subsequent expression in a tale. For example, books by authors such as Andrews,[7] Castaneda,[8] or Storm[9]—by virtue of being tales of power themselves—may facilitate shifts in the readers' consciousness, which can then be used by readers as the basis for their own tales of power. (Storm's books can be seen as particularly powerful medicine in this context.) In this way they may help to create a point of departure, an opening to the numinous or nagual.

The experiences to be embodied in tales of power thus have to be of something that is felt as larger than the range of experiences controlled by the conscious purpose of wakeful, consensual consciousness. They may also be called a connection with some archetypal level or an opening to the unconscious or the supraconscious. In any case, individuals will usually describe them as "powerful." They are characterized by a lessening of the controls of the ego and social self so that something outside of these boundaries can be experienced. This clearly happens with Castaneda's inconceivable leap, in which he is able to suspend his usual "internal monologue" (the analytical/discursive thought processes, which maintain the consensual world view) and, by doing so, achieve an "act of power"— a personal action beyond the limits of what is considered possible in ordinary reality.

The experiences preserved in tales of power can basically be of anything within the realm of the numinous that the individual, by creating a tale of power, infuses or tries to infuse with meaning. Thus I restrict the use of this term either to experiences that deal directly with the spiritual and mythical, or to those which at least set individuals on the road to "the larger." Oftentimes these experiences involve a feeling of awe in the face of something that very clearly is outside the controls of ordinary purposive consciousness. Tales of power may be created as part of a spiritual discipline during which experiences of the larger are likely to occur; but they may also guide individuals who have not yet found their path toward an appropriate spiritual discipline.

Any experience of the larger can be viewed as a point of choice. If no tale of power is created around the event, then the individual has made a choice to regard it just like any other experience that does not stand out in any particular way; at best it is curious, at worst nonsensical and silly. On the other hand, if a tale of power is created, then a choice has been made to use it in some fashion to give meaning to life; this is true whether the meaning is clear or only vaguely sensed, and even when it is jarring or disturbing and cannot be understood immediately.

Integration through Shamanic Tales of Power

The experiences reflected in tales of power are not just interesting occurrences; they are part and parcel of the process of individuation. Oftentimes they can be regarded as the first call on the hero's or heroine's journey.[10] They are then the beginning of the initiation, the beginning of the journey toward individuation. By forming tales of power, individuals consciously mount on the adventures of internal and external exploration that lead to integration of the "shadow" elements of the psyche.

These stories have their power because they are unique and individual and, as such, deviant from the social selves and collective expectations of everyday reality. Moreover, they are deviant because they have a power of uniqueness that stems from a movement into the individuals' creative center. Because of this, tales of power always have a "crazy" edge to them.

This is the price to be paid for stepping out of the collective of consensual reality in Western technological societies. Castaneda, for example, over and over reports how he felt pushed to the brink of insanity by his experiences.

Keen discusses the process of individuation in some detail.[11] He refers to the result of an individual's move into autonomy as "the outlaw," because it involves a "re-membering" of the dangerous knowledge that has been exiled in the unconscious.[12] The development of tales of power is thus the act of inviting the outlawed elements of the psyche into conscious life. Individuals step into their center of power, into their uniqueness, by deconstructing the social scripts that have guided them so far. In telling a tale of power, I therefore claim my individuality and take all the felt risks that go with it, acknowledging and accepting my own creative power.

In this sense, tales of power are a response to a call, a decision for self-transformation. They guide individuals on their path of transformation, serving as beacons that structure their experience, guide decisions, and pull the individual along. As in the reading of poetry, their meaning unfolds over time as the individual continues to live and develop additional perspectives—as it did, for example, through four consecutive volumes in Castaneda's works.

As the name suggests, tales of power are primarily preserved verbally. Nevertheless, there are other adjuncts—for example, artifacts or rituals—that may serve as a way beyond the verbal and help an individual to retain and activate the memory of the experience serving as the basis of the tale of power. In fact, these adjuncts may be a crucial ingredient in the unfoldment and working with a tale, serving as mementos and strengthening ties to the unconscious, the mythical, and spiritual. The medicine bundles or shields of the American Indians are a good illustration of this principle. Drawings or pendants are other examples of nonverbal representations of tales of power. It should also be noted that tales of power by no means have to be public; they may be told to another individual or to a group, but this is not necessarily desirable. At times it may even be good or necessary that these tales be kept to oneself—for example, in a diary.

Harvesting a Shamanic Tale

The following tale is an illustration of the process of work with a powerful experience by way of a story. The description of the visionary experiences in this narrative has gone through a number of drafts, which not only indicate work on the presentation, but also a deepening understanding of the cohesiveness of the visions and well as their symbology and details. In this story, the process of remembrance and integration occurs on a smaller scale than the momentous experiences and recollections that Castaneda reports in the examples mentioned previously, but it shows how continued work and rewriting of a particular experience facilitates integration.

> The visions started last night under the cottonwood trees as I went out of bounds carried by the intensity of the vibrations around me. . . . I am flying before I have even descended into the canyon. As I descend into the earth, the rocks provide me with bounds only so that I go out of bounds further. . . . And all the while the ravens are with us. Messengers of Mother Earth. . . . And then the ravens appear right in front of me, and I fly with them. I look into their eyes and *know* their energy, and I *see* how I can jibe my energy with theirs. . . . Never before have I felt the energies of the world in this manner, with this degree of clarity. . . . Then the baby spirit that has been hovering over me becomes clear. She wants to return. The feeling is seductive, her presence overwhelming. . . . And then another veil is lifted and I am told: "You need to step into your creativity."

This first version of this tale of power was written shortly after the experience. The following description, written somewhat later, indicates how the author has paid more attention to the events and remembered more detail, how connections between different parts of the vision have become clearer, and how phenomena that must have seemed incidental at first have received an added depth or dimension. For example, the meaning of the energies of the place—"Spider Woman's Place"—has been uncoded; while initially the power of the place had received no attention, its relevance for the visions is now understood. Also, the description of the appearance of the spirit of the dead girl has by now led to an enriched understanding of a custom of some tribal cultures. The reimmersion into the original visionary experience, in general, has led to clarifications and added detail.

> This place was a special place indeed. It was Spider Woman's dwelling place. And it was into her crevices that I was venturing in order to learn more about my true humanity. . . . The visions had started last night as I had gone out of bounds carried by the intensity of the vibrations around me. . . . I was flying before I had even descended into the canyon. Thoughts and things rushed by like some movie running at fifty times the normal speed. It

was hard for me to stay centered and observe, and I knew it would take me a long time to decipher what I saw while out of bounds. . . . And all the while the ravens were with us— messengers of the Kachinas. And there was a small down feather also which we received as a present from Spider Woman. Then the ravens appeared right in front of me, and I flew with them. I looked into their eyes and I *knew* their energy and I *saw* how I can jibe my energy with theirs. Never before had I felt the energies of the world in this manner, with this degree of clarity. . . . And then the spirit of the friend's girl who had died recently pushed down on me: She was the baby spirit that had been hovering over me. . . . It seemed that she had a very hard time adjusting to her new state, and it was clear that she wanted to return immediately. . . . The feeling of her presence was seductive, overwhelming. I understood why some tribal cultures take a year before they mentioned the names of deceased persons again. They do not want to disturb their spirit journey, they do not want to distract them from their path. They want to let them live in peace to do whatever it is that they needed to do. . . . And then another veil lifted and I was told: "You need to step into your creativity."

I have chosen the example of this developing story to indicate why it is a tale of power and to show how it provides guidance and is used by the narrator to facilitate a process of growth and individuation. In this regard we should note first that the act of writing and rewriting—using the rational mind of the tonal to capture the trans-rational, numinous reality of the nagual—allows for the conscious harvesting of an apparently intense, dense, and profound experience, as well as helping to build a bridge between the tonal and the nagual that prevents the fleetingness and subtlety of the experience from being buried in oblivion. The author, as an explorer of the nagual, "the ground of being," has apparently worked intently at understanding the experience.

Second, this tale of power contains a number of suggestions that can provide guidance for future action—for example, the suggestion that deciphering the message will take a long time, that this is connected with learning more about the narrator's "true humanity," that there is a possibility of learning to sense and use energies in a new way and to harmonize with the energies of other living things, and that creativity should be developed. Clearly, the acceptance of these suggestions may entail a fundamental process of self-transformation. Thus the discipline of writing and rewriting entails a decision for a movement toward the center of power of the individual.

In interpreting an act of power as embodied in a tale of power, it is useful to determine the salient images. Often it is helpful to reimmerse oneself in the imagery in order to remember and understand additional detail. Familiarity with mythological material may guide one to a deeper understanding. In order to use the guidance contained in such tales, it is important to determine the basic message(s) contained in the shamanic experience. As a next step, it is crucial to be aware of the feeling and thinking responses to this message.

The awareness of internal and/or external obstacles is helpful in understanding what may keep one from using the power contained in the tales. Subsequently, artistic representations of the experience (for example, drawings, shields, sculptures, found objects, and so forth), Gestalt dialogues, journal work, imagery, and other human potential techniques can be helpful in garnering the contents of a tale. The determination of possible action in consensual reality to preserve, enhance, and live a tale of power are crucial as a follow-up.

Shamanic Stories as Bases for an Evolving World View

The world view inherent in the tale of power just discussed is one that is at odds with the prevalent Western scientific story, for it does not reflect an intent to control or manipulate realities, be they internal or external, as in our present paradigm. Rather, this tale reflects a dance with these realities. It puts its author further into a unique circle of power, a uniquely constellated individuality. It is a tale that is concerned with experience, not explanation. The individual felt more empowered after this work, even though the experience had an edge of unreality and craziness. From it emerged a clarification of the direction of the person's life.

Shamanic traditions are built on such tales of power, and we can clearly sense their relationship with mythology and legends. The techniques available to shamans allow them to travel continuously to the creative ground from which our everyday consensual reality and rationality have emerged. These powerful acts, be they shamanic journeys, healings, divinations, or other phenomena connected with contact with nonordinary reality, are reflected in the continuously developing narratives which attempt to capture their essence.

These stories also create a matrix for continuous change in consensual social reality. This change starts with individuals who build their lives as sequences of tales of power. Thus shamanic stories can serve as a model of how individuals may construct their own uniquely evolving and fluid world views as a basis for creating communities that dance with internal and external realities. Shamans may be able to show us ways to create a narrative universe that contains a multiplicity of stories and that can contain a level of ambiguity higher than the one the current scientific story can bear.

But all this is not an argument against science. Rather, it is an argument against science as the dominant and ultimate story. If we are looking for ways to rebuild the stories in contemporary Western societies, it appears that we will have to begin with the stories of individuals and encourage them to "be their own prophets" by forming their own tales of power. As a result of that empowerment, we may then find new ways of choosing from among the numerous individual life stories as well as societal stories. Hence this narrative universe will most likely find its own way to contain, change, and dance with the scientific story.

All this means that we do have alternatives to the cynicism and anarchism often associated with attempts to deconstruct the scientific paradigm and other social scripts underlying our Western consensus reality. Indeed, there are better and worse stories to create and participate in. Those which empower the individual, those which do not further domination and control, those which do not seek explanation at the expense of experience—those, I would hold, tend to be the better stories. Implicit in this view is a continuous evolution of narratives that does not allow for dogmatism.

If we can agree that emancipation of the individual and emancipated social conglomerates (of whatever nature) are meaningful goals and values, then we need to seek the coincidence of the rationally known with the felt sense of rightness (wisdom). This is an aspect of *alignment*, a term that refers to the alignment of the elements within human beings—for example, an open dialectic between the intuition, intellect, emotions, sexuality, and body—as well as between human beings and between humans and their environment.

This alignment occurs when members of our species acknowledge their fundamental likeness to each other while at the same time retaining an appreciation of their unique differences in language and culture. Thus the question of alignment appears to me to be the crucial test for the quality of our stories. The starting points for alignment are individuals and the unique tales of power that they create. The way shamans construct their individual life stories, as well as the way in which they participate in their social groups, are models that we can fruitfully explore as the "discourse of modernity" edges closer and closer to its limits.

NOTES

1. J. Kremer, "The Human Science Approach as Discourse," *Saybrook Review*, 6, no. 1 (1986): 65–105; "The Shaman and the Epistemologer," in R.-I. Heinze, *Proceedings of the Third International Conference on Shamanism and Alternative Modes of Healing* (Berkeley: Asian Studies Center, 1987).

2. Terry Williams, *Pieces of White Shell* (Albuquerque: University of New Mexico Press), p. 5.

3. Carlos Castaneda, *Tales of Power* (New York: Simon & Schuster, 1975).

4. Carlos Castaneda, *The Second Ring of Power* (New York: Simon & Schuster, 1977).

5. Carlos Castaneda, *The Eagle's Gift* (New York: Simon & Schuster, 1981).

6. Carlos Castaneda, *The Fire from Within* (New York: Simon & Schuster, 1984).

7. L. V. Andrews, *Medicine Woman* (San Francisco: Harper & Row, 1981).

8. Carlos Castaneda, *The Teachings of Don Juan* (Berkeley: University of California, 1968).

9. H. Storm: *Seven Arrows* (New York: Ballantine, 1972); *Song of Heyoehkah* (San Francisco: Harper & Row, 1981); *Mentor und der magische Kreis (Mentor and the Magic Circle)* (Munich: Boer, 1986).

10. Joseph Campbell, *The Hero with a Thousand Faces* (Princeton, N.J.: Bollingen, 1949).

11. S. Keen, *The Passionate Life: Stages of Loving* (New York, Harper & Row, 1983).

12. Ibid., p. 140.

Shaman's Journey, Buddhist Path[1]

JOAN HALIFAX

T HE INTERFACE of shamanism and Buddhism is hardly new. Vajrayana, for example, was seeded in the ground of the Bonpo shamanic religion of Tibet. This is also the case for other Buddhist sects, such as the Zen Chogye order of Korea. We are not investigating the virtues or nonvirtues of either Buddhism or shamanism, but rather examining some curious overlaps that occur between these two traditions from a number of different perspectives.

My own practice has been in Zen and to a lesser extent in the Vajrayana tradition. Although I have practiced Zen for many years and have been a student of shamanism for nearly two decades, it never occurred to me that Zen was particularly influenced by this older tradition. One day, however, I had an unusual experience during a Zen chanting retreat *(kido)*. It was then that I decided to look more closely at my own Buddhist practice, and there I discovered many shamanic elements.

Prophecy

Let us for a moment digress into prophecy, a problematic area but nonetheless a cultural phenomenon. The Buddha himself is reputed to have said to the goddess Vimala that twenty-five hundred years after his death the highest doctrine would be spread in the "country of the red-faced people." It has been 2,500 years since the Buddha's passing.

Guru Rinpoche, who brought Buddhism to Tibet in the eighth century, is reputed to have said the following: "When the iron bird flies and horses run on wheels, the Tibetan people will scatter like ants across the world and the Dharma will come to the land of the red man." This indeed seems to have happened. The Tibetan people have scattered across the world, the iron bird flies, horses are running on wheels, and the dharma has come to North America, or "Turtle Island," the land of the red people.

What do the "Earth People of Turtle Island" say about this? There are many prophecies and myths related to two brothers of the Sun Clan, the younger who stayed on Turtle Island and the older one who traveled far away to some distant country in the East. The return of the older brother from the East has been long awaited for. There is an interpretation of this Hopi prophecy that looks forward to a red-garbed man who will help to reestablish the correct way of life. Various Hopis have indicated a Tibetan connection. Certain Lakota prophecies talk about the coming together of teachings and traditions from the East and from Turtle Island.

Hence there is an apparent synchronicity. To stay in the ethnographic suprareality, we could say the prophecies of the Tibetan people and of the Buddha, and the prophecies of the people of Turtle Island indicate that some kind of alchemy may be occurring. When I read Chögyam Trungpa Rinpoche's *Shambhala: The Sacred Path of the Warrior*,[2] I found that the teachings contained there were quite familiar. The phraseology and many of the instructions had been given to me years ago by Meso-American and Native North American teachers. It was like reading a distillation of twenty years of study with old medicine men and women. This overlap between Buddhism and shamanism has been noted by other teachers as well.

Weaving Together Earth and Sky

In the past few years, I have endeavored to look at those areas where the traditions of Buddhism and shamanism merge. I am not interested in creating a unified tradition or theory of Buddhism and shamanism. The traditions have important differences that put them in a complementary relationship to each other. Yet some of the overlaps and differences might be useful for us contemporary Western people to notice in the particular dilemma in which we find ourselves today.

I have characterized shamanism as an "earth tradition." The four worlds of Grandmother Earth—the mineral, plant, animal, and human worlds—are in harmony and balance with each other, as symbolized by the teachings of the Medicine Wheels. Shamanism is not, strictly speaking, a revealed religion but a tradition based on a dialogue with nature. Nature is perceived to be an uncontrived display of the Great Spirit, and as such is Truth. We can say, then, that shamanism is primarily a dialogue with Truth through the vehicle of nature.

Shamanism in general is also not an institutionalized religion. There is usually no corpus of formal teachings. Rather, the teachers are Death and Change, the Sacred Rocks, White Buffalo Woman of the plant realm, and the realm we know as Sweet Medicine—the animal realm.

It is interesting to note that in Buddhist teachings the animal realm is characterized as an environment of ignorance, whereas in the Native American tradition it is, on the contrary, the realm of wisdom. Why? Because for the shaman the world of creatures is the uncontrived, the uncooked, the raw: it is the realm where thought does not interfere. One never sees a wolf stumble or a hawk falter in the sky. They are naturally what they are, completely and utterly. The bear is just bear. The jaguar is completely jaguar and stays thus, unnamed. It is a very crucial relationship that the shaman cultivates with the world of creatures, the world of uncontrived mind. This is an interesting distinction between Buddhism and shamanism.

We can find other differences as well. For example, tobacco is a sacrament among Native American people, regarded as a gift from the plant world. The smoke of the tobacco rises to the sky carrying the prayers of those who offer the tobacco by smoking it. Alcohol is considered to be a nemesis among the people of Turtle Island, whereas alcohol in Vajrayana is a sacrament and tobacco is a nemesis. There are a number of other distinctions of this nature, but both traditions share a common interest in the uncontrived, in an experience beyond language, something that we call in Zen "direct knowing," the experience of stopping the mind, of "stopping the world."

If shamanism is an earth tradition, then it can be said that Buddhism is a "sky tradition" in the sense that the emphasis is on mind and space. But the curious thing about this description is that although shamanism is an earth tradition, it nevertheless takes its followers into the experience of ecstasy, of transcendence, of flight, and is involved with the spiritualization of matter, whereas the spacious sky tradition of Buddhism brings one down to earth to the world of the ordinary.

The Wilderness of the Zendo

In both traditions the relationship with human teachers has some notable similarities. A neophyte or a would-be shaman goes to a great teacher and says, "I come to you because I desire to see." The old man or old woman points to the wilderness and says,"Before we get involved in too much, go out there. Do your job out there." But basically, going "out there" means an encounter with the wilderness within, with all the uncooked stuff of the psyche. In the most fundamental sense of the word it is an encounter with fear, the first enemy of the shaman.

In Buddhism, there are innumerable yogis, such as Milarepa, who have sought this quality of freedom of mind, of unobstructed awareness, in wilderness settings. It is an ancient tradition in Buddhism, and we could say that the meditation hall is a form of wilderness. One goes there and sits, which does not mean that one is going to get enlightened; but after a while the "uncooked" mind reveals itself. This practice is quite subtle. But one could say that the meditation hall is an environment that performs a similar function to the shaman's wilderness.

Enlightenment as Accident

The neophyte shaman, after going through trials of an inner nature (which are frequently projected into the external world and perceived as external experiences) is—at least ideally—purified by his or her experience. These experiences, which have been described in my book *Shamanic Voices*,[3] are very unpleasant—some of the worst kinds of experiences one can have—but seem to be necessary stages on the path.

It is not possible to sign up for a weekend course in shamanism and "get it." It is not possible to dream it up, pay for it, or study it. In fact, you cannot really seek it; rather, it seeks you. In a similar context, Richard Baker-roshi once said, "Enlightenment is an accident. Practice makes you accident-prone." Becoming a shaman is the same thing. Going on vision quests, making offerings, doing the Sun Dance—none of this makes a person a shaman. Going for days and days without food and water in the coldest and harshest of climates—none of this confers shamanhood. Something has to break open inside of you; and then that which is discovered within is found to be raw and absolutely naked. It is a mind that some healers know, and which some people know who leave no tracks on their way. It is rare, and it is cultivated in the wilderness.

Mind Transmission

After that, the neophyte returns and learns the craft of ceremony from the teacher, refines the knowledge gained in the wilderness, and refines the relationship between teacher and apprentice. My own teacher, Don José Matsuwa, a very old Huichol Indian, once said to me, "Juana, you have seen the flower of vision on my face." He was reminding me of a ceremony up in his village of Colorin many years ago, where many

Indians and myself had ingested peyote. It was a very challenging experience for me. At one point I looked up into Don José's face and I saw the *nierika*, I saw his mind as flower—an unending flower of generations and generations, of all those who have been touched by wisdom.

Years later, with a Tibetan teacher in Bhutan, a similar moment also occurred, which might be called "mind transmission." After that I realized that in both Buddhism and shamanism something profoundly intimate could transpire between disciple and teacher, between neophyte and shaman—a mixing of minds.

Silence

Silence as a spiritual value is of extraordinary importance in the tradition of shamanism—the moving beyond words into the wilderness. It is not only the silence of the space of night on top of a mountain or in a vast desert, but also the silence of an unmoving mind that ushers in the process of the shaman's journey. The shaman works thus with song and silence, with space and beauty. Silence in the practice of Buddhism is also important. By literally stopping the "tongue gate," the meditation hall becomes a display of what can potentially unfold within our own minds as authentic experience.

Stopping the Mind, Stopping the World

It is understood by shamans that the only way to tame the mind is to make the mind an ally. To become a master of the visionary realm, a master of ecstasy, a master of these exotic and relative states of altered awareness, one must die to the ordinary discursive mind, which is culturally conditioned.

There are many ways this is done. In the world of the shaman, the most obvious is through extended periods of isolation: by entering the vision pit, the cave, the desert. This awakens the senses and breaks the perceptual and conceptual habits conditioned by culture.

In the Tibetan tradition three emotions are used in this process of shock in order to help facilitate realization. The first is that of shame or extreme embarrassment, the second is grief, and the third is fear. Thus it is said that some of the cleverer Old Ones deliberately create situations that cause their charges' minds to stop by inducing shame or grief or fear. This is also the case among shamans. We are talking about shock at the level of the self, at the core of the psyche, beyond an idea.

The Practice of Giving Away

Both shamanism and Buddhism have to do with what Native Americans call the giveaway. From the point of view of Native American shamanism, everything is understood as a process of giving away, of exchanging and interchanging. For example, one takes no plant or animal for oneself without giving an offering. One constantly makes offerings to one's neighbors. One has the sense that one owns nothing. Thus every official holder of a sacred prayer pipe will tell you, in referring to the ceremonial pipe with which he is entrusted, "I don't own this."

Likewise, the first *paramita* (perfection) in Buddhism is the perfection of generosity *(dana)*. Suzuki Roshi put it succinctly: "To give is the practice of nonattachment."[4] In the Native American world, there are three ceremonial aspects of the giveaway: one is the activity of purifying, of making oneself empty; the second is the activity of blessing, praying for the well-being of others; and the third is the activity of sacrificing, of giving up one's connection to everything, even to death.

Interdependence

The notion of interdependence is exemplified by Grandmother Spider, Spider Woman. It is she who spins the stuff of life from the very center of her being; it is she who is the ultimate networker, the connector of all there is. In the Native American world, this realization of the interconnection of all living beings is extremely important. One day Don José took me down to the ocean and said, "Juana, this is your mother. She is the source of your life. And if you realize that, you won't throw trash into her." Then he proceeded to construct a kinship diagram: the sun is your father, and so on. We could not exist without all our relations being in correct relationship with us.

For this reason, when we enter the sweat lodge, we say we are doing it not just for ourselves, but for the Rock People, for Earth Mother, for our brothers and sisters the plants, for White Buffalo Woman, for all the different animals and peoples and ancestors. All are our kin. In many other shamanic traditions this quality of intimate relationship is stressed, until one suddenly realizes that one cannot be separate from the elements and the four worlds of Grandmother Earth.

One day I heard the venerable Zen master Thich Nhat Hanh talk about interdependence. He held up a piece of paper and said, "What do you see?" He paused and then quietly continued, "When I see this paper I see a cloud." And suddenly one could see the cloud that yielded the rain that watered the forest floor and flowed into the roots of the trees that the lumberjack cut for the paper mill and finally arrived in the hands of our teacher.

Everything from this perspective is the Medicine Wheel. Everything is teaching you that it is connected to you and everything else. There is an Ojibwa chant sung by a hunter who has killed a bear. He chants over the bear: "When you fall, I fall. When you suffer, I suffer. We are both in the same boat."

Ceremony in the world of the shaman is therefore a re-membering of where we have been dismembered from nature, from the ground of our life. In this way it takes us home again. It reminds us to remember our relations so we may come into a direct realization that from the earth grows the grass upon which the deer grazes before being shot by the hunter who eats the deer and one day himself dies and returns to the earth. Thus we begin to see the cycle of life, the dance of impermanence within this dance of interdependence.

NOTES

1. This chapter is based on a lecture given at the Naropa Institute, Boulder, Colorado, in February 1986. A transcript of the lecture was published in *The Vajradhatu Sun* 8, no. 4 (April–May 1986): 9.

2. Chögyam Trungpa, *Shambhala: The Sacred Path of The Warrior* (Boston and London: Shambhala, 1985).

3. Joan Halifax, *Shamanic Voices* (New York: Dutton, 1979).

4. Shunryu Suzuki, *Zen Mind, Beginner's Mind* (New York: John Weatherhill, 1970).

To Paint Ourselves Red

BROOKE MEDICINE EAGLE

I N Lakota ways, as well as many other native traditions, medicine people and conductors of special ceremonies used ochre (red paint) to redden their hands as an indication of their sacred calling and dedication to the "blood of all the people" in service. The use of red paint is thus symbolic of their commitment to Spirit, to "All-That-Is," for the purpose of serving one's relations through oneself. It represents the awakening of Spirit through "doing hands."

In this chapter I want to suggest that we in the modern world can benefit by learning to "paint our entire body red." This means acknowledging and experiencing that our body is the repository of Spirit. Such an attitude calls forth the understanding that Spirit lives within each tiny cell of us as physical beings.

Much of my work with people is about this very thing—embodying Spirit, bringing Spirit to full manifestation in this body, right now. I believe that it is important not only for our spirits but for our very survival today that we understand that the "heaven" we can truly expect is not a faraway place to which we will go when we leave the "mess" we have created here, but is instead a light that will shine forth from *within* us to join joyously with others in re-creating a garden of Mother Earth. The challenge lies not in gaining "new parts" of ourselves but in awakening to and using well the parts that we already have.

The Second Great Power

Lakota ways acknowledge four Great Powers: (1) the Power that created the earth and all things, (2) the Power that lives in everything, (3) a

209

mysterious Power of healing and awareness in the West, and (4) the Power of Heyoka—of laughter, of turning things around to see anew. Here I want to focus on the Second Great Power, that which lives in everything. It is important to understand that *everything* includes not only all our relations upon the earth around us, but it also includes us—that is, our physical body right down to our very cells. That Power is not separate from us; it vibrates from within us and through us.

Shamans have long understood that we need go nowhere but inside ourselves for our transformation. Even journeying "out of body," awakening the dreamer to "magical flight," and other such phenomena are accomplished *through* the body. Focus of attention within ourselves is the first step. To touch and unfold our shamanic will,[1] to stop the seemingly endless internal dialogue, to find our power—all happen within us. Too often, however, we begin by looking outside ourselves for understanding, wisdom, spirituality, and transformation, whereas the first step is always to acknowledge that what we need lies inside. We wait for secrets to be told to the mind, yet it is really a matter of getting to the body. Mother Earth and Father Spirit are not apart from us.

Our usual daily reality *and* the alternate reality of Spirit both lie in the interior dimension of ourselves: this is the twin-pronged horns of the shaman's symbolism. Speaking metaphorically, it can be said that an individual in the prevalent culture develops the "right side"—that is, the left brain, ordinary reality, *tonal*—while keeping his head butted firmly against a tree to prevent the growth of the horn on the left side—that is, the right brain, intuitive/dream reality, *nagual*).[2] After finally stunting his growth, he staggers back, exhausted, underdeveloped, and imbalanced, wobbling through life with much less than half his capacities available.

Somewhere within us, of course, we are aware of our incompleteness and seek to fulfill ourselves. But too often we do this by trying to escape our physical body—to quiet ourselves by "getting away from ourselves" rather than through developing inner stillness. Indeed, our very seeking is framed by the language of our one-sidedness, which confuses us into thinking that body and spirit are separate. The very fact that we have two distinct words, *body* and *spirit*, implies that they are two different things; whereas in reality they are woven together so closely that they are one.

For this reason the great teachers of many traditions emphasize the body and its connection with Earth as primary, as the basis of all development in the human form. Thus Don Juan admonishes Carlos Castaneda to clear and strengthen himself;[3] Agnes and Ruby press Lynn Andrews to become strong, toned, and capable physically.[4] Such teachings are a challenge to all of us to call into wakefulness this Second Great Power. The finest martial artists and shamans learn to open their perception by awakening each and every part of themselves; they can see what is behind them because they have aroused the ability to perceive in every cell, and thus do not rely solely upon their eyes. When we kindle and accept this Great Power within us, we will be opening the most useful, powerful, and magical energy available.

Therefore the most abundant and powerful resource for us to develop on Mother Earth is not fossil fuel or nuclear power or even solar energy; it is the light from Father Spirit and Mother Earth which we can allow to pour through us unrestricted, and which will produce miracles beyond our present imagining. When we stop looking outside oursevles for answers, we will stop tearing and using up our Mother Earth. And then we will create beauty before us and all around us in our Earth Walk.

The Belly

What one of my southern lineages refers to simply as "the belly" is the mysterious center point within the geography of the human body and within the Spirit. This lies in the body one or two finger-widths below the navel. This is the home base for an integrated walk in everyday life *and* for the unfolding of the mysterious power of the will, which leads to opening the dreamer and the nagual. We call this point "Mother's Mind within us," meaning that this is where the invisible umbilical cord that joins us to our true Mother, Mother Earth, connects to us. This cord attaches us to Mother and thus, through similar cords, to all Earth's children, whether two-legged, four-legged, winged, swimmers, green growing ones, or stone people.

This kind of base-level intelligence is what we are to develop in our first few years on Earth. Thus our Lakota people asked new mothers to spend at least one full year focused on teaching the new infant about a good and full relationship with All-Our-Relations upon Mother and in the heavens. This deep connection, without abstract words or concepts, forms the flowing interface with Mother and all her children that is the true basis of power. So it is very important that we not rob our children and ourselves of that encompassing knowledge; we must not assume that knowledge lies solely in words, books, schools, and our heads.

A story is told about a meeting in the early days between a white man and an old Indian man. The white man remarked that Indian people seemed to have known about the circle for a long, long time; why then did they not develop the wheel? The wise Indian replied, "We have known of the wheel for a long, long time as well. We knew, however, that it would take us up and away from our Mother Earth. That would be a disservice to our children, for children cannot become fully human unless they are in intimate contact with Mother Earth."

A way for those who missed the recognition and development of this connection with all things is to develop it through first accepting its existence (in the face of the fact that "experts/scientists" tell us we are separate from everything), and second, by an attentive "toning" of their bellies, their centers. Regarding the latter process, the first resistance to overcome is the idea that you may feel foolish focusing your attention two finger-widths below your navel. Another obstacle is our heavy cultural conditioning to keep our minds "above the belt," which starts as our sexuality emerges. These crippling restrictions need to be cast aside before the work can truly begin.

In this it is useful to find time alone to explore the body and find one's center. The middle finger of the left hand can be used to feel and press until the spot is discerned. Even though one may not be at all confident of its exact location, the intuitively chosen spot can still be used. Later, after work with the belly through exercise and practice, its location will be felt clearly—it is not necessary to wait for certainty.

My suggestion is to use the following breath exercise. First, pull in your stomach powerfully as you expel your breath from your open mouth; then take a deep breath down fully into the bottom of your lungs, and finally expel it with your belly, getting the feeling of blowing your breath out with the snap of your belly inward. You may find that initially just a few of such deep breaths are tiring. This is quite normal. Just begin where you are and work upward to five, ten, twenty, and so on. Then, consciously, press your belly against your world. Feel your world through that part of your mind which has been with two-leggeds all the way up through our evolutionary development, and give that little slice of fore-brain (which came relative to human time on earth *very* recently) a break. It is not meant to do all the work.

To understand the importance of toning the belly, it is necessary to say something about our relationship with our children. Children are born from our bellies. Whether referring to the mother or the father, the energy of creation comes from this lower part of our bodies. And every parent feels a bond with his or her children that goes beyond what words can explain. It doesn't have to do with logic or reason; it is a bond deeper and fuller and more mysterious than that—a connection through the energies of this belly center. This is the kind of connection that we will have with All-Our-Relations on Mother Earth as we develop a deep awareness of Mother's Mind within us and awaken to the incredible bond which exists between ourselves and all things.

It is imperative for us to become aware of and develop this "gut reaction" in a good way. Modern disciplines give us another view of it. In Neurolinguistic Programming, for example, we are shown that there are many internal modalities used in making decisions. In other words, when someone asks what we want to order for dinner, we may picture *(see)* the foods on the menu, internally *hear* our mother remind us that too many sweets are not good, remember the *taste* of a steak, or *smell* onions cooking. Yet whatever process we go through, we will come to our kinesthetic sense, our *feeling* sense, to make the final check and say yes or no. The gut feeling, the kinesthetic sense, is the most important, then, and this is the same belly reaction and wisdom of which native teachers speak. The quicker and clearer we can come to this belly-level feeling response, the more elegant our decision-making process.

However we state it, this awareness of Mother's Mind within us is what we are working toward regarding questions of either destroying and damaging our other relations upon Mother Earth or learning to live in harmony. Our deep bonding will not only naturally block destructive attitudes and actions, it will also give us the intelligent connection with all of life that provides us harmonious and *truly* ecological solutions to the issues we face today. We will finally come to understand White Buffalo Calf Woman's sacred pipe law: We are all One; whatever we do to any other of Earth's children, we do to ourselves.

So to paint this "belly" place within us red, to awaken spirit and aliveness within it, has very powerful implications to our life on earth at present and for our ability to live the Creator's one law given as the worlds were formed: *You shall be in good relationship with all things and all beings.*

Healing Metaphors in Action

The idea of "painting our bodies red" can be approached from another perspective as well. Studies from many cultures remind us that movement is the key to life. Whether we learn from the ancient lineage of shamanism, from modern physics, or from studies of bodily motion such as those of Moshe Feldenkrais or Joseph Chilton Pearce, we are shown again and again that actual physical movement—use of the human body—is the basis of intelligent human life and can be deeply healing and transforming as well. In my work I call this focus on embodying spirit *healing metaphors in action.*

As I suggested in the beginning paragraphs, we must learn to paint our *entire* body red, to acknowledge our whole body as a repository of Spirit, aliveness, knowledge, and wisdom. When we do this, many possibilities open. One very potent area is the use of bodily movement in transforming a person's total experience: physical, mental, emotional, spiritual. In intellectual traditions, these "parts" of ourselves are split and thought of as separate. Shamans understand them as one, with varying descriptions and viewpoints. When we work with any one, we are working with all, with the whole. But since this body, this earthly part, is what we live through on this level of existence, it is very powerful to work directly with it.

It is very easy to demonstrate to oneself the strong influence the body has even on one's emotional states. As an experiment one can try walking around slumped over with head hanging down and feet dragging, and then try to feel happiness and joy. It is very difficult to do. Or one can throw one's arms up, open the chest/heart area, skip and dance, and try to feel depressed or upset. Again, it is very difficult. By such experiments we can vividly realize that what we choose to do with the body makes a profound difference in how we feel, in our emotional and mental state.

To elaborate further, the body can be "programmed" through physical movement to carry out complex agendas in the larger world. For instance, if a person comes to me needing to make a "leap" in his life, to leave his safe branch and try to fly a bit more, it makes sense to take him to an appropriate place and have him take an actual physical leap. The picnic table or whatever he chooses to stand on can represent "where he is now" and the ground can represent the new job, the new relationship, the year of world travel, or whatever fits his particular situation. It is likely that the person who cannot easily take a metaphorical leap in his larger life will be able to make only the smallest actual leap comfortably. If he can only jump from the curb onto the street, that's fine. He can start from there and work up until he is truly taking a good leap. This will do a surprising amount to ready him on all levels to make the move he wishes to make in his life.

Still on the subject of leaping, I use another healing metaphor in action called the Warrior's Leap with almost every group I teach. The basic idea is for ten or twelve people to line up, five or six on a side, with arms extended to make a body-sized "net." The leaper stands back fifteen feet or so and holds strongly in mind the idea of what she wants to "go for" in her life. Keeping that thought in mind, she runs and leaps into the arms of the supporting group, who bounce her gently over onto her back and roll her up in a full-body hug to each side before standing her on the ground. For some people it takes a lot of courage to make this leap, yet it gives great rewards in terms of helping them set up their nervous system to go for what they want and instilling the idea that they will be supported and loved in the process. And, of course, it is fun besides—an important and often forgotten aspect of growth and transformational work. More important, however, is the fact that one can sit around talking and catharting and being counseled all day without accomplishing the powerful transformation brought about by ten minutes of these intense whole-body exercises, the self-transformational possibilities of which are virtually endless.

For example, many people may need to "cross a bridge" in their lives—move to a new city, get out of a poor relationship, or whatever. In that case it can be very powerful to take them for a walk across a bridge, assigning the beginning side as "where you are now" and the other side as "where you want to be." Or, if they want to "get to the top" of their profession, one may pick a high hill in the area and walk to the top of it with them. If they think other people will be in the way, you as helper can get in their way and try to stop them. In moving around these obstacles and coming to the top, they will set a powerful program in their system. It is the same with "getting to the bottom" of an issue—one finds a downward slope and gets to the bottom of it, and so forth.

This same kind of practice can be seen in our native cultures as well. To use examples from books well known to students of shamanism: Don Juan didn't teach Carlos Castaneda a powerful night-running technique by describing it to him in words; he took him on walk after walk to practice it, then got him in a frightening situation and ran away from him in the night.[5] Carlos found out that he knew the running step when he needed it! Again, Agnes did not simply talk with Lynn Andrews about strengthening and toning her body; rather, she set her tasks of carrying and walking and riding horses to do this.[6] And old Plenty Coups, our last Crow braid chief, talks of being trained by an elder to develop self-reliance and courage in the face of sudden danger. Grandfather called them out early on a cold morning with a bundle of peeled sticks in his hand, some elegantly carved. "These are horses," he said, throwing them into the icy river. "The boy who gets the finest bunch will be honored." And the boys jumped without hesitation into the freezing water.[7]

To use more mundane examples, many of us in our daily lives find ourselves very much out of balance, with too much work and too little enjoyment, with too much doing and too little dreaming, spending too much time on the children and not enough on ourselves, and so on. In this situation, most people will find that their actual physical balancing ability is upset. For instance, if they attempt to balance and walk along even a one-foot-high curb they will fall off. For these folks, I suggest a very childlike practice: walk on anything that can be found that will give practice in balancing. Begin with something easy and continue to increase the challenge. The greater the challenge, the more that can be transformed in the human system, for the strongest programs are set in the nervous system under high emotion. For me and for many native shamans and healers, such growth techniques are extremely powerful and useful tools that help us create fuller, more harmonious lives for ourselves and All-Our-Relations. In this search it is important to remember to open ourselves more and more to the Spirit, to the Mother's Mind, and to everything else we need that lies within us, acknowledging that life within every cell of our body. By turning our attention again and again to the awakening and embodying of this Great Spirit in our everyday lives we will truly learn to paint ourselves red.

NOTES

1. By *will* I do not mean a stubborn emotional state; I refer rather to a mysterious state beyond our usual daily patterns that can unfold, interact powerfully with the world, and foretell the future.
2. I am using the terms *tonal* and *nagual* in the senses delineated by Don Juan as described by Carlos Castaneda in his later books, for example, *The Eagle's Gift* (New York: Simon and Schuster, 1981).
3. Carlos Castaneda, *Tales of Power* (New York: Simon & Schuster, 1974), p. 239.
4. Lynn V. Andrews, *Flight of the Seventh Moon* (San Fancisco: Harper & Row, 1984), preface.
5. Castaneda, *Tales of Power*, p. 16.
6. Lynn V. Andrews, *Medicine Woman* (New York: Harper & Row, 1981), p. 81.
7. Frank Linderman, *Plenty Coups, Chief of the Crows* (Lincoln, Neb.: Bison Press, 1962), p. 25.

Shamans, Yogis, and Bodhisattvas

GARY DOORE

T HE TRIBAL SHAMAN driven into a trance by the sound of loud
drumming may seem to be doing something quite different from the
Zen monk sitting in silent meditation or the yogi repeating a *mantra*. A
closer examination, however, reveals that each of these individuals shares
an interest in investigating a certain psychophysical process known as
entrainment—a state of consciousness in which nonordinary reality may
be accessed for the purpose of helping oneself and others in various ways.

Although mystics of different schools, such as Buddhists and shamans,
may use quite different terms to describe their experience of entrainment
states, these differing descriptions need not lead us to the conclusion that
such individuals are talking about fundamentally different states of consciousness. Indeed, it seems more reasonable to conclude that the mystical
journey—however it is be described in a particular language and culture—
is phenomenologically the same, differing only at a verbal level. This is
strongly suggested by evidence relating to the shamanic origins of yoga
and by a comparison of the stages of entrainment in shamanism and yoga.

Definition of Entrainment

In this chapter the term *entrainment* will be used to refer to the induction
of altered states of consciousness by the fixation of attention on a regularly
repeating pattern of stimuli—for example, percussion sound. Research by
Lex, Neher, and others has provided clues to why concentration on
repetitive "driving" stimuli produces entrainment, indicating that it may
have to do with such factors as the blocking, through sensory overload, of
the sequential processing function of the left lobe of the brain (the function

217

responsible for logical, rational thought processes), thus keeping activity of that hemisphere constant.[1] Otherwise stated, entrainment is what Castaneda's shamanic teacher Don Juan refers to as "stopping the world" and what yogis call "stopping the oscillations of mind" *(citta vritti nirodha)*. However we choose to describe the phenomenon, it means bringing a halt to the ordinary consensus reality created by the rational, analytical mind.

In the shamanic tradition, entrainment is generally induced by absorption of attention on the sound of rhythmic drumming (sonic driving) or by other methods, including dancing and singing, and it may also be enhanced by fasting and isolation. Contemporary neo-shamans have added still other methods, such as photic driving (strobe light), "new age" music, active-alert hypnotic induction, and flotation tanking.

In the classical Indian systems of yoga, as well as in Buddhism and several other Eastern traditions, entrainment has traditionally been induced by a wide spectrum of practices, including concentration on a rhythmically intoned mantra, on internal sound currents, on a regular breathing pattern, on visualizations of rotating mandalas or pulsating inner lights, or (as in *jnana yoga*) on the subtle vibration of the current of self-awareness. Contemporary meditation research also confirms that the rhythmic driving stimuli necessary to produce entrainment need not be external but can be merely imaged or internally perceived and still result in significant physiological changes.[2]

Shamanic Origins of Yoga

Michael Harner has proposed the idea, with which I agree, that shamanism gave birth to yoga at the time of the rise of city-states and state religions in the East, when loud drumming became dangerous because it alerted the inquisitors of the official religion, who were interested in protecting their monopoly on divine revelation against the threat posed by the shamans' religious egalitarianism.[3] Harner argues that it was this oppression of shamans that forced them to develop the silent, undetectable methods of altering consciousness that later evolved into yoga and other "occult" (or "concealed") spiritual paths.

It appears that the first clue to have been pursued by the proto-yogis in their search for a more sophisticated mystical technology was the observation that each state of consciousness is accompanied by its own specific kind and quality of *breathing*. Patanjali, for example, notes correlations between breathing disturbances and disturbed states of mind.[4] Using such facts as springboards for further research, the reciprocal influence of breath and mental states was then systematically explored. By experimenting with various ways of controlling the breath, they found that altered states of consciousness could be induced.

One of the most powerful ways of influencing the breath was discovered to be through the use of certain bodily postures. The early yogis noted that by placing the body in certain positions that stretched, bent, twisted, inverted, and otherwise manipulated the hardware of the human machine in particular ways, they could change breathing patterns and states of consciousness at will. As Felicitas Goodman reports, the physical postures found in certain shamanic spiritual traditions, such as that of the ancient Aztecs and other Amerindian groups, may also be used to induce altered states of consciousness. (See her chapter on page 53.)

Although the yogic postures, or *asanas*, are generally regarded today as a kind of Hindu calisthenics designed to promote health, it is clear from Patanjali's comments that the production of health was not the primary reason the ancient yogis developed these postures. As he notes in the *Yoga Sutras*, the main purpose of the *asanas* is to bring about a condition of imperviousness to "assault from the pairs of opposites"—which in this context means the ability to switch off the impressions that constantly bombard the mind from the external world through the channels of the five senses. Of course, the health-promoting benefits of the *asanas* were no doubt also appreciated, since the physiological and psychic stresses produced by the yogi's intense work in states of deep trance demanded, as it did also for the shaman, a high degree of bodily fitness. Moreover, the postures served the purpose of physical purification, helping to eliminate toxins that produce bad visions—a cleansing process that had always been the prerequisite of shamanic initiation. Nevertheless, their primary importance still lies in their ability to alter consciousness by lessening the input from the external senses. This appears to be connected with the rechanneling of certain very subtle energy currents in the central nervous system.

When the ability to withdraw from external sensory distractions was achieved, the early yogis found that the heightened concentration it facilitated enabled them to penetrate into deeper and deeper altered states. Thus Patanjali speaks of *asanas* and *pranayama* (control of the breath) merging into the fifth limb of yoga, *pratyahara*, which is the capacity to completely switch off the exterior senses, accompanied by the most intense activity of the inner senses—the imaginal power of "magical flight" referred to by shamans. This enabled the yogi, like his shamanic predecessors, to enter the stream of entrainment and perceive the subtle phenomena of nonordinary reality.

Advanced Stages of Entrainment in Shamanism and Yoga

Having succeeded in reaching absorptive states of concentration, the yogis next experimented with deepening such states by the use of internally imaged driving phenomena—the mantras, visualization, and other techniques mentioned—which they now found were as effective as the drum in producing the final stages of entrainment. These final stages became known in yoga as "fixation" (*dharana*) and "absorption" (*dhyana*), which shamans referred to as passing through a dark tunnel. In Buddhism it was called "entering the stream" (of meditation). Although shamans spoke of emerging from the tunnel into another world, yogis and Buddhists used the word *samadhi* to describe their experience. In this way, the silent yogic methods enabled shamanic work to continue even in the midst of unfavorable outer conditions.

Based on their preferred method of induction into entrainment states, several new mystical traditions then branched out from the original shamanic roots. The labels attached to the stages of the entrainment process in these schools naturally differed according to local traditions of language and mythology. Thus psychics speak of *trance*, Christian mystics refer to *ecstasy*, Sufis use the word *fana*, alchemists and certain other Western occultists talk of *astral travel*, and so on. But there is an essential overlap of phenomenological content in the states of consciousness these words describe.

This can be seen by comparing the shamanic journey with the stages of yogic *samadhi*, which reveals that the entrainment state called *savitarka samadhi* in yoga—the first stage of *samadhi*—corresponds to the altered state of consciousness in which shamans make their metaphoric "journey to the Lower World." This explains why yogis and shamans respectively describe *savitarka samadhi* and the shamanic Lower-World journey as states of consciousness involving vivid mental imagery of "particular" or "concrete" *(tarka)* objects of sensory or extrasensory experience—for example, "spirits," "astral beings," "power animals," "*devas,*" and so forth.[5] In terms of the mental "vehicle" through which this stage of entrainment is accessed, both *savitarka samadhi* and the Lower-World journey of the shaman can be described as modes of the "lower" or empirical mind *(manomaya kosa)* and its imaginal power.[6]

The next stage of entrainment is known as *savichara* in yoga, which refers to the universalizing or conceptualizing function of the mind *(vichara)*. In shamanism this mental function and its corresponding stage of entrainment can be observed in the symbolism of the shaman's journey to the Upper World to communicate with spiritual teachers. Although the state of consciousness thus represented is expressed using symbols or archetypes derived from the imaginal function of the lower mind (for example, in the imagery of a "dialogue with a teacher"), the "dialogue" in question can be seen as representing the abstract, conceptualizing activity of the "higher" mind which is active in this stage—the mental vehicle known as *vijnanamaya kosa*.

The next stage of entrainment is referred to in yoga as *sananda samadhi*, which means literally, "samadhi with bliss" *(ananda)*, referring to the ecstatic nature of contact with the intuitive mind *(buddhi)* through which this stage of entrainment is accessed. In shamanism this aspect of the mind is represented by the shaman's mystical "flight to the sun" in the initiatory journey or vision quest. In the course of this flight the neophyte gains access to intuitive wisdom, although he or she may, again, symbolize it in ordinary reality by means of the images and concepts of the pre-intuitive levels of mind.

Having transcended even the intuitive mental vehicle, the yogi then enters into the stage of entrainment known as *sasmita samadhi*, from the Sanskrit *asmita*, which refers to the feeling of self-existence, one's sense of individual "I-ness." Here entrainment occurs on the subtlest oscillation of consciousness between the two poles of subject/object duality, the seeming perception of a distinct "I" and "not-I."[7] This is the last stage of "objective" *(samprajnata) samadhi*, because the mind is still focused on an object of knowledge *(prajna)* and has not yet gained the power to abide in the nonobjective field of pure awareness underlying the dualisitc fluctuations of the mind. In shamanism it may be described variously (depending on the culture) as entrance into the kingdom of the Sun God, ascent to the highest heaven, and the like.[8] It is a realm of indescribable bliss and perfection, but still within the realm of dualistic phenomena, and therefore ultimately subject to suffering. Thus in yogic mythology it is said that even the gods in the highest heaven of Brahma must be reborn when their good karma wears out.

In order to find freedom beyond even the last realms of suffering, the shaman must journey beyond the highest heaven or the realm of the Sun God, into a deep level of trance known in yoga as *nirbija samadhi*, which gives access to an undifferentiated, nonobjective mode of awareness in which every "vehicle" of consciousness has been transcended and consciousness alone remains, beyond all distinctions of subject and object. In shamanism we find reference to this stage in descriptions of the shaman's "dismemberment" by demons or predatory animals in the initiation process, symbolic of the destruction of ego. It is the last stage prior to "rebirth."

Nevertheless, the undifferentiated state of entrainment is still not the ultimate stage because it remains an "introvertive" trance in which there is no awareness of or ability to function in the external world of ordinary reality. "Rebirth" occurs when the scattered parts of the initiate's worldly personality are put back together again in a new arrangement capable of establishing a connection between the worlds of ordinary and nonordinary reality. It is then that the shaman acquires magical powers such as telepathy, clairvoyance, healing ability, and so forth—referred to in yoga as the *siddhis*. In this final integrative stage, enlightenment is "brought down," as it were, from the remote peaks of nonobjective consciousness into the mundane world of ordinary reality. This is the stage of "active *samadhi*" in yoga; in Buddhism it is the realization of *nirvana* in the midst of *samsara*. In each case it marks the end of the candidate's novitiate and entry into the life of active service for the benefit of others, whatever the specific means adopted for that service may be.

The Rhythmic Basis of Entrainment

We have noted that entrainment in both shamanism and yoga is facilitated by concentration on repetitive driving stimuli. But what about the spiritual techniques of Buddhism, which seem to involve no obvious attention to rhythmic phenomena? Does this mean that when Buddhists refer to *samadhi* they mean to indicate a different kind of entrainment state than that referred to by shamans and yogis? And does this therefore point to a different sort of spiritual experience and realization by Buddhists?

It should be noted first that attention to externally produced rhythmic phenomena *is* incorporated into Buddhist practice in several schools—for example, in Korean Zen, where the *moktak*, a wooden percussion instrument, is used in conjunction with the rhythmic chanting of *sutras*. (It is also interesting to note in this connection that Korean Zen gives more attention than most other schools of Buddhism to exploring visionary phenomena of the sort reported by shamans. This may be due to the close association of shamanism and Buddhism in Korean society, where native shamans can still be found practicing today.) It is true, however, that many forms of Buddhist meditation give the appearance of not incorporating any methods utilizing rhythmic phenomena. Nevertheless, this appearance is deceptive, for even in the so-called "formless" types of Buddhist meditation—for example, those found in Soto Zen and southern Buddhist *vipassana* meditation—meditators report experiencing a definite regularity or "beat" to the dance of transitory phenomena in advanced stages of meditation. The rapid procession of "empty thought-instants" *(ksana)*, which are perceived to flash before consciousness from moment to moment, serves in itself as repetitive driving stimuli. Hence, by absorption of attention on this oscillation—the basis of phenomenal existence itself—the Buddhist meditator is driven into the higher stages of entrainment just as surely as the shaman who enters those stages through the regular beat of the drum.[9]

The method of "formless" meditation does not appear to have been thoroughly discussed in the modern literature on yoga, although Pantanjali himself refers to it in his chapter on the *siddhis*, or psychic powers. There he says that the threefold process *(samyama)* of fixation, absorption, and entrainment on the arising and passing away of the *ksana*, or thought-moments, gives the power of perceiving the distinction between self and nonself.[10] The precise implication of the Sanskrit here is that the fundamental dualistic illusion *(avidya)* from which all suffering arises is actually a rapid oscillation or flickering of consciousness *(citta vritti)* between the two basic poles of phenomenal reality—namely, subjectivity and objectivity, or the awareness of a distinction between an "I" and a "not-I." For this reason, the highest stages of yogic meditation involve the same process as the formless varieties of Buddhist practice, in which entrainment is produced by fixing attention on the dualistic fluctuation of phenomenal existence itself—the basis of the flow of time. Thus *nirbija samadhi*, which occurs when there is transcendence of even this fluctuation, is characterized by timelessness and "nonobjectivity."[11]

Shamans too, of course, are well acquainted with the timeless state of undifferentiated consciousness beyond the flux of phenomenal existence, as reported for example by E. Nandisvara Nayake Thero among the renunciate Australian aboriginal elders, whose spiritual practices he specifically refers to as a "type of yoga."[12] Hence, we can say that shamans, yogis, and Buddhists alike are accessing the same states of consciousness, although each utilizes different methods to induce the initial stages of entrainment.

The Ultimate Path

With proficiency in the art of entrainment and the ability to enter higher states of consciousness at will, the paths of the shaman, the yogi, and the Buddhist blend into one—a path that we might call the Way of Compassionate Action—whose goal is to relieve the many kinds of suffering to which human beings are subject.

In this task, each of these practitioners uses specific powers gained through entrainment in order to diagnose and treat particular types of human problems, whether these problems are manifesting primarily at a physical, emotional, mental, or spiritual level. Of course, since there are many types of human beings and many kinds of suffering, the specific means used to help relieve it will vary from school to school and even from one individual to another within a single school; and therefore the uses to which practitioners put their knowledge of entrainment will vary.

For example, in shamanism and *hatha yoga*, which "start from the body" and are traditionally regarded as putting more emphasis on the healing of physical illness, entrainment is frequently used to develop powers such as psychic diagnosis, clairvoyant perception of auras or *chakras*, nonordinary reality "extraction" techniques, and so forth; whereas in Buddhism and *jnana yoga*, the emphasis is more on using entrainment to penetrate to the psychic root of all forms of psychophysical dis-ease—namely, the basic dualistic illusion of an ego or separate self. Nevertheless, the importance of the emotional and egoic components of illness is clearly recognized in shamanism and *hatha yoga* as well, which is reflected in the holistic approach to the treatment of psychophysical disorders in the practice of those who have become proficient in these disciplines.

Hence it is dangerous to postulate any fundamental distinction between the aims of shamans and the so-called "contemplative" schools of mysticism such as Buddhism and yoga. The Buddha, of course, was referred to as the Great Physician, and many yogis in India are known as healers, often operating naturopathic clinics in conjunction with their ashrams. Moreover, when yogis are referred to as "taking on the karma" of their disciples to help them overcome problems (a frequent explanation for the illnesses of yogis), this can be seen as a variety of the common shamanic technique of healing by "sympathetic resonance" with the patient's problem, reflecting the ancient belief that "the shaman cannot treat any disease he doesn't know." Indeed, from the standpoint of the yogi, the "wounding" of the true psychic healer is not a one-time occurrence but is, rather, a continuous process wherein each new illness dealt with brings another wounding.

Thus it would be misleading to suggest that followers of the contemplative paths are preoccupied with the quest for their own enlightenment at the expense of altruism. This may be true of some novices, but not of those who have mastered their discipline. For the same reason, the prevalent idea that a shaman is a healer and community servant but not a seeker of enlightenment also needs qualification. If a particular shaman is not a seeker of enlightenment, this may be because he or she has already found it. Yet the quest for enlightenment is no doubt still important in the earlier stages of the shaman's training. For it is, indeed, only by following the shamanic discipline to the end and finding the "shaman's light of brain and body" that the true shamanic practitioner acquires the ability to activate the self-healing powers of others.

NOTES

1. See, for example, Barbara W. Lex, "The Neurobiology of Ritual Trance," in E. d'Aquili (ed.), *The Spectrum of Ritual: A Biogenetic Structural Analysis* (New York: Columbia University Press, 1979); cf. Andrew Neher, "A Physiological Explanation of Unusual Behavior in Ceremonies Involving Drums," *Human Biology* 34 (2): 151–160.

2. See H. Benson, J. F. Beary, and M. P. Carol, "The Relaxation Response," *Psychiatry* 37 (1974): 37–46. Quoted in Jeanne Achterberg, *Imagery in Healing* (Boston: Shambhala, 1985).

3. "The Ancient Wisdom in Shamanic Cultures: An Interview with Michael Harner Conducted by Gary Doore," in *Shamanism: An Expanded View of Reality*, compiled by Shirley Nicholson (Wheaton, Ill.: Quest Books, 1987), pp. 3–16; cf. Harner's *The Way of the Shaman* (New York: Harper & Row, 1980).

4. See Patanjali's *Yoga Sutras*, I, 31. There are at least two English translations and commentaries available in paperback: Swami Hariharananda Aranya's *Yoga Philosophy of Patanjali* (Albany: SUNY Press, 1983), and I. K. Taimini's *The Science of Yoga* (Wheaton, Ill.: Quest Books, 1973).

5. For a detailed explanation of the stages of *samadhi*, see Taimini, *The Science of Yoga;* for the shamanic journey and the shamanic state of consciousness, see Harner, *The Way of the Shaman.*

6. Cf. Taimini, *The Science of Yoga*, p. 37ff.

7. See Hariharananda Aranya, *Yoga Philosophy of Patanjali*, p. 44.

8. See, for example, Larry G. Peters, "The Tamang Shamanism of Nepal," in Nicholson (ed.), *Shamanism: An Expanded View of Reality*, pp. 161–180.

9. Alexandra David-Neel hints at this in her *Secret Oral Teachings in Tibetan Buddhist Sects* (San Francisco: City Lights, 1969).

10. Patanjali, II, 52.

11. See Patanjali, I, 18.

12. E. Nandiswara Nayake Thero, "The Dreamtime, Mysticism, and Liberation: Shamanism in Australia," in Nicholson (ed.), *Shamanism*, pp. 223–233.

Index

127; and return to true nature,
137; role of faith in, 107; sacredness
and prayer in, 130–132; shamanic,
25, 75, 80, 90, 107–113, 47–51, 119;
in shamanic counseling, 184; spiritual and community aspects of, 111
healing model, shamanic: of Cuna
Indians, 104, 105; of María Sabina,
102; of Pima Indians, 111; of Rolling
Thunder, 108. *See also* healing,
shamanic
healing model, Western. *See* medicine,
Western
heaven, 35, 221
hell, 167
herbs, in shamanic treatment, 136, 156
hierophonies, 153
high blood pressure, 95
Himalayan shamanism. *See* shamanic
cultures
hippies, 74, 78, 80
Hmong shamanism. *See* shamanic
cultures
holistic health movement, 81, 118
holistic world, 44, 50
holotropic therapy, 161–175
Hopi Indians. *See* shamanic cultures
Horus, 23
Huichol Indians. *See* shamanic cultures
human potential movement, 74
Huna. *See* shamanic cultures, Polynesian
Hunt, Howard, 157
hyperventilation, 162, 163
hypnosis, 50, 131, 133
hypnotherapy, 101

ideology, shamanic, 33. *See also* cosmology, shamanic; shamanic world
view
ike papaha, 44, 50
ike papakahi, 44, 46
ike papakolu, 44, 49
ike papalua, 44, 47
illness. *See* disease

imagery: in pain treatment, 141–142;
and shamanic stories, 197
imagination: in healing, 123; influence
on bodily processes, 123
power of, 122, 141
immune function, 96
impermanence, 207
inaduledi, 104
Indian tribes. *See* shamanic cultures
initiation, shamanic, 219
inner healer, 109
integrated medicine, 132–133
interconnectedness, 82, 101, 115;
concept of, in Huna shamanism, 46;
concept of, in neo-shamanism, 79;
and shamanic world view, 129; of
triple worlds, 26
interdependence, 12, 47, 206, 207
intuitive wisdom, 221
isolation, 218; in pain treatment, 145–
146; and resolution of depression,
146; in treatment of schizophrenia,
146

Jesus, 23, 79
Jívaro. See shamanic cultures, Shuar
jnana yoga, 218, 224. *See also* yoga
journal work, 197
journey, shamanic, 7, 8, 12; as heroic
journey, 193; induction with psychedelic drugs, 12; compared with
samadhi, 217–225; as out-of-body
experience, 36. *See also* magical flight
Jung, Carl Gustav, 162, 174

kachina, 196
kahuna, 158
kantule, 104
Kardec, Alan, 155
kauyumari, 105, 106
Keen, S., 194
Khan, Pir Vilayat Inayat, 18
krakophonies, 153
ksana, 222–223
kundalini, 171